W9-BZL-319

African Dimensions

AFRICAN DIMENSIONS

Essays in Honor of William O. Brown

Edited by

Mark Karp

African Studies Center, Boston University 1975

Published in 1975 by the African Studies Center,
Boston University
10 Lenox Street, Brookline, Mass.

Library of Congress Catalog Card No.: 74-84802
ISBN 0-915118-05-X

Printed in the United States of America

Preface

A common fault of multiauthor works is their lack of unity. The editor may strive for at least a semblance of unity by imposing a common theme, tone, and style on the contributors to a book. But he seldom succeeds. It is practically impossible, and most people would agree that it is not even desirable, to smother individual differences in interests and ways of thinking, with the result that these differences more often than not manage to frustrate the editor's efforts to impart a sense of continuity and purpose to the volume he has undertaken to put together.

In this book no attempt has been made to achieve unity. Except for the fact that they all deal with Africa, the twelve essays that make up this volume have nothing in common. They have been contributed by Africanists with different disciplinary and other interests. All of them, however, were at one time or another close associates or disciples of William O. Brown, one of the most prominent figures in the struggle to promote African studies in the United States. Professor Brown's main objective was to correct the widespread tendency, especially in America, to view Africa in greatly oversimplified terms. He did not believe that this could be done by relying on a single discipline or a single approach to African studies. Though a trained sociologist, he tried to encourage others to study Africa from other points of view as well as that of the sociologist. With so many dimensions to the reality of Africa and its populations, he believed that only through serious studies at the university level could one hope to break the

v

myths dominating the public mind and begin to travel the long road to genuine understanding. Diversity was the keynote to Professor Brown's approach to African studies, and it seemed appropriate that a collection of papers prepared in his honor should try, at least symbolically, to express it.

Strict objectivity and painstaking attention to details are most evident in Philip Gulliver's description of traditional methods of handling and settling a land dispute in East Africa. His paper typifies the research methods of a social anthropologist working along conventional lines. Another distinguished anthropologist, Elizabeth Colson, makes a powerful plea for change not in methodology but in the research orientation of anthropology, especially in the choice of topics for investigation, in view of the political changes Africa has undergone during the last two decades.

Historians are generally concerned with the reconstruction of Africa's past, but their methods and emphases vary. Relying on European sources, Harold Marcus covers a segment of Ethiopia's diplomatic history. Norman Bennett sketches the career of a relatively obscure African chief in nineteenth-century Tanganyika. He tries to show that the European interpretation of Africa's past need not be the only valid one and that certain events take on a different meaning when viewed from an African standpoint. George Brooks focuses on the tiny island of Goree to demonstrate that there is no necessary continuity between past and present. Goree, which once played an important commercial role in West Africa, no longer does so today, and for that reason its history risks being neglected. On the other hand, Douglas Wheeler emphasizes the ancient roots of the current unrest in Angola.

In discussing the troublesome racial scene of South Africa, Newell Stultz, a political scientist, offers the thought-provoking thesis that the greater the external pressure on the South African government to adopt a liberal racial policy, the more likely is that government to harden its attitude toward the Black African population under its control. In a carefully documented paper citing the experience of Katanga, Edouard Bustin points out that post-colonial governments are no less uncertain and ambiguous in their attitudes toward native cult movements than were colonial governments. Another political scientist, John Montgomery, examines some of the lessons and wider implications of American development aid in sub-Saharan Africa.

Economic development is Idrian Resnick's concern as well. What specifically interests this economist is the conceptual framework for manpower training—an important issue in underdeveloped countries. Elliot Berg, a specialist in labor problems, presents a comparative analysis of labor unions in Ghana and the Ivory Coast during the colonial period. He shows how the different traditions of British and French labor unions influenced the development of labor organizations in Africa. While Berg thus focuses on the impact of Western ideas on African institutions, the editor, in a paper relating the religiously motivated economic conduct of a Moslem brotherhood in Senegal to Max Weber's discussion of the role of the Protestant Reformation in Western economic development, tries to show how the analysis of African institutions can sometimes be used to reexamine interpretations of Western experience.

The editor wishes to thank professors Adelaide Gulliver and Daniel McCall for their help in the preparation of this book. Unfortunately, the book could not be presented to Professor Brown, who died suddenly while it was in preparation. It is hoped that his numerous friends and the general public will accept the book as a fitting posthumous tribute.

MARK KARP
African Studies Center
Boston University

Contents

A Land Dispute in
Arusha, Tanzania

by Philip H. Gulliver

The Arusha, living on the slopes of Mount Meru and the surrounding
lowland plains, are divided among locally autonomous parishes, aver-
aging some two square miles on the mountain slopes and containing
about 2,000 people. The adult males of a parish are arranged into
corporate age groups occupying the grades of retired elders, senior
elders, junior elders, senior *murran,* and junior *murran.*[1] For ritual
and political purposes senior elders are linked with senior *murran* and
junior elders with junior *murran* in the idiom of "fathers" and "sons."
Each age group has several spokesmen, all of whom, together with their
age-mates, constitute an assembly to deal with parish affairs and disputes, with the seniormost spokesman of the junior elders acting as
chairman.

Land rights are held individually by homestead heads and are in-

---

1. *Murran:* from *ilmurran* (s. *olmurrani*), which means "younger men," in contrast to *ilwayiani,* which means. "elders." See Philip H. Gulliver, *Social Control in
an African Society. A Study of the Arusha: Agricultural Masai of Northern Tanganyika* (Boston: Boston University Press, 1963), pp. 26–27.

herited patrilineally. Close agnates—brothers, father's brothers, cousins
—comprise an inner lineage in which there is continuous mutual assistance. A number of inner lineages form a maximal lineage. If a dispute
breaks out, the members of a maximal lineage select one, sometimes
two, of their number to act as counselor—that is, as advisor, negotiator,
and advocate. A number of such lineages make up a subclan, which,
however, is not a corporate unit. Disputes can be discussed in an ad-
hoc "moot," in which each disputant is actively supported by his counselor and by other patrilineally linked kinsmen who live reasonably
near. A moot is a semiformal meeting in which there is no adjudicator,
and decisions are reached by negotiation and bargaining. An even less
formal and smaller conclave for the same purpose includes only the
counselor and a few close agnates of the disputant. A disputant can
usually choose the forum he prefers from among parish assembly (if
both disputants belong to the same parish), moot, and conclave. Recourse is also available to local government courts, though the Arusha
dislike this for settling private disputes.

The dispute discussed below occurred in 1957. In following its discussion, the reader may find the accompanying genealogy and sketch
map helpful. Three hearings were held: the first in the parish assembly, the second in a conclave, and the last again in the parish
assembly.[2]

First Hearing in the Parish Assembly

A senior *murran*, Saruni, raised a plaint at the regular weekly
assembly of a mountain parish. He asked the assembly to acknowledge
his rights to a certain piece of land of about two acres. The occupant
of this land, a tenant named Kewa, wished to vacate it, for he had
recently inherited a larger farm some distance away. Kewa made no
claim to the land; he only wanted to obtain the customary compensation for the coffee bushes he had planted there and for improvements
he had made to the irrigation system, to hedging, and to fencing.
Saruni explained that he had reversionary rights to this land by inheritance from his father, Olorishon, who had originally cleared the
virgin woodland adjacent to the farm of his father, Saruni's grandfather, Rikoyan. Saruni stated that he had no quarrel with Kewa and
that he was prepared to pay him proper compensation; but he had

2. The author was present at all three meetings.

SKELETON GENEALOGY TO ILLUSTRATE
RELATIONS BETWEEN PARTICIPANTS IN THE DISPUTE.
Only people directly relevant to the case are shown.

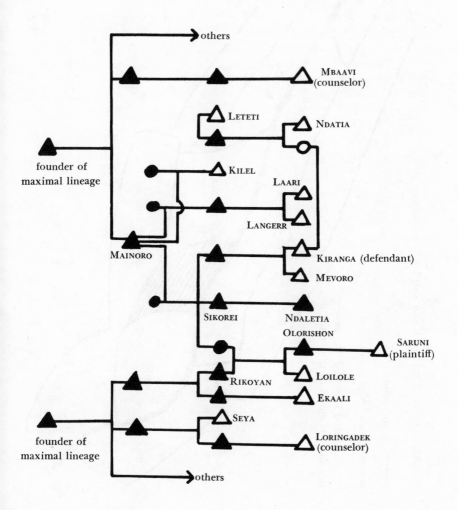

SKETCH MAP OF DISPUTED LAND AND ITS ENVIRONS

— farm boundaries

━━ main irrigation channel

Disputed land is shaded: the new
boundary is shown by the dotted line.

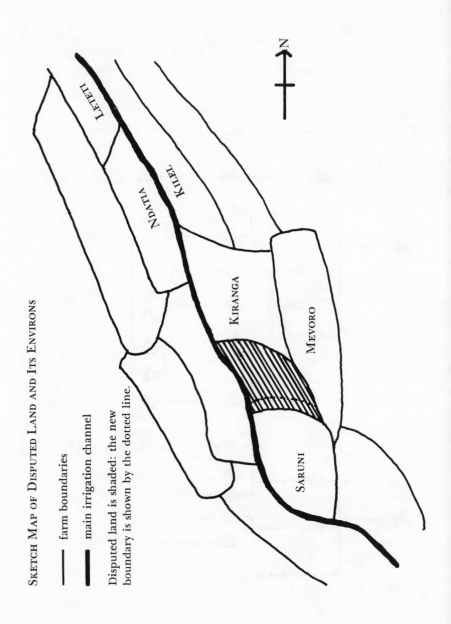

LETETI

NDATIA

KILEL

KIRANGA

MEVORO

SARUNI

N

4

discovered that the land was being claimed by another neighbor, Kiranga, who had already offered compensation to Kewa. Saruni declared that Kiranga would be a thief if he took the land, and he asked the assembly to prevent Kiranga from interfering further.

When Saruni sat down, Kiranga, a junior elder, came to the center of the assembly and explained his claim to the land. By his account, the land in dispute, together with much more now occupied by himself and his agnatic kinsmen, was originally claimed by his grandfather Mainoro as first pioneer. As had been the custom, Mainoro had laid claim to more land than he immediately needed in order to allow for later expansion. The disputed area along with other land including that now occupied by Kiranga was allocated to Mainoro's son Sikorei, and the still uncleared part was later lent by Sikorei to his sister's son Olorishon, father of the plaintiff. On Sikorei's death his land rights were inherited by his son Ndaletia. When Ndaletia died without sons or brothers, the inheritance went to Kiranga.[3] In reply to a question by Saruni, Kiranga admitted that Kewa had been granted his tenancy by the plaintiff but, he claimed, only with the explicit approval of Ndaletia. Kiranga explained that he now needed the land because his family, including a widow and daughters of Ndaletia, was growing. He would not have sought to evict Kewa, he said, but Kewa wanted to leave as soon as he obtained proper compensation. The amount had been agreed upon, and Kiranga was ready to pay it. He planned to take over his inherited land and incorporate it into his existing farm. He ended by telling the assembly, "Everyone knows that Mainoro was the big man long ago in this part of the parish." "This truly is the estate of Mainoro, and we are his grandsons. Saruni is our affine, so how can he say this land is his?" He then sat down among his fellow junior elders in the assembly.

The assembly's chairman—a senior spokesman of the junior elders, Kiranga's own age group—then said that this was not a real dispute, for clearly the land belonged to Kiranga. This was just an instance, he stated, of the senior *murran* (Saruni's age group) trying to make trouble for their superiors "as usual." Senior *murran,* spokesmen, and others immediately protested, and one appealed directly to the senior elders present. A senior elder spokesman called out, without rising to his feet, that the case should be discussed. "You junior elders do not know the proper ways of an assembly," he said. "You cannot say there is no

3. Kiranga was the senior surviving member of the same *olwashe* as the deceased Ndaletia. See Gulliver, *Social Control,* p. 72.

dispute. Let us hear all the words. Then let us discuss them." There were calls of agreement.

"All right," replied the chairman, "let these *murran* ask their fathers [senior elders] to speak for them. They are only young and they know nothing, for they are not yet elders." And turning to the *murran,* he told them to ask their "fathers" to speak on their behalf. The senior *murran* protested indignantly, and one of their spokesmen stood up and declared that "we are like elders now. We are no longer youths. We know things and we know how to speak." After further similar exchanges during which the senior *murran* grew increasingly angry, it was agreed that the senior elders should speak with, rather than for, their "sons."

Evidence was next given by two old men—Kilel for the defendant, Seya for the plaintiff. Both claimed personal knowledge of the past, but they merely reiterated the conflicting claims already made. A junior elder spokesman gave the opinion that Seya was too old for his memory to be trustworthy, but that Kilel was not senile and had truly seen what had happened in the old days. "Look," said the spokesman, turning to the senior *murran,* "do you not believe your father who tells you the truth?"

Leteti, a senior elder spokesman, declared his belief in what Kilel had said. He mildly suggested that "my son, Saruni," was mistaken and misguided. "Is not Kilel the youngest son of Mainoro? Yes. So that is how he knows. You *murran,* how can you know these things if you do not listen to your fathers? And how can Seya know? He did not live here but, as today, he lived over there, a long way away."

Leteti's remarks brought dissenting cries not only from senior *murran* but from some of his senior elder age-mates. The junior elders sat quietly and watched. It became clear that although Saruni had the unanimous support of his senior *murran* age-mates, their "fathers" were divided and thus their support weakened. Eventually, a senior elder spokesman suggested that the case should be taken to a moot, for it was not a matter to be dealt with in the parish assembly. Kiranga and a junior elder spokesman rejected this. "Are we not all neighbors here?" Kiranga inquired. "This is a matter of neighbors, the people who know. Those kinsmen of Saruni, what do they know about it? They have always lived far from here. I say we have discussed this enough. But if Saruni has more words, then let him bring them here."

The chairman called out that the matter could be discussed further at the next meeting of the parish assembly. Saruni protested that he could not be prevented from seeking a moot, and several of his age-mates shouted their agreement. Leteti, the senior elder spokesman, said that of course his "son" could do that but that he advised him not to take it farther. The assembly chairman called out that the discussion was finished and ostentatiously asked for the next plaintiff to start his case before the assembly.

Hearing in the Conclave

Saruni was clearly unwilling to lose his claim by default, as his opponents perhaps had hoped. Because the counselor of his own maximal lineage lived more than eight miles away, Saruni went instead to consult with Kiriama, the counselor of a collateral lineage of the same subclan who lived conveniently nearby, in the next parish. Kiriama advised Saruni to continue to argue his case in the parish assembly because it would be difficult to convene an adequate moot. He pointed out that only one member of Saruni's inner lineage resided locally, while the rest of his near agnates lived in relatively distant parishes in the plains. Furthermore, Saruni could not rely entirely on their support as he had no brother and was on poor terms with his father's brother because of disagreement over a herding contract.[4] In addition, only a few members of his maximal lineage lived within four or five miles of Saruni's homestead. Saruni would have to ask agnatic kinsmen to come fairly long distances to attend a moot on his behalf. The counselor thought that Saruni might not be able to obtain a strong body of supporters for a moot; and he himself may have been unwilling to accept the responsibility of acting as a leading advocate for Saruni, who did not belong to his own maximal lineage.

Believing that the parish assembly was weighted against him, Saruni persisted in the idea of trying to advance his claim in a different forum. He finally persuaded the reluctant Kiriama to try to arrange a patrilineal conclave. Kiriama went to see Mbaavi, the counselor of Kiranga's maximal lineage. After some argument, Mbaavi and Kiranga acceded to the request, and a conclave was held in Saruni's house. There, supporting Saruni were Kiriama, Kiriama's brother, and two members of Saruni's inner lineage, Seya and Ekaali. Supporting

---

4. Loilole, the father's brother, had agreed to keep Saruni's cattle on his lowlands farm in return for milk and gifts of bananas from Saruni's mountain farm. But Saruni had been asked to remove his animals, though he had not yet done so.

Kiranga were his counselor Mbaavi and the whole of his inner lineage
—Mevoro, Kilel, Laari, and Langerr—as well as Leteti. Leteti was not
an agnate, but he was a most influential man in the parish who
claimed knowledge of early land rights.

Kiranga and his supporters immediately pointed out Saruni's supporters' lack of intimate local knowledge other than by the old man
Seya. Kiriama was in a poor position to refute this argument for he
had never lived in the parish nor was he an agnate of Saruni's. He
could not claim first-hand knowledge of what had taken place in the
days of Saruni's father; he had not even been a counselor then. All
he could do was argue that Saruni's inheritance of his father's land
some twelve to fifteen years before had been undisputed. Kiranga and
Mbaavi retorted that Kiriama had no personal knowledge of the facts
and was merely repeating Saruni's allegations. They repeated that the
testimony of Kilel, Mbaavi, and Leteti was much more credible than
that of old Seya. Mbaavi added that it was not merely a matter of the
land occupied by Kewa, for Kiranga also had a good claim to the land
occupied by Saruni himself. Saruni, of course, strongly rejected this
view. Leteti then urged Kiriama to agree that the dispute be resumed
in the parish assembly. No settlement seemed possible in the conclave,
and the meeting ended after little more than an hour. It left Kiriama
as uncomfortable about the case as he had been before the conclave
met. He strongly advised Saruni to present his case again in the
parish assembly and added that if Saruni did not wish to take his
advice he should consult with the counselor of his own maximal
lineage.

A day or two later Saruni went to see his own counselor, Loringadek.
While declaring himself willing to arrange a moot if Saruni insisted,
Loringadek pointed out the probable weaknesses of Saruni's position
in a moot. Finally, he repeated Kiriama's advice that Saruni return to
the parish assembly.

Second Hearing in the Parish Assembly

At the next meeting of the parish assembly Saruni raised his claim
again. The chairman, a junior elder spokesman, told him that he
must wait another week, till the next regular meeting, for people were
not ready for his case; and, in any event, the assembly had all the
business it could conduct at that session. A spokesman of the senior

murran (Saruni's age group) protested that the junior elders were merely seeking to delay the matter to prejudice Saruni's case. The chairman denied this but pointed out that some of Kiranga's supporters were not present because "they did not know that Saruni is still trying to take Kiranga's land." A senior elder spokesman declared that "these junior elders are acting like Europeans. They listen to no one and try to tell us what to do." The senior *murran* spokesman called out, asking him to support them in arranging a special meeting of the parish assembly on the site of the disputed land in order to deal specifically with that dispute. After further exchanges the chairman announced that such a meeting would be held four days later at midday.

The parish assembly met at the appointed time in the open space next to the house of Kewa, the tenant. First Saruni presented his case in full. This time, however, he gave more attention to the land he himself already occupied. He stated that it had been virgin woodland lying between lands cleared by Rikoyan, his grandfather, and Mainoro, Kiranga's grandfather. There had never been any understanding that Saruni's father, Olorishon, had received the land as a loan from his mother's brother Sikorei, son of Mainoro, or that Olorishon was a tenant. Had he been a tenant, said Saruni, Olorishon would have made annual gifts to his mother's brother at harvest time, and this he had never done. Nor had any such claim been raised at Olorishon's death, when Saruni inherited. It was he, Saruni, who had permitted Kewa to occupy and use the disputed area, which had until his death been occupied by Saruni's brother. Never before had Kiranga claimed that land, nor had the previous holders of Kiranga's land, Ndaletia and Sikorei.

Kiranga spoke next. He reminded the assembly that his grandfather Mainoro had been a "big man," one of the earliest pioneers and a founder of the parish. Mainoro had laid claim to all the land now occupied by Saruni, Kewa, Kiranga, Kiranga's brother, and Kilel. He had been the chief architect of the main irrigation channel that ran along the western edge of this land. The area now occupied by Saruni sloped up slightly from this channel and, therefore, had not been cleared by Mainoro, unlike the rest of the land, which was more favorably situated for irrigation; but Mainoro's claim had extended up that slope to the crest of the low ridge where it met the boundary of the land of Rikoyan, Saruni's grandfather. Later Sikorei had allowed Olorishon, Saruni's father, to clear that slope for a farm. Sikorei

had never demanded harvest gifts in formal recognition of this because, said Kiranga, that is only done when landholder and tenant
distrust each other and Sikorei and his sister's son Olorishon had been
very friendly, "as everyone here remembers." Nor had Sikorei's heir,
Ndaletia, objected to Saruni's inheritance of Olorishon's tenancy
rights. "Why should he? Were they not kinsmen—neighbors and
friends? Today I do not wish to move Saruni off that land where his
house and fields and bananas are. That would be unfriendly. But
Saruni has not used this land here and I have need of it. It is the
engithaka [estate] of Mainoro and I am his grandson, his heir."

As in the previous hearing, Kilel affirmed the correctness of Kiranga's claim and stressed his own credentials as Mainoro's son. A
spokesman of Saruni's senior *murran* age group questioned both the
veracity and the impartiality of Kilel, and he reminded the assembly
of evidence to the contrary given by Seya, who was not then present,
in support of Saruni. The spokesman then appealed to the senior
elders, "who know these things of the old days." A junior elder called
out that Kilel was a senior elder, but the *murran* spokesman ignored
that.

There was a pause. Then a junior elder spokesman declared, without standing up, that there were no senior elders who knew better
than Kilel. A senior elder spokesman stood up and went to the
central open space to speak. "Land is scarce nowadays," he said, "and
we cannot agree to people being driven off the land which they have
always cultivated because his neighbor wants to take it. What do we
know now about the old days? It was all different then; there was
much land and people were friendly." He described how men had
been generous and had allowed others to use areas which they themselves did not need. Perhaps Sikorei had allowed his sister's son to do
this; or perhaps it was untouched land that Olorishon had cleared as a
pioneer, thereby establishing legitimate right to it for his heir. In
either case, Kiranga could not now drive Saruni away. Saruni had
planted bananas, hedges, and coffee bushes, and no one had ever
interfered with all this. The spokesman ended his address to the
assembly with an emotional appeal to parish unity and peace.

Leteti followed. He agreed that Saruni should not be asked to give
up the land he occupied, even though it might be part of Mainoro's
estate. But Saruni should give up his claim to the land occupied by
Kewa, for that land had been cultivated by Mainoro, as proved by
the irrigation channels on it leading off the main channel. "Let

Saruni stay where he is," he said. "That is good and we agree. But
let Kiranga take this land here, for that is not Saruni's."

Leteti was thus seeking to show the support for senior *murran*
expected of a senior elder and a spokesman and at the same time to
induce Saruni to accept a compromise—to give up his claim to Kewa's
area in return for affirmation of his security on the land he already
occupied. Leteti also tried to show that Kiranga, being neither greedy
nor antagonistic to Saruni, was willing to accept the suggested compromise. Full consideration of Saruni's claim was thus deliberately
obstructed by Kiranga's counterclaim on Saruni's title to the land he
already occupied. Saruni had certainly not expected any questioning of
that tenure and was put at a disadvantage. Now he was in danger of
seeming greedy and unwilling to compromise, while what might seem
a compromise for him was not one for Kiranga, who made no real
claim for more than Kewa's land.

A junior elder spokesman accepted the compromise suggested by
Leteti. Kiranga, of course, voiced his agreement. Saruni protested that
his land was not in dispute, although several junior elders declared
that it was. Saruni persisted, saying that Leteti's solution was no
solution at all since it ignored Saruni's original claim. He asked
why Leteti was supporting Kiranga, a junior elder, instead of Saruni,
a "son" (senior *murran*). Leteti replied that he was seeking to show
his "son" a way of settling the matter. Saruni then asked why Kiranga
wanted the land—for his own use or for another purpose? Kiranga
merely replied that he needed it, but a senior *murran* called out that
Kiranga intended to pledge it to his brother-in-law. The chairman
said that this was irrelevant, since a man could do as he wished with
his own land. After more exchanges of this kind it seemed clear,
though not explicitly admitted by Kiranga, that he wished to pledge at
least part of the land to his wife's brother Ndatia in lieu of bride-
wealth debt of two cattle.

This, said Saruni, was why Leteti, Ndatia's father's brother, was
supporting Kiranga instead of his "son"—Leteti himself would benefit
if Kiranga gained the land. Leteti denied this and argued that he acted
as a spokesman of the parish seeking a workable solution to the dispute. He had, he pointed out, supported Saruni's continued right to
the land he occupied. A *murran* spokesman declared that his age-mates
were being deserted by their "fathers" (senior elders). "We know," he
said, "that you, our fathers, have been angry with us about your wives,
but you cannot desert us here. Are you trying to punish us all for

what some of us have done to you?" He was referring to compensation claims by senior elders for alleged adultery by their wives with some senior *murran*. The adulteries may or may not have occurred, it being customary for senior elders to make such claims when senior *murran* were beginning to prepare for eventual ritual transfer to elderhood. It was a standard method of emphasizing the corporate authority of senior elders over their "sons."

A junior elder spoke about the unruliness of the senior *murran* and their inexperience. He urged the compromise suggestion of Leteti, and Kiranga again voiced his assent. Senior elders were divided some for and some against, but none seemed strongly in favor. One suggested that the dispute ought to go to a moot, but no one took up the idea. Another senior elder proposed that the men should "walk and look at the land," the recognized implication being an inspection with a view to division of the land between the disputants. The age groups consulted among themselves in whispers. After some time, a junior elder spokesman said that his age-mates saw no value in the proposal; but then a senior *murran* spokesman said that his age-mates agreed to it. There was a pause, more whispered consultations, and then a senior elder spokesman stood up and commended the wisdom of his "sons." He began to move out of the seated cluster of men, followed by some, while others remained sitting. Junior elders conferred again, and eventually they too got to their feet. There was confused movement, as many men seemed not to know what was happening. The chairman of the assembly took the initiative and called out: "Let us go and look over there, beyond these bananas." He moved that way accompanied by his age-mates, including Kiranga. Thus Kiranga and his age-mates tacitly agreed to some division of the disputed land. By following, Saruni and his age-mates indicated that they also accepted this.

Between the banana grove and the boundary of Saruni's farm to the south was a field of about half an acre. "Let Saruni take this field," said the chairman. Kiranga showed agreement, while Saruni and his supporters conferred among themselves. The chairman repeated his words, and the senior *murran* remained silent, thus indicating absence of disagreement. "These are the words. The matter is finished," called out a junior elder. There was no dissent. The parish headman said that the new boundary should be marked out with hedge shoots, and the chairman ordered some *murran* to do this. The rest of the men returned to the place where they had been sitting and began to drink beer supplied by both Kiranga and Saruni.

Implications

In this dispute no unequivocal evidence was produced nor was a firm decision reached concerning the first pioneering claims to the land. It is possible that at that time, over seventy years ago, no well-defined rights and boundaries were established, as land was then plentiful. The manner in which this dispute was handled can be seen as part of a general process of determining formerly undefined land rights. Lack of clear definition, tolerable in the past, was no longer acceptable. What may have been a tacit working arrangement among kinsmen and neighbors was no longer tolerable among their heirs who were but distantly related.[5] Some compromise solution is typical of the Arusha in cases involving conflicts over what has become, in modern times, a critically scarce commodity. Population density exceeded 1,000 persons per square mile in 1957, and land was becoming increasingly valuable for cash crops.

On the other hand, land rights and arrangements in earlier years may have been quite well defined. But even established rights can be challenged or circumvented, and they may be authenticated and defended with varying adequacy. What is clear is that the conduct of the hearings and the eventual solution depended inevitably on the negotiating skills and power of the disputants and their supporters. In other circumstances the evidence might well have been scrutinized and weighed differently. Though both parties to the dispute appealed to accepted norms and reasonable expectations, these norms and expectations could not be decisive in the absence of an adjudicator or arbitrator. Saruni obtained only about a quarter of the disputed land, mainly because of his weak negotiating strength.

Saruni's weak position had several sources. In the first place, he had very few close agnates and other patrilineal supporters in and near the parish. Secondly, his maximal lineage counselor and the members of his inner lineage, some of whom were poorly disposed toward him, all lived at a distance. Thirdly, he was only a senior *murran* and had rather inexperienced spokesmen and age-mates. They failed, for example, to put enough stress on the previous occupation of the disputed land by Saruni's brother and on the fact that Saruni had granted the tenancy to Kewa; they allowed themselves to be rattled and discon-

5. Neither disputant attempted to make a claim on the other in terms of kinship, so slight was their relationship in that sense.

certed by the junior elders' tactics and to be hurried into a final division of the disputed land at the conclusion of the assembly. Finally, the senior *murran* were already in some conflict with their logical and experienced allies, the senior elders, who therefore failed to give them undivided support.

Kiranga's relative strength lay in his having several agnates in the parish and a united inner lineage behind him; his being a junior elder strongly supported by his experienced spokesmen and age-mates in opposition to their rivals, the senior *murran;* and the valuable assistance given him by Leteti, probably because Leteti stood to gain from Kiranga's intention to pledge land to Ndatia. The senior elders' already weak support of the senior *murran* was further reduced by Leteti's disruptive action. Full consideration of the claim originally raised by Saruni to the land occupied by Kewa was successfully deflected by the stratagem of questioning Saruni's rights to his own farm, as this enabled Leteti and the junior elders later to make much of their readiness to acknowledge his rights there.

Throughout the dispute the junior elders took every opportunity to belittle and harass their structural inferiors and rivals, the senior *murran.* This was done both to weaken and obstruct Saruni's case and to emphasize their own superiority in the continuous conflict between structurally and chronologically adjacent age groups.

Finally settlement of the dispute was reached, publicly witnessed, and affirmed by the planting of hedge shoots along the newly agreed boundary. It would be extremely difficult for either side thereafter to raise the issue again. And to that extent, at least, it was a successful settlement.

Changing Anthropology in Africa

by Elizabeth Colson

Every generation is critical of the work of its immediate seniors, though it may not always know the reasons for its disquiet. On the whole, this discontent is a good thing. A discipline is alive only if it continues to change, finding new problems to investigate and new solutions for old problems. This is as true of anthropology as it is of any other discipline, but the young anthropologist has more reason than do specialists in other fields to query the relevance of old problems and old solutions for the organization of his own research. After all, the societies and cultures that we study are changing rapidly and the approaches and assumptions that dominated work done in earlier years may no longer be appropriate or feasible. Changes occurring in Africa and elsewhere with the removal of colonial rule and the coming of independence are forcing us to give careful consideration to what we have been doing and to reconsider some of our basic assumptions.

In part, the realization of the need for self-analysis is due to the growing hostility to anthropology in many of the countries where we have worked. If we wish to continue to base our discipline on the whole range of human societies rather than on that limited portion represented by Europe and the United States, we will have to under-

15

stand and deal with this hostility. In doing so, we may learn some things of value about the theoretical implications of some of the assumptions that have guided us in our research, and this, in turn, may help us in our search for new and better formulations.

Now, in part, our unpopularity is a fashion of the moment, voiced by many who have probably never attempted to read an anthropological account dealing with the region from which they come. It is enough for them that too many of us continue to speak of primitive peoples and that we illustrate our books with photographs emphasizing the exotic. We will have a difficult time living down our current reputations as students of the primitive even if we see that future publications are so written that they do not offend in this respect. Nevertheless, this is only a minor matter. Such editing would not force the future anthropologist to abandon any of the present methods of work or require him to alter any of the formulations handed down to him by his teachers. He could continue to work in the same way as did his forerunners.

Some of our unpopularity, however, stems from a characteristic much more fundamental in determining the nature of our research. In a century in which the leaders of newly independent countries are trying to develop a sense of national unity based upon citizenship in a common territory, the anthropologist has taken as his basic unit for the organization of research something we usually call "tribe." There are many definitions of "tribe," but all of them carry some assumption of homogeneity based on common language and common descent. They also carry the implication of a limited development of political institutions. The definitions also imply something about size—that the tribal population is too small to sponsor a full-scale state. In Africa today the new governments and their political leaders are attempting to minimize the importance of smaller ethnic units, and they decry both tribes and tribalism. If anthropology continues to be associated with either term or appears to emphasize the importance of either phenomenon, it continues to be an unacceptable form of research in the new countries.

We would therefore be well advised to ask ourselves why we have chosen to study tribes and whether it is necessary for us to continue to phrase our research in these terms. Now certainly Africa, like any other part of the world, has within it a multiplicity of languages, and common language in the past has often encouraged the creation of a social or political entity worthy of examination. But our emphasis upon tribe probably stems more from the founding fathers of anthropology than it does from African realities. They were very much a part of the intellectual milieu of the Western world of their period. The question of nationalities was the dominant political question in nineteenth-century Europe, gave rise to the doctrine of the self-determination of nations in the twentieth century, and continued to haunt the European scene into the first years of World War II. For Europe and for the social scientists of the Western world the nineteenth and twentieth centuries were the centuries of nationalism—a nationalism of a peculiar kind. In Great Britain and the United States, where political unity had been attained at an earlier period, a nation was seen as created by a state organization; people born within the territory controlled by the state were its citizens and thus members of a nation.[1] The rest of Europe, led by German humanists, developed quite another conception of nationalism. "German nationalism," as Hans Kohn said, "substituted for the legal and rational concept of 'citizenship' the infinitely vaguer concept of 'folk,' which first discovered by the German humanists was fully developed by Herder and the German romanticists."[2] It was the romanticists who "established a distinction between State and nation: they regarded the State as a mechanical and juridical construction, the artificial product of historical accidents, while they believed the nation to be the work of nature, and therefore something sacred, eternal, organic, carrying a deeper justification than works of men."[3]

These words strike an answering echo in the minds of anthropologists. We began as a study of the "folk" in the German sense. We sought a natural unit lasting through time, having an organic unity, capable of being analyzed as a natural system. Commonalities of language and custom were to us a sign that we had found such units and that they implied political and social organization. Assuming that they were natural systems that would persist through time, we set to work to understand them.

The predilection given to anthropologists by their concern for cultures as patterned wholes or societies as integrated systems was fostered by the fact that they entered an Africa dominated by colonial powers whose political thinkers had also been influenced by the idealization of

1. See Sir Lewis Namier, *Vanished Supremacies* (New York: Macmillan, 1963), p. 32.
2. Hans Kohn, *The Idea of Nationalism* (New York: Macmillan, 1946), p. 331.
3. Ibid., p. 249.

the nation or the folk. It was the European administrations that
organized the political units of twentieth-century Africa. The administrators were fully aware that the countries they had created
through the carving up of Africa were artificial units. They did not
expect that the new countries would necessarily persist in the form of
the moment. But within the artificial states they sought to sponsor the
development of what they regarded as the natural units of African
societies either by using existing political structures persisting from
the pre-colonial African states or by creating new units on the basis of
what they perceived as ethnic unities. No attempt was made to cater
to ethnic identities where they were at odds with international boundaries, but within the new countries the administrations tried to make
local political divisions coincide with ethnic or tribal divisions. No
doubt this reflected the awareness of European administrations of the
problems caused in Europe by the nationalities question and the
demands for national unity on the part of peoples speaking a common
tongue. The new administration sought to prevent similar problems
from arising and disturbing the future peace of Africa. Where possible,
therefore, district or provincial boundaries reflected linguistic or cultural boundaries. Local governments were treated as the embodiment
of tribal or ethnic polities and indeed were customarily called
native authorities. The tribe or nation rather than the territorial
district was regarded as the ultimate reality, for nationality was
assumed to be inherited. Men were regarded as tribal members
wherever they might happen to be living. They were recognized as
having a legal claim only in the territory dominated by the tribe into
which they had been born. Each member of a tribe was assumed to
have an inherited culture received from his ancestors and passed on to
his descendants. His natural associates were those who shared this
same mystical bond with past and future.

The anthropologist was thus encouraged both by his own discipline
and by the current political scene to use the tribe or national polity as
his reference points, whether he came to Africa expecting to study
culture, as did many American anthropologists, or to study a society,
as did many trained in Britain. From the people inhabiting a common
area with their multitudinous relationships and actions he abstracted
a tribal entity for study, and his statements about society and about
culture referred to this entity.

When African leaders began to challenge the colonial regime, they
changed the definition of nationalism. They did not see their own

development as a prolongation of the history of Europe. When they organized for the future, they chose to employ the territorial state as the natural political unit, and within the state they emphasized common residence as the basis for common citizenship. They ignored the nations or the tribes as politically irrelevant or noxious. The anthropologist who studies tribes is to them as outmoded and pernicious as the colonial officials who sought to entrench the small societies of the past as permanent groups with unchanging boundaries.

Until this happened, few anthropologists had sought to defend their choice of the tribe or its culture as a research focus. The choice seemed to them in many instances to be a self-evident one, though Schapera had already argued in the 1930's that the student of social change should study the various relationships and institutions represented within an area and that trader and missionary were as much a part of the local scene as the chief. Even where this was accepted by anthropologists who were beginning to talk about social systems and action fields rather than societies and cultures, in actual practice the tribe continued to be the focal point.

Conditions in Africa often encouraged this. Until after World War II, communications were usually difficult. Like most residents of Africa at that time, the anthropologist tended to be tied closely to a small locality and had little opportunity to move widely about the countryside. Until the improvement of communications, the rise of national political parties, and the new stress on economic development, it was usually not only possible to ignore what went on within the country or district at large, it was also difficult to obtain much information about what was occurring beyond one's immediate purview. Commercial and industrial centers might exist in the same district in which the anthropologist was working, but their impact was not constantly before him. The few who did study urban life—and such studies mostly date from very recent years—found that African areas of the town were set apart physically, socially, and politically from areas inhabited by the ruling peoples. The local political system of the native authority differed in kind as well as in membership from the administrative system of the district office or the national political system. The anthropologist who worked in the rural areas could go for weeks and sometimes months without seeing an official from the wider political system, although he might hear of official actions that impinged on the local people. He would see material goods brought into the countryside and used there, and he would hear of the sale of cash crops and of men going to work for cash wages, but many of the economic transactions he observed took place in a local exchange system governed by other principles than market exchange. Some of the children might be in school, but before World War II most of them were educated at home by parents and guardians preparing them for the same way of life they themselves knew. As late as the 1950's it was entirely possible for anthropologists to work in areas with no nearby schools and where it was difficult to find anyone with more than a bare minimum of literacy.

In the late 1940's, when I first worked in the southern province of Zambia, then the colonial territory of Northern Rhodesia, most of the people I knew were mainly concerned with village life. For many the political horizon stopped at the district level, and the district commissioner was regarded as wielding independent power. The provincial commissioner and the territorial governor were distant figures in whom the local residents had little interest. The legislative council of the territory meant little or nothing. Settlers, traders, missionaries, and administrative and technical officers were occasionally seen, but usually only when one visited a township, farm, mission, or administrative station. Such people were discussed more than seen, for a constant theme of conversation was the differences between Europeans and Africans.

Village people saw Europeans as foreigners with their own manners and customs. They distinguished between their own institutions and those of the foreigners, and even when they attempted to model themselves on the foreigners they did not regard the new way of life as representing their own custom. Insofar as I learned to see through local eyes, their attitudes certainly influenced me. I suspect most other anthropologists who worked during these decades were similarly influenced.

We accepted the local view all the more easily because for many reasons it was convenient to compartmentalize our thinking and to attempt to isolate a tribal or local system from a wider system for the purposes of analysis. Even though social anthropologists sought to deal with contemporary life and with social change, our analytical models at this period were such that we were happiest when we could create a working description that included only sets of relationships that could be observed by the investigator. Given the difficulties of transportation and of following sets of transactions over any wide area, we sought the most convenient cutoff points, which left us with the local scene as an independent world of events related only vaguely to external happenings.

Whether we intended it or not, this method of working led to an archaizing of our descriptions, for the organic model we were trying to preserve was our model of the tribe as a culture-bearing natural unit. This tribe had a past, and we paid disproportionate attention to the more immediate past in reconstructing what we thought of as the traditional culture, not always realizing that to claim something as traditional was sometimes the only way to legitimating innovation. We emphasized old customs or older types of institutions that we regarded as characteristic of the tribe and gave only a very summary attention to the new schools, the developing group of clerks, technicians, and teachers, the discontent of the young, and the creation of new forms of association. All these might be recognized as present, but they were not part of the "tribal" picture. If they entered into our description, they did not form part of our analysis of the ongoing system of institutions.

In many parts of Africa tribal society, if it ever existed, has long been a thing of the past. Today almost everywhere the more natural unit for observation, and certainly the one that most easily reflects the rapidity of change, is the territorial one. Teachers, traders, clerks, and local government officials transfer from one part of the country to another; men seek economic advantage where they can. Today it would be more realistic to concentrate on the heterogeneity of the actual local scene rather than to attempt to reconstruct the assumed homogeneity of the past. Of course, if we are to do this we will have to develop new methods that can deal with heterogeneity and rapid change. Such a shift will guide us away from some of the errors involved in the old forms of research based on the assumption that the tribe existed historically over a long period of time.

Our adoption of the tribe as a natural unit also had other implications. Unconsciously we were all Darwinians, for we wrote as though acceptable change took place only through the slow accumulation of small variations. Only then could the natural system absorb change and continue as an integrated system. Violent change or violent confrontations were seen as harmful or dangerous. Indeed, attempting to describe too faithfully the various rapid changes that might be occurring put in jeopardy our theoretical model. Changes as rapid as those we might encounter could not be related to one another in an integrated system; perhaps we were no longer studying an integrated system. The result of such speculation was to challenge the validity of our local study. The only possible escape from the impasse was to disregard as much as possible the impingement of the outside on the local scene, to allow only that much to be reflected in our descriptions as permitted us to continue with the assumption that we were studying a society with an organized way of life in which the various actions of its members were somehow harmonized.

The overemphasis on the past and on "native culture," as opposed to the growth within local society, was also conditioned by the anthropologist's audience. He was certainly not writing for the local people, though he might claim to be writing for their children and their children's children. But he was much more conscious of his immediate audience, composed of other anthropologists and various Europeans with interest in Africa—administrators, technicians, missionaries, traders, and settlers. In writing for such an audience there were certain things the anthropologist could assume his readers knew. They knew about schools, stores, prices, the color bar, the colonial system, and the organization of technical and administrative services. Thus, much detail important for an understanding of the contemporary scene could be mentioned briefly, for the readers wanted material unfamiliar to them described and explained. Inevitably the anthropologist wrote of customs as though they were strange and stressed the exotic, not necessarily because he himself found them strange by the time he wrote his report but because he was trying to explain local institutions to foreigners. If an African belonging to the local society had written an account of the same scene for his own people he would have written in different terms. He could have assumed their knowledge of such things as the kinship institutions, the marriage rules, the meaning behind religious rituals. On the other hand, he might have dwelt at length on such matters as the administrative organization, the school system, and the peculiarities of the trading stores.

Both accounts would have been equally true, though neither would have been complete. But the fact remains that for thoughtful African observers anthropological accounts usually appear either as distorted or as pretentious discussions of the commonplace.

Today our audience is much more varied. It still includes anthropologists and a variety of Europeans and Americans concerned with Africa. But today we are increasingly aware of African colleagues and the educated men and women of Africa who are deciding if we have anything to offer them. In a period of rapid change in which each country is developing along its own lines as it is freed from the uniformity imposed by the colonial system, it is no longer possible to assume that our audience either from outside Africa or inside the continent is familiar with the general framework of national political, legal, and economic institutions within which a particular local area operates. Of necessity we will have to pay greater attention to national institutions than we have in the past. At the same time, learning to write for this new audience may compel us to a new rigor in presentation. In deciding what to write about we can no longer ask ourselves the easy question—what is familiar and what is unfamiliar? We will have to ask ourselves the much more demanding question—what features must be included if we are to describe this system adequately, or what variables must be included if this hypothesis is to be tested? In this, of course, we also meet the drive from within anthropology for a more rigorous sense of problem.

For anthropologists who expect to judge and use earlier accounts of an area there is an implicit warning in what has just been said. They can expect to understand the implications of the earlier research only if they know what the writers assumed their readers to already know.

Emphasis on the tribe as the natural social unit and on the unknown rather than the familiar had advantages during the colonial period that were more or less consciously recognized by those conducting the research but that do not apply in contemporary Africa. Both emphases permitted the fieldworker to avoid violent collision with the local power structure. The tribal political system was prevented from having any direct influence on the national political scene. It was permitted to deal only with local issues and local events, and this under the guidance of district officers or magistrates who came from outside the tribe. The anthropologist might be suspected by administrators and settlers as a possible troublemaker whose actions questioned the validity of the color bar and the existing distribution of wealth and privilege. He was almost certainly an irritant, with his claims to superior understanding of the local people and their aspirations based on the fact that he lived among them. But so long as he made no attempt to comment on the administration and did not publicly challenge the existing structure of relationships in too blatant a fashion, he could usually work without much interference. As long as his writing dealt with the remnants of the pre-European political structure or with the religious or social life of the local people it was not considered dangerous, although it might be dismissed as irrelevant to practical problems. Administrators, settlers, and missionaries had little reason to feel threatened by the anthropologist's work because it did not deal with their own customs and policies.

It was fair enough, perhaps, to ignore the kinship system of settler and administrator, but in ignoring the local administration and its involvement with a larger system of power relationships, the anthropologist was working in a political vacuum. This he realized, but it was a compromise required of him if he were to continue to carry out his research within Africa. Attempts to widen the scope of investigation and include the local political officer and his staff ended in disaster. Attempts to include local settlers as objects of research might meet with outright refusal of cooperation.

This limited scope may have mattered little for some of the problems anthropologists were investigating before the late 1950's. Indeed, it may have been an advantage since it permitted the fieldworker to concentrate on a manageable field of observation. I suspect, however, that the limitation contributed to the continued use of the organic model of society, with its emphasis on harmonious functioning of institutions for the maintenance of society. Already this was preventing advances into research on more complex social systems and was limiting the examination of the problems of maintenance, as well as of problems of change. It led to an expectation of stability and continuity and to a failure to perceive the actual forces at work. We were, in fact, examining dependent systems as though they were independent systems. In analyzing a political system, we did not deal with that portion of the system that controlled the use of force save in the most casual fashion. We consequently played down the degree to which men manipulate events and seek their own interests. We paid little attention to the clash of irreconcilable differences. The functional model led us to emphasize sets of ideal relationships or immutable custom rather than the degree to which men manipulate their fellows to attain their ends. Such conflict as we reported was usually repetitive conflict seen as absorbed by the system or as working to maintain it. Our descriptive statements might contain information on the discontents of people and the breakdown of this or that accommodation, but our analytical models stressed the continuation of relationships and the maintenance of the existing system. The radical changes that have taken place in Africa within the last ten years have helped to discredit the old theories of the bases for social systems. Only now are we beginning to develop the tools for a study of conflict that allow us to deal with rapid change. Indeed, the shift from a study of equilibrium to the study of conflict is one of the significant developments within anthropology in the last decade and a half.

It is uncertain that this new development will help us very much in the immediate future in making ourselves acceptable as students of Africa. Central governments and national political parties today dominate the local scene both in towns and in rural areas as they never did in earlier years. Local and national political leaders are interchangeable; they belong to the same universe, as they did not in the past. Local and national elites share in the same social and economic institutions in a way new to Africa and to the anthropologist attempting to describe and analyze the processes of contemporary African life. There are no sealing-off points at the moment to remove the local from the national scene either for the purpose of constructing convenient analytical models or for the purpose of producing descriptions of political and social processes that can be regarded as innocuous by those in power. What the anthropologist is describing as true only of the most remote rural area may affect the position of a national leader. Earlier, local European settlers and administrators had the political power to prevent themselves from being subject to study by a foreign observer; today African leaders have stepped into the positions of power and they can prevent studies that include them as part of the scene. Although Africans objected to the type of study that emphasized the harmony of life and the continuity of relationships insofar as this seemed to imply a continuance of colonial society, today they may object even more to the examination of situations wherein men come into conflict and the way in which men seek to manipulate one another.

The new theoretical interests of anthropology, therefore, are not always such as bring them willing acceptance on the part of those who have power. What else have they to offer? Foreign anthropologists working in Africa have lost advantages that formerly accrued to them because they were foreigners of the same type as those who composed the ruling group. Once they could serve as interpreters and intermediaries between the local peoples, with whom they lived, and the foreign administration and foreign institutions, which the people saw as threatening. Frequently the anthropologist won a welcome because with his entrée to the society of those who held power he could be used by the local people to their own ends. For this, if no other reason, it was wise to court him and to assist him in his research. An anthropologist in these circumstances might be seen as someone who could become at least a partial confidant of those in many ranks of local society. Today this is no longer true. The people of the local area usually have more access than does the anthropologist to administrative and political circles in which decisions are made. They have no need of the anthropologist in the role of intermediary.

In the new Africa the anthropologist will probably be welcome only if he can find a new role for himself and a new set of research problems. He will no doubt have to accept that he is no longer committed to the holistic approach to culture and society, which has long been regarded as the hallmark of his profession. He may retain the fundamental conviction that actions can best be understood in context, but he cannot expect to know the total context. Probably the approach was never realistic; today it is inappropriate. The stage on which people move is too large; their contacts extend over too wide an area; they are aware of themselves in a new fashion as citizens not only of a new country but also of a new earth. When in 1965 I visited the villages where I had lived in the 1940's, I found their people visiting here and there throughout Zambia, at school in Europe and America, attending conferences in other parts of Africa and in Australia. Where I once found none who had gone beyond the primary school, there are now university graduates. Where the political horizon was once the district, it is now the country of Zambia and the United Nations. Already they are finding their own voices and are writing their own books in which they speak for themselves about their lives, their culture, their society. They no longer feel the need for a foreign interpreter.

Probably the same changes have taken place over much of Africa. The people who are aware of themselves as never before have no wish to be studied as objects, though they may still welcome the outsider who is prepared to respect their ways. The anthropologist can no longer expect to become the expert on a people, the unique exponent of their way of life. He now shares the stage with many other interpreters, some of whom are permanent members of the cast of the drama he watches. It is no longer enough to describe the strange, to analyze the unfamiliar. We must say something significant in local terms if we are to be welcome. On the other hand, the anthropologist can find new advantage in this change. He no longer needs to feel that he alone is responsible for the collection and presentation of data. As his work has been made more difficult in one direction, so it has been eased in others. Increasingly he can rely on colleagues in the area who have collected much of the relevant detail that formerly he had to record himself. Perhaps the anthropologist today has a greater chance to speculate, to explore a range of problems, because there are others who can provide data and check his results. If he will accept the new era, he can speak with more assurance of his intellectual findings because he no longer must cite himself as the sole authority. Increasingly we work among people with a known history, with a file of records, with a written literature. Increasingly they are able to comment on our results.

To sum up the changes which a changing Africa is forcing upon anthropological research: We can no longer consider ourselves as students of primitive peoples or of tribal culture. We cannot study people as people, for they see this as turning them into objects of research. We are increasingly dealing with contemporaries who are able and only too willing to criticize our work. But a genuine concern for comparative religion, law, economics, kinship, and other social phenomena will still give us entrée to the society of people who, like us, are concerned with the diversity of the human record and seek to understand it.

The British and the
Ethiopian Railway

by Harold G. Marcus

After the Fashoda crisis, when France decided that "schemes of territorial conquest should be abandoned . . . and attention should center on the realization of the economic possibilities of the territories already in French hands,"[1] she found the way to economic predominance in Ethiopia already open. A French company held a concession to build a railway from Jibuti to Addis Ababa. French officials thought that, should this railway be successful, "the commerce of Harrar and Abyssinia would very naturally use the railway from Jibuti,"[2] thus making Jibuti vital to the Ethiopian economy. Commercial predominance was bound to bring with it a measure of political control.

Britain's need to protect the Nile affluents meant that she could not allow any potentially dangerous European power to gain influence at Menilek's court. Sir John Lane Harrington, Great Britain's first am-

1. J. B. Christopher, "Ethiopia, the Jibuti Railway and the Powers, 1899–1906" (Ph.D. diss., Harvard University, 1942), p. 52.
2. Silvain Vignéras, *Notice sur la Côte Française des Somalis* (Paris: Imprimerie Paul Dupont, 1900), p. 78.

29

bassador in Ethiopia, strenuously opposed the attempt to make Ethiopia a French preserve. He favored an open door policy, which he regarded as compatible "with the maintenance of the territorial integrity of Abyssinia which the British Government was anxious to see preserved."[3]

The Railway Concession of 1894

The long and complex story of the Ethiopian railway began in 1897. Alfred Ilg, who later became Menilek's chief foreign adviser, constructed a model railway to show Menilek, then King of Shoa, what modern transportation could mean for the future of Ethiopia. Remembering that the British had built a small railway for moving troops into Ethiopia at the time of the Mak'dala expedition, Menilek felt that he should not build anything so strategically dangerous; moreover, he believed that the Emperor Yohannes would never approve such a project. When Menilek became King of Kings in 1889, however, Ilg again suggested that the possibility of a railroad be studied, and on 11 February 1893 Menilek issued a decree allowing Ilg to do so.

Ilg chose Jibuti as the coastal terminus for the proposed railway and then sent Leon Chefneux—a friend of Ilg's in Ethiopia, where he was variously a merchant, a trader in guns and munitions, French consular officer, Ethiopian consular officer in Europe, and adviser to Menilek—to Europe to investigate the cost of materials and possible sources of capital and to find a contractor for the job. Chefneux returned in late 1893; he reported that the projected plans for the railway were feasible and that funds for the venture would be available in France.

On 9 March 1894, Menilek granted Ilg a concession that allowed him to form a company to build a railroad.[4] Though the concession stated that the line was to be built in three sections—the first from Jibuti to Harer, the second from Harer to Int'otto (Addis Ababa), and the third from Int'otto to Kafa and the White Nile—it only dealt with the line from Jibuti to Harer. The validity of the concession extended from the date of signature until ninety-nine years after "the day

3. T. Lennox Gilmour, *Abyssinia: The Ethiopian Railway and the Powers* (London: Allston Rivers, 1906), p. 11.

4. Conrad Keller, *Alfred Ilg, Sein Leben und Seine Werke* (Frauenfeld and Leipzig: Verlag von Hüber und Co., 1918), pp. 131–34.

when the construction is finished and operation begins." The concession further stipulated that no other railroad company would "be authorised to construct concurrent lines, from either the shores of the Indian Ocean, or the Red Sea to Ethiopia, or from Ethiopia to the White Nile." However, if construction of the railway did not begin within four years of the date of signature, the concession would be nullified.[5] Upon the concession's expiration, the railway's equipment and fixed installations were to become "the property of the Government of Ethiopia without indemnity." To aid it in meeting its expenditures, the company was allowed to collect a ten-percent duty on all merchandise "coming or going" on any usable portion of the railroad, and the emperor undertook to order that all goods leaving Jibuti "ought henceforth to be transported by the railway," with the proviso that troops or war materials of the Ethiopian government would be carried at low cost in times of peace and free of charge in times of war.[6]

On 12 January 1896, the Paris firm of Duparchy and Vigouroux signed the contract to build the railroad line.[7] But in order to start construction at Jibuti, the concessionaires needed the French government's permission. Since the outcome of the Italo-Ethiopian war was then not yet certain, the French government, though it aided Menilek with arms and ammunition, did not wish to provoke Italy further by authorizing the construction of a strategic railway through French territory. Moreover, an Italian victory would have doomed the Addis Ababa-Jibuti railway project, since the Italians could then be expected to insist that any railroad to Addis Ababa start in Eritrea. In light of these considerations, the French government withheld its permission to build a railway until shortly after the Battle of Adwa.[8] A formal convention giving the Imperial Railway Company of Ethiopia the right to lay a railway to Harer over French Somali territory, to build the necessary appurtenances in Jibuti, and to collect in Jibuti the

5. A supplemental statement of 5 November 1896 gave the company an additional three years within which to start construction. F.O. 403/334, Law Officers of the Crown to Foreign Office, 16 February 1903.

6. Governo Italiano, Ministero degli Afferi Esteri, *Trattati* (Rome, 1906), I, 415; and F.O. 403/299, 1900.

7. Gouvernement de France, Tribunal Civil de la Seine, *La Concession du Chemin de Fer Franco-Ethiopien* (Paris: Librairie Générale de Droit et de Jurisprudence, 1924), p. 1.

8. Angoulvant and Vignéras, *Djibouti, Mer Rouge, Abyssinie* (Paris: Librairie Africaine et Coloniale, 1902), p. 334; F.O. 403/275, Letter of Mr. Guiyesse, 27 April 1896.

ten percent duty stipulated in the Concession in 1894 was not signed until 12 March 1897.[9]

British Financial Involvements

The Railway Company estimated that the 300 kilometers of the Jibuti-Harer section of the line would cost about 30 million francs. They "knew from the first that construction of the railway would be expensive [but] they casually assumed that they could procure with ease the large sums required."[10] By mid-June 1897, the Railway Company had gathered 4 million francs by subscription, 1 million of which was paid in.[11] Among the subscribers to this first bond issue was a British firm, the New Africa Company, Ltd.[12] Most of the big firms in France, however, did not invest as much as the Railway Company had hoped they would; they regarded the railway as a political instrument rather than a commercial undertaking, and they felt that they could not count upon the backing of the French government, whose attitude in regard to the project was unknown to them.[13] Thereupon, the Railway Company decided to create 85,000 obligations worth 500 francs each. Of the 76,500 obligations immediately issued, the concessionaires bought 56,700 for only 250 francs each. They succeeded in selling about 2,000 more, and the remainder was given to Duparchy and Vigouroux as an advance for their work. Thus, of the 38 million francs that could have been realized from the obligations issued, only 15 million were actually obtained. Even with the 4 million it received from the first bond issue, the Railway Company was still about 10 million short of the 30 million francs it needed. In December 1897 it finally obtained a loan for the balance in France.

New financial difficulties arose in 1899. This time the Railway Company was unable to raise a loan in France and it turned to British investors for help.[14] On 29 June 1900 the chairman of the New Africa Company intimated in a public speech that for commercial reasons his

9. Carlo Rosetti, *Storia Diplomatica dell'Etiopia* (*durante il Regno di Menelik II*) (Turin: Società Tipografica Editrice Nazionale, 1910), pp. 139–40.

10. Christopher, *Ethiopia*, p. 26.

11. Angoulvant and Vignéras, *Djibouti*, pp. 333–39.

12. Christopher, *Ethiopia*, p. 37.

13. Ibid., p. 46.

14. F.O. 403/322, memo. of Sanderson, 28 June 1902.

firm might aid the Imperial Railway Company of Ethiopia,[15] and in August the New Africa Company agreed to lend the Railway Company 2 million francs at six percent interest. In the following year Oceana, Ltd., and the New Egyptian Company also invested heavily in the railway.[16] In July 1901 the three British companies together with a few French investors pooled their interests and formed the International Ethiopian Railway Trust and Construction Company, Ltd.,[17] which immediately assumed control of the Imperial Railway Company. The trust took four of the eight company directorships. It also acquired options on 30,000 company bonds, or 15,000 shares. The company agreed not to issue any further obligations or shares without first obtaining the trust's agreement, and the trust held the contract for constructing the railroad line from the 225th to the 245th kilometer. In addition, the trust obtained from the company exclusive rights for constructing any of its future lines in Ethiopia.[18] Thus, by the middle of 1901 the Railway Company, though French in name, was largely controlled by British capital. This fact caused concern in French colonial circles, who immediately began a vigorous campaign to secure the French government's intervention in the building of the railroad,[19] and the Trust Company reacted by seeking the British government's protection.

Fears of French Domination

The Trust Company knew that the British government had evinced concern as early as 1898 over the possibility that French government involvement in the railway would result in French political and economic predominance in Ethiopia. At that time Sadler, the consul in the British Somaliland Protectorate, had written to Creagh, the

15. Gilmour, *Abyssinia*, p. 18.
16. The New Africa Company, Oceana, Ltd., and the New Egyptian Company, each organized to make overseas investments, held each other's shares and had interconnecting directorships. Together they held interests in the Transvaal, South Africa, Mozambique, Congo, Egypt, and Sudan. See Woolf, *Empire and Commerce in Africa* (London: Labour Research Department and George Allen Unwin, n.d.), p. 206.
17. Rosetti, *Storia Diplomatica*, p. 141.
18. F.O. 1/41, memo. by Lansdowne to Salisbury, 26 June 1901.
19. Gilmour, *Abyssinia*, pp. 20–21.

resident in Aden, warning him of the possible consequences of the railway for the Somaliland Protectorate:

> I do not think it is too much to say that, if the line is completed and no counteracting steps are taken by our Government the trade of southern Abyssinia and the Galla country [to] Zeyla will be doomed . . . [and] we should in fact lose the very means [customs duties] upon which we rely to develop the Protectorate and make it a paying concern.[20]

And Harrington, the British ambassador to Ethiopia, warned London that the railway would enable France "to lay hands on Harrar and the surrounding country should a favourable occasion occur." He also informed London that a British "group" was willing to underwrite a railroad from Zeila to the trunkline below Harer. He thought that both Ras Makonnen, Manilek's viceroy in Harraghi Province, and the emperor would prefer a line with branches to both the English and the French seaboards, "as thereby they would feel themselves more independent of one or another power"; and the "group," he reported, believed that a connection between Harer and the English seaboard would "improve the prospects of the Railway Company in all respects."[21]

The Foreign Office wrote to Sadler about the suggested Harer-Zeila line to be built under British government guarantee.[22] The British government, though unwilling to take any concrete official action, was ready to "view with approval arrangements to facilitate a line from Berbera to Zeyla and Harrar."[23] Sadler, however, felt that a British railway to Zeila, though politically expedient, could not be justified commercially. "It has . . . yet to be shown," he wrote, "that a railway would result in a large increase of trade to the Protectorate . . . [since] trade would naturally follow the best route and find its exit at Jibuti." If the railroad could have its one terminus at Berbera, instead of at Jibuti, it might succeed, but he did not "think that the French would . . . readily acquiesce in a measure that would spell ruin to their Colony unless they are prepared to abandon it, of which I

20. F.O. 403/284, Sadler to Creagh, 4 June 1898.
21. F.O. 403/275, memo. by Harrington, n.d.
22. F.O. 403/275, Foreign Office to Sadler, 14 October 1898. In this letter the name of Alfred Ochs, general manager of the New Africa Company, was mentioned. In December, Ochs wrote to the Foreign Office (F.O. 403/275, A.L. Ochs to Foreign Office, 3 December 1898). From this correspondence it is fairly clear that Harrington's "group" was made up of agents of the New Africa Company.
23. F.O. 403/275, Salisbury to Cromer, 19 December 1898.

see no present indication."[24] Harrington agreed that there was no
room for two lines, and he suggested that the best method for England
to ensure against French predominance in Ethiopia would be to take
over the French railway.[25]

Harrington had already written in November 1898 that "the more I
see of this country the more convinced I am that it is to our interest to
pay a considerable sum for Railway communications with Harrar, or
to prevent France alone having it."[26] To him the whole issue was
simply a "question of rendering British influence paramount in Abyssinia or not, [and] the chances of our making our influence paramount
are at the present moment most favourable."[27] British capital was already deeply involved in the railway, and Harrington felt that the
most obvious step would be for the British government to back a
British financial group in taking over control of the existing railway.[28]

By this time Harrington was gaining some support in his growing
concern over the railroad. Lord Cromer, while believing that "Harrington overstates the case," wrote that he "would much rather the French
should not occupy the predominant position in Abyssinia, which the
construction of the railway will probably give them. They are sure to
cause us trouble of one sort or another."[29] When Harrington warned
Menilek that the railroad concession was a monopoly which "had
placed practically the whole future commercial development of his
country in the hands of the French," Menilek replied that the concession did not interfere with British interests, since "he had only
written in the Concession that no other railway would be permitted
'near' the French railway, and that he had never intended a monopoly."[30] Harrington then asked London for a legal interpretation, and
in August the Law Officers of the Crown reported their

> opinion that the effect of the Concession granted to M. Ilg is to debar the
> Emperor from granting any Concession for the construction of a railway
> in Abyssinia which would be a competing line with that authorised by
> M. Ilg's Concession. The question whether any proposed railway would
> so compete would be a question of fact, but it would appear clear that

24. F.O. 403/298, Sadler to Salisbury, 29 March 1899.
25. F.O. 1/36, Harrington to Rodd, 22 April 1899.
26. F.O. 403/275, memo. by Harrington, 7 November 1898.
27. F.O. 403/284, memo. by Harrington, n.d.
28. F.O. 403/298, Harrington to Cromer, 14 April 1900.
29. F.O. 403/298, Cromer to Foreign Office, 15 May 1900.
30. F.O. 403/299, Harrington to Salisbury, May 30, 1900.

any line running from the coast of British Somaliland to Harrar would
be both "competing" and "near."[31]

This statement persuaded the British government that a railroad
line from Harer to the British coast was out of the question from a
legal as well as from an economic standpoint. It also aroused Menilek's
fear of France, whose friendly motives he had not previously suspected.[32] He turned to the British in hope that they would find a way
of circumventing the concession. The British Trust Company, too,
solicited the support of its government in its effort to keep control of
the Railway Company out of the hands of the French government.

The Convention of 1902

Meanwhile, the Comité de l'Afrique Française, which "considered
British designs on the railway part of a gigantic plot to expel the
French from East Africa and install British hegemony over Ethiopia,"[33]
was making some headway in its campaign to secure the support of
the republic in ridding the railway of British interventionists. To gain
the support of the comité in the forthcoming general elections, the
Waldeck-Rousseau Ministry agreed to give financial aid to the Railway
Company,[34] which by the end of 1901 had run out of funds with only
220 kilometers of rail completed.[35] On 6 February 1902, the French
government and the Railway Company signed a convention that had
the effect of making a private enterprise, as one writer put it, "the
official protégé of one state, operating in another equally sovereign
state, but without the consent of the second party."[36]

The convention provided for the transfer of the title to the railway concession from Alfred Ilg to the Railway Company. It also
stipulated that the company should have its permanent headquarters
in Paris and be governed by French law. Henceforth, the company
could assume no obligations without the approval of the French
ministers of colonies and finance. The directors of the company had to
be French and their appointments subject to approval by the ministers
of colonies and foreign affairs, who could, if they deemed this to be in

31. F.O. 403/299, Law Officers of the Crown to Foreign Office, 31 August 1900.
32. F.O. 403/312, Harrington to Lansdowne, 12 January 1901.
33. Christopher, *Ethiopia*, p. 73.
34. Gilmour, *Abyssinia*, p. 21.
35. Gouvernement de France, *La Concession*, p. 1.
36. Christopher, *Ethiopia*, p. 140.

the public interest, replace them at any time. The company could not change any of its statutes without the permission of these two ministers, nor could it cede or lease any of its property without their approval and the advice of the minister of finance. The convention granted the company a fifty-year annual subvention of 500,000 francs and the right to charge whatever rates the company found necessary to make a profit and repay its debts, as long as these rates were not so high as to drive trade away from Jibuti. The company was required, however, to share its profits with the government of French Somaliland. These provisions were to be in force for ninety-nine years from the time the railroad was completed to Addis Ababa; thereafter the rights of the concessionaires to the line between Jibuti and Dirre Dawa were to be turned over to the government of the French Somaliland Protectorate, which was also given the right to buy the concession and the part of the line between Jibuti and Awash anytime after 1 January 1920. Only in the last of its eighteen articles did the convention make any reference to Ethiopian sovereign rights: it simply noted there that any of the stipulations regarding the Ethiopian sections of the railroad would require the approval of the Ethiopian government.[37]

Since the convention made it virtually certain that France would eventually control the railway not only within its own Somaliland territory but also within Ethiopia, the British government reacted negatively and instructed Harrington to bring the terms of the convention to Menilek's attention.[38] Harrington told the emperor that

> it was now acknowledged by everyone official and private that the object of the railway was political and not commercial . . . [and] that this convention was an usurpation of his Sovereign rights, and showed a great want of respect for him on the part of the nation who had always posed as the great friend of Menelek.

He then suggested the possibility of neutralizing the "political effect of the French line by a competing line which Menelek could build to the British frontier." The concession's restriction against competing commercial railroads might be evaded, he added, if the additional line were built by the Ethiopian government, and he advised Menilek to seek a loan for such a project from the British government. On Menilek's request, Harrington promised to draft a telegram to London requesting such assistance.

37. Governo Italiano, *Trattati,* p. 673 ff.
38. F.O. 403/322, Lansdowne to Harrington, 18 March 1902.

The French minister resident in Addis Ababa, M. Lagarde, did not immediately send Menilek a copy of the convention. Harrington took advantage of the delay by securing a second audience with the king to explain the exact terms in his own way. Menilek was dismayed. If the French expected to control the railway as far as Awash, he said, "they might as well tell me to prepare for war at once." He could see that the final article, requiring his agreement for the Ethiopian part of the line, was merely intended "to smooth it all over." For, if the French had really wanted his agreement, they would have shown him the convention beforehand. He could not help wondering why France, who had always proclaimed her friendship for him, had acted so "arbitrarily."

Harrington replied:

> If you believe friendships exist between Governments, you are very much mistaken. Friendship between Governments depends on community of interests and . . . no Government will make a considerable sacrifice for another unless it is to their interest to do so.

He told Menilek then that the British government feared that the railway as a political instrument in the hands of the French would become

> a danger to his independence which it was to our interest to maintain. . . . The present situation unless neutralized or averted in some way or other, was to my mind the beginning of the end . . . the day of spheres of influence in Abyssinia was approaching . . . [and] if nothing was done by him to counterbalance the situation . . . [which] French Government control would create, then I should fail in my duty did I not do the utmost to urge my Government to come to terms with France, as regards spheres of influence before the railway could make her position stronger than our's or Italy's.

He went on to point out that if Great Britain helped him in this issue, she "did so because it was to [her] interest to do so, and not out of friendship or philanthropy."

Menilek urged Harrington not to send the telegram he had drafted earlier but instead to sound out unofficially the London government's views on the railroad problem. Harrington informed London that Menilek promised in return

> that he would sign no agreement about the railway with Lagarde without giving me beforehand a copy of any proposed arrangement, and the

necessary time to submit the same for any remarks or suggestions that my
government might wish to make. Consequently time has been gained and
we have what at present looks like a very fair chance of neutralising the
French railway if we want to and we play our cards carefully.[39]

Since Menilek wanted London's advice on what action to take,
Harrington wondered

whether, should he act on that advice, [Great Britain] will be prepared to
support him. Further, he asks, whether, should he give a partial consent
to the Convention, His Majesty's Government would lend him money for
the construction of a line from Harrar to our frontier, and themselves
construct a line from Berbera to join his, at the same time guaranteeing
him possession of Harrar against the French.

Harrington recommended that the British guarantee £2,000 to cover
the interest on the capital required to build the line from Berbera to
the Ethiopian frontier. He also suggested that they lend Menilek the
capital to build a line from Harer to the proposed British railway. "It
is hardly likely," he added, "that a better opportunity for establishing
our influence will occur than is offered by the present situation."[40]
It is well to note at this point that several French authors have
claimed that Menilek's hostility to the railway convention was due to
Harrington's activities and his dislike of the French.[41] Other writers
believe, however, that the French had only themselves to blame for
underestimating Menilek's intelligence.[42] Be that as it may, the London government decided to move cautiously. The Foreign Office took
the position "that King Menelek's proposals are of a nature which
require careful examination before they can be entertained. They
would involve us in heavy expenditure and in far-reaching responsi-
bilities."[43] Harrington, who had found an ally in Captain Ciccodicola,
the Italian minister resident, in trying to induce Menilek to continue
to withhold recognition of the 1902 Convention, to withdraw the
original railway concession, and "to give French influence a set back,"
complained to Ciccodicola that His Majesty's Government would
probably not build a railway line, "as apparently both he [Ciccodicola]
and I attached much more importance to the political importance of

39. The preceding questions are based on F.O. 1/40, Harrington to Boyle, 5 April
1902.
40. F.O. 403/322, Harrington telegram in Cromer to Lansdowne, 12 April 1902.
41. Notably Pierre-Alype, L'Empire des Négus (Paris: Librarie Plon, 1925), p. 107.
42. Keller, Ilg, p. 152; Gilmour, Abyssinia, pp. 30–31.
43. F.O. 403/322, Lansdowne to Cromer, 14 April 1902.

the French railway than those who were not personally acquainted with the political situation actually existent here."[44]

Harrington continued to press his point of view on London. He wrote:

> the question, in my opinion, is largely one of political finance, and unless we are prepared to run the risk of seeing the French in the near future paramount politically in Abyssinia, eventually Mistress of Harrar and southern Abyssinia, and in a position to divert trade from the Berbera hinterland, then it is obligatory on us to ascertain what the cost of neutralising such a situation would be.[45]

He sent Lord Lansdowne a letter he had received from Swayne, the consul in Berbera, who wrote:

> Looking far ahead I cannot but feel that after all our sacrifices in South Africa and Uganda, and the Soudan, it would be fatal to the general African interests if we allow a hostile power (France is always hostile when we are in trouble) to get a preponderating influence in Abyssinia, and at a time when we were involved in trouble in the Soudan, she might and would use her influence to make Abyssinia actively hostile to us in the Nile Basin.[46]

Lord Cromer supported Harrington's views on the British inaction concerning the railway. He feared that the French would try to extend the railway to the Upper Nile and was concerned that the Somali protectorate would suffer a considerable loss of revenue if there were no connecting line to Harer.[47]

Nonetheless, the British government continued in its reluctance to build a railway from Berbera to Addis Harer (Dirre Dawa). They felt it would be too expensive an undertaking, besides being of dubious legality.[48] Moreover, they apparently were not at all certain that it was desirable to encourage Menilek to cancel the railway concession, since they would then be practically obliged to take over the construction of the line from Harer to Addis Ababa[49] and would also risk antagonizing France at a time when the two powers were moving toward the

44. F.O. 1/40, Harrington to Boule, 3 May 1902.
45. F.O. 403/323, memo. by Harrington, n.d.
46. F.O. 403/323, Swayne to Harrington, 7 May 1902.
47. F.O. 403/323, Cromer to Lansdowne, 17 October 1902.
48. F.O. 403/323, Law Officers of the Crown to Lansdowne, 17 November 1902; F.O. 403/334, Law Officers of the Crown to Foreign Office, 23 February 1903.
49. F.O. 403/323, Lansdowne to Cromer, 24 November 1902; F.O. 1/43, Sanderson to Cromer (initialed by Lansdowne), 17 March 1903.

entente cordiale.[50] Great Britain's ultimate object in Ethiopia continued to be the safeguarding of vital British interests in the Nile Valley and, therefore, to ensure that Menilek and Ethiopia not fall under French hegemony. These aims could be achieved by sustaining Menilek in his defiance of the 1902 Convention, thus blocking further construction of the French railway until such time as France agreed to guarantee the interests of the other European powers in Ethiopia.

Harrington was therefore instructed "to dissuade King Menelek from signing the French Convention, pointing out to His Majesty the very serious effect that will be produced by his doing so."[51] The instructions added, however, that Harrington should not "put too much stress on the assistance we can render as regards railways . . . [since] the issues are scarcely of sufficient gravity to warrant expenditure of millions."[52] Harrington wrote to Lord Cromer that he would, as the London government had directed, continue working for the neutralization of the French railway. He added that if he had appeared "too eager," it was because he had to deal with the railway issue from the local and not from the imperial point of view.[53]

Menilek now tried to force the British government into an active commitment regarding the railway by sending a personal telegram:

As I have been advised by His Majesty's Government not to accept the proposed French Government Convention, I am ready, provided that His Majesty's Government agree to support me in the question to make no arrangement with the French Government in connection with the Railway question without the advice of and except in agreement with, His Majesty's Government.[54]

Although the British government had already rejected a similar proposal a year earlier, Harrington again supported Menilek, because he believed that the emperor would "make undesirable terms with the French Government unless he receives assurances of support from His Majesty's Government."[55] The British, however, again rejected the idea, this time because

50. A. J. P. Taylor, *The Struggle for Mastery in Europe, 1848–1918* (Oxford: Clarendon Press, 1954, 1957), pp. 412–13.
51. F.O. 403/334, telegram to Harrington in Lansdowne to Cromer, 20 February 1903.
52. F.O. 1/43, Sanderson to Cromer, 17 March 1903.
53. F.O. 1/43, Harrington to Cromer, 20 March 1903.
54. F.O. 403/334, Menilek telegram in Harrington to Cromer, 10 April 1903.
55. F.O. 403/334, Harrington to Cromer, 10 April 1903.

it is almost certain that the French Government would claim the right of
holding direct discussions with the Emperor Menelek on the subject of
the Railway Convention, and would maintain that they cannot admit
the right of any other Power, which has only indirect and secondary interests, to intervene in the matter.[56]

In June 1903, the emperor in a last attempt to gain British aid sent
Harrington a letter summarizing his views on the railway. He explained that

> originally the Emperor gave the Concession to a private business on the
> understanding that no government should take part in the enterprise.
> . . . His Majesty, the Emperor, is opposed to the French government par-
> ticipating in the enterprise because he does not wish to give preferential
> treatment to one power at the expense of others. . . . French control of
> the railway . . . will necessarily give them an exclusive advantage in the
> trade of all the eastern parts of Ethiopia. His Majesty does not like this to
> happen. His Majesty believes that such control of the railway by a single
> power is a direct threat to the independence of his empire . . . [and] a
> breach of good faith on the part of the original concessionaires. . . .
> The Emperor does not want the French to enjoy much more influence in
> his empire than the other powers.

He then again suggested that the British should build a railway from
Berbera to the Abyssinian border and that he in turn would construct
the line from there to Harer. "There is only one problem here: it is
a financial one. It can, however, be solved by the British Government
itself."[57]

When this letter received no more response from the British government than his previous ones had, Menilek proceeded to take his own
steps to block further railway construction by the French. He had
already shown his displeasure with the Railway Company by refusing
to attend the inauguration of the first section of the line, 310 kilometers
between Jibuti and Addis Harer, which was completed in December
1902.[58] He then damaged the company's borrowing power by with-
drawing its privilege of collecting a ten percent levy on merchandise
in transit, because "he had originally granted the privilege to a private
company and not to a foreign government."[59] He also withdrew his

56. F.O. 403/334, Lansdowne to Cromer, 23 April 1903.
57. F.O. 1/43, Menilek to Harrington, Sene 6 1895 E.C. (approximately 13 June
1903), translated by Getachew Tebicke.
58. F.O. 403/334, Monson to Lansdowne, 24 February 1903.
59. Christopher, *Ethiopia,* p. 210.

agreement to channel all goods requiring transport between Jibuti and Addis Harer toward the railway,[60] thus causing the railway's traffic to drop to such a low level that the company's receipts could not cover current expenses and pay the interest on bonds. Finally, the emperor refused to sanction the construction of the second section of the railway line, from Addis Harer to Addis Ababa, and the company was forced to stand by idly eating up its capital.[61]

Pressures for Internationalization of the Railway

The Railway Company had procured 11,300,000 francs from an insurance company that had bought up the subvention of 500,000 francs a year granted in the 1902 Convention. Three million of this was used to pay back the English lenders, who continued, however, to hold the bonds they had bought. The remainder was used to finish the first section of the line. Because of Menilek's continuing refusal to agree to the convention the company could not procure additional funds in Paris, and so from 1902 on it suffered an annual deficit of more than 1 million francs.[62]

The plight of the Railway Company brought the Trust Company once again into the picture. The Trust Company helped the Railway Company to meet interest commitments with several large loans[63] and it sought in other ways to harmonize English and French interests in the area. The Ochs brothers felt that many influential circles in France wanted to come to an agreement with Britain on outstanding Franco-British problems in Ethiopia, and they told the British government to rely on the Trust Company's influence to induce the administration of the railway to come to a suitable arrangement.[64] Alfred Ochs was certain that the French government could also be brought to terms "if Menelek refuses to allow them to continue their line, which, if he is sure of support, he will do, [and then] they [the French government] will accept the situation without any real fuss."[65]

The British government instructed Clerk, their chargé d'affaires

---

60. Sylvia Pankhurst, "The Franco-Ethiopian Railway and Its History," *Ethiopia Observer* 1 (1958): 381.
61. Gilmour, *Abyssinia*, p. 35.
62. Gouvernement de France, *La Concession*, pp. 1–2.
63. F.O. 401/11, memo. on the Railway Situation by Gilmour, 1 January 1908.
64. F.O. 1/43, Ochs Brothers to Sanderson, 31 July 1903.
65. F.O. 1/43, Harrington to Sanderson, 20 November 1903.

in Addis Ababa, to start negotiations for the establishment of a connection between the Ethiopian railway and a proposed British line
from Berbera to the British Somaliland border. The British had
shown earlier that it really had no intention of building this link.
Menilek knew this, but he apparently fell in with the British maneu-
ver so that he could tell the French "that he has been advised by
[the British] to withhold his consent from any proposals to which he
is not pledged under the existing contract, pending the result of this
negotiation."[66] Possibly he also still hoped to involve the British in
the building of the rail connection, since Harrington was again pressing London "for . . . a pledge of our support to Menelek and a
pledge to commence construction of a competing scheme."[67]

The government in London was beginning to be annoyed with
Harrington's continued opposition to its policy on the railway issue,
particularly while the Anglo-French *entente* was being negotiated.
Cromer warned Harrington on 28 November 1903 not to exceed his
instructions. In reply Harrington hinted that he was willing to take
the risk. In another letter Cromer pointed out to Harrington that,
while it sought to prevent French predominance in Ethiopia, Great
Britain was not willing to go to war with France to achieve that objective.

Cromer thought that the solution to the railway problem lay in
an agreement between France and Great Britain.[68] Lord Lansdowne
went a little farther:

In Lord Lansdowne's opinion [it would] be better that the line should be
an international undertaking or at all events that England, France, and
Italy should all have a share in the direction and management rather
than it should be under Anglo-French control.[69]

Explaining this suggestion, Lord Cromer wrote to Sanderson that

what is meant by internationalisation . . . [is] I think . . . an equal control by all the three powers interested over the railway throughout its
course, and perfect equality of commercial treatment in respect to all
goods landed at Jibuti for transit.[70]

The Trust Company apparently convinced the British government

66. F.O. 403/334, Lansdowne to Cromer, 13 November 1903.
67. F.O. 1/50, memo. by Harrington, 24 January 1904.
68. F.O. 1/50, Cromer to Sanderson, 14 January 1904.
69. F.O. 1/50, memo. for Cromer (initialed by Lansdowne), 29 January 1904.
70. F.O. 1/50, Cromer to Sanderson, 6 February 1904.

that France would ultimately consent to the internationalization of the railway. In early February, Albert Ochs, general manager of the Trust Company, told Cromer that the colonialist group in the French Assembly would accept an Anglo-French arrangement on the railway.[71] Later, in a memorandum sent to the British government to explain what terms the French colonialist group would accept, Ochs said that "the Company would become international; it would be administered by Frenchmen, Englishmen, and Italians in equal number. The President would be French."[72] In early March he informed the British that the Colonialist party in the French Assembly saw the hopelessness of obtaining from the French government enough capital to complete the present railway, "and they are therefore ready to give their support to any reasonable proposal for giving the Company an international character and thus distributing the burden."[73] Further evidence of an apparent French *volte-face* on the subject of the railway appeared when Deloncle, one of the leaders of the Colonialist party in the Assembly, came to the British Embassy and stated that he was "well aware" that Britain would continue to block a railway "under exclusively French auspices," and "to avoid this . . . the bulk of the Colonial Party desire to come to terms with England, and if need be, with Italy also, with a view to internationalizing the railway."[74] In 1904, however, during preliminary talks with the British about the Tripartite Agreement, the French did not mention the possibility of internationalization[75] and, contrary to the statements of Trust Company officials, never seem to have seriously considered such a move. Deloncle's statement was apparently no more than a reflection of the impatience of the colonialist group in the assembly. The French government clung to the idea of a "French" railway with great determination and rapidly convinced Lord Lansdowne that they would never give up their proprietary rights over the railway.

On March 25 Menilek and Chefneux signed an agreement to extend the railway to Addis Ababa. Clerk immediately went to Menilek and "complained of the breach of faith to Harrington and myself."[76] Menilek replied that Chefneux "had suddenly offered to accept any

71. Ibid.
72. F.O. 1/50, memo. by Albert Ochs, 25 February 1904.
73. F.O. 1/50, Monson to Lansdowne, 4 March 1904.
74. F.O. 1/50, memo. by Mr. de Bunsen, 8 March 1904.
75. See Harold G. Marcus, "A Preliminary History of the Tripartite Treaty of December 13, 1906," *The Journal of Ethiopian Studies* 2 (1964).
76. F.O. 403/364, telegram to Clerk in Cromer to Lansdowne, 1 April 1904.

conditions His Majesty wished to impose, and that it therefore seemed to be a good opportunity for a favourable settlement of the whole railway question." He added, "by the preamble all previous Concessions and Agreements had been cancelled." Clerk was openly skeptical and asked to see the agreement. He found that

> the actual meaning was that the Agreement about the section from Kaffa to the White Nile (a matter of complete indifference at the present moment) only was cancelled. . . . All reference to the existing railway was left out, and His Majesty thereby tacitly assented to the Convention between the Railway Company and the French Government of the 6th February, 1902.

After he explained the deception to Menilek, he recommended that the emperor recall the document before it was signed by Ilg, the third contracting party, and that he should "make it quite clear that he would acknowledge no Agreement or Concession unless his own intentions were therein expressed in language of whose meaning there could be no doubt."

Clerk suggested three possible explanations for Menilek's ill-conceived and precipitous behavior: first, "His Majesty . . . has an unshaken confidence in his own astuteness as a maker of Treaties and Conventions, and will not believe that any one can get the better of him in such matters"; second, "His Majesty is apt to get wearied of questions which he is constantly being urged to settle, and is sometimes inclined to finish them off at any cost, in the hope he will thereby be troubled no more"; third,

> M. Chefneux . . . [probably] confessed to the Emperor that the greater part of the indemnity paid after Adowa by the Italians to His Majesty, and by him entrusted to M. Chefneux, had been invested in the Railway [Company]; if the extension was not granted, the Railway Company would go bankrupt and His Majesty would lose all his money. This reason, if true, would be quite sufficient to account for the action of His Majesty, to whom a threatened loss of actual cash appeals with especial force.[77]

At the end of March Menilek's secretary called at the British Legation to tell Clerk that the emperor had retrieved the agreement from

---

77. The two previous paragraphs except for specific references have been drawn from F.O. 402/346, Clerk to Lansdowne, 2 April 1904. See also F.O. 403/346, agreement signed by Menilek and Chefneux, 25 March 1904, and the amended agreement, 27 March 1904.

Chefneux and that he desired Clerk's suggestions for possible amendments. Clerk's suggestions were incorporated into a revised draft under whose terms

> all monopoly is done away with, no interference on the part of any Government will be admitted without Menelek's consent, and equal treatment on the railway will be granted to all nations. This solution of the question, though not the best, should insure, at least, the independence of Abyssinia, if His Majesty is firm in resisting French pressure.[78]

The British chargé d'affaires thus blocked Chefneux, who, however, refused to accept the amended agreement.[79] In August Lagarde explained to Menilek the importance of a letter authorizing the construction of the second section of the railway. He pointed out that the company's troubles would lead to bankruptcy if Menilek did not provide some assurance that the company would be allowed to continue the work, and he told the emperor that such a letter "would have no effect on the negotiations now in progress in Europe." Lagarde received the letter he wanted on 8 August. When Harrington saw a copy on 26 August, he told Menilek

> that the wording of the letter, doubtless unintentionally, ignored the fact that the railway question was now being discussed at home, and tended therefore to complicate matters very considerably, unless His Majesty made it quite clear that, of course, his consent to the continuation of the railway was conditional on the agreement of the three powers . . . thereto.

Menilek thereupon wrote another letter to Lagarde stating that his commitment in the letter required the consent of Italy and Great Britain. Lagarde refused to receive this letter, but Menilek was satisfied that he had seen its contents.

Harrington was quite upset about Lagarde's action, since Lagarde had promised to do nothing regarding the railway until a conclusion had been reached in Europe, "an undertaking which I reciprocated and observed." Since the French had already "trapped" Menilek twice, Harrington requested and received from him a letter granting the British government the right to construct a line from Berbera, through Ethiopia, to the Sudan.

> This letter not only renders the intrigues of my French colleague or of

78. F.O. 403/346, telegram by Clerk in Cromer to Lansdowne, 1 April 1904.
79. F.O. 403/346, telegram by Clerk in Cromer to Lansdowne, 2 April 1904.

any one else here comparatively harmless, but should also enable your
Lordship to insure France coming to reasonable terms on the question of
internationalisation, as the existence of a British line from Berbera to
Harrar, even if continued no further, would suffice to wreck the French
railway.[80]

Lord Lansdowne then asked Cambon, the French ambassador in
London, to request his government to restrain Lagarde from further
separate negotiations with Menilek about the railway while the general
talks between England, France, and Italy were in progress.[81]

The Ethiopian State Bank and the Railway

In his next attempt to find some way out of the railway stalemate
and to provide himself with greater bargaining power in relation to
France, Menilek informed Harrington that he would be willing to
grant a British firm a fifty-year concession for a state bank with exclusive privileges.[82] Cromer was delighted with this idea, which would
provide Great Britain with some control over Ethiopia's economic life
and might provide Menilek with enough capital to build the second
part of the railway. He immediately telegraphed Harrington that the
Bank of Egypt would send an agent duly authorized to study and
negotiate the details of the question to Addis Ababa.[83]

On 10 March 1905 Menilek signed the concession for the bank.[84]
The charter gave the bank a capital of £500,000 and stipulated that
the head office was to be in Addis Ababa. The bank was incorporated
for fifty years. It was to be the only bank in Ethiopia, had the sole
right to issue bank notes, and had to be consulted whenever the government undertook to mint coins. All Ethiopian government funds
had to be deposited in the bank, and the bank was to be given
preference for all government loans. The charter further stipulated
that after expenses had been paid, ten percent of the profit should be
placed in reserve and a seven percent dividend paid to shareholders.
Of the remainder Menilek would get twenty percent and the bank

80. F.O. 403/346, Harrington to Lansdowne, 31 August 1904; Menilek to Lagarde,
28 August 1904; Menilek to Harrington, 28 August 1904.
81. F.O. 1/50, memo. initialed by Lansdowne, 16 September 1904.
82. F.O. 403/346, Cromer to Lansdowne, 20 December 1904.
83. F.O. 403/346, Cromer to Lansdowne, 28 December 1904. See also F.O. 401/8,
Cromer to Palmer, 24 December 1904 and Palmer to Cromer, 27 December 1904.
84. F.O. 401/8, Cromer to Lansdowne, 14 March 1905.

could use the rest as it saw fit.[85] Even though several nationalities were represented on the board of the bank and stock had to be sold on the open market, the number of Englishmen in the administration was sufficiently large to give Britain control.[86] Harrington wrote to Cromer:

> I sincerely trust that there may be no hitch in the formation of this bank, as I am firmly convinced that it will be of inestimable value to the development of Abyssinia, and the fact that it is under English direction is an asset of great value in the political situation here.[87]

MacGillivray, whom the National Bank of Egypt had sent to make the survey of Ethiopia's banking needs, had reported that the proposed bank would act essentially as a ministry of finance, even though during its first few years of existence it would do little more than cover its expenses. He also saw that the second section of the railway could be built with the funds Menilek had in his treasury reserve along with a loan from the bank.[88] Apparently MacGillivray made Menilek aware of this fact, or else the emperor had foreseen the possibility of using the bank's resources as a threat to obtain concessions from the French. On 1 April he asked Harrington to

> tell your government that after the experience I have had of French policy in my country, I fail to see the value to me of any Agreement whereby the French Government have control of a railway to my capital, and that, failing internationalization of the railway in my territory, I shall myself undertake the construction of the line.[89]

On April 11 he called the ministers of France, Italy, England, and Russia and a number of Ethiopian dignitaries to a meeting. He told them:

> for three years now work [on the railway] has ceased and you know the reasons; time passes in sterile discussions. . . . It is with great regret that I see the months and years slip away without our friends being able to come to an accord on this question. . . . It is to put an end to this state of affairs that I called you here today. I come to ask you to inform your governments [of] the decision that I desire to take relative to this question of the railway. . . . I would be happy to see the guaranteed construction of the railway as soon as possible by an agreement between the several powers giving to each of them the necessary guarantees. Up to

85. F.O. 401/8, The Bank Charter, 11 March 1905.
86. F.O. 401/8, memo. by Sir Palmer, 20 April 1905.
87. F.O. 401/8, Harrington to Cromer, 14 March 1905.
88. F.O. 401/8, report by MacGillivray, 14 March 1905.
89. F.O. 401/8, Harrington to Lansdowne, 1 April 1905.

now, I have received no proposition on your part. If I receive no proposition from your Governments, nor any plan reconciling your . . . interests, which puts an end to this conflict, I would see it necessary, to assure the construction of the railway to undertake the construction myself, without asking nor accepting agreement from any part.

In reply to Menilek's statement, Harrington said that the best way to solve the problem would be to allow all interested nations to share in the capital required for the construction of the railway. Lagarde remained silent, and Menilek berated him and his government for signing the 1902 Convention, which had brought on the railway impasse and endangered his sovereignty. The Italian representative stated that his government favored the internationalization of the railway, while the Russian minister, who supported Lagarde, merely said that he would make Menilek's intentions known to his government.[90]

The Tripartite Treaty

Despite Harrington's statement at the meeting, the British government did not want to see Menilek take over the railway. By this time safeguards for British interests in the Nile Valley had been gained from France and Italy, and Britain no longer cared who controlled the railway so long as there was no discrimination on the line.[91] When MacGillivray left Egypt to become director of the new bank, Harrington was instructed "to prevent his doing any thing by which Menelek might be encouraged to reject the proposals which the British, French, and Italian governments have laid before him,"[92] and in February 1906, when some of the local bank directors tried to take over the railway, the British made every effort to block their action.[93] They were convinced that Menilek's speech on the railway and the bank's actions that followed were the direct result of MacGillivray's influence, and in March 1906 Lord Cromer wrote to Grey "that the inevitable recall of Mr. MacGillivray is necessary."[94] But he stayed, because Harrington felt that "to recall him would be a fatal mistake, as the Emperor would

90. Gouvernement de France, *La Concession,* pp. 3–6.
91. See Marcus, "A Preliminary History."
92. F.O. 401/8, Cromer to Lansdowne, 1 December 1905.
93. F.O. 401/9, Cromer to Grey, 7 February 1906.
94. F.O. 401/9, Cromer to Grey, 19 March 1906.

thus be convinced that the bank is a political institution, as he hears on all sides."[95] Cromer, still concerned

> that the Emperor Menelek . . . [would] take the railway in hand himself . . . [suggested] that it might be well for Sir John Harrington to receive . . . instructions to use all his influence with the Emperor to dissuade His Majesty from taking any definite action on his own account until the termination of the political negotiations now in progress.

He added that the governor of the Bank of Egypt should send similar instructions to MacGillivray.[96]

In late June Menilek suddenly interrupted an audience with Harrington to announce that the time limit for a railway settlement had passed and that he would now build the railway himself. Harrington was able to persuade him to wait a few more days and wrote to Grey that unless some agreement was arrived at soon, he would not be able to restrain Menilek.[97]

The Tripartite Treaty, reconciling the differences of England, France, and Italy, was initialed on 4 July 1906,[98] making it unnecessary for Menilek to take over construction of the railway. The treaty recognized the right of a French company to continue the railway from Dirre Dawa, on condition that the railway practice no discrimination "in . . . matters of trade and transit." Great Britain, Italy, and Ethiopia were each granted the right to have one of their nationals on the board of the French company, and France was given the same right on any future British or Italian railways that might be built in Ethiopia. The treaty did not reconcile Menilek's differences with the French, making further negotiations between Ethiopia and France necessary. But it satisfied Great Britain's political aims in the area.

95. F.O. 401/9, Harrington to Cromer, 23 March 1906.
96. F.O. 401/9, Cromer to Grey, 5 April 1906.
97. F.O. 401/9, Harrington to Grey, 29 June 1906.
98. F.O. 401/9, Grey to Lister, 4 July 1906.

Isike, *Ntemi* of Unyanyembe

by Norman R. Bennett

By the middle of the nineteenth century the African and Arab trading network reaching from the East African coast to Lake Tanganyika and beyond was able to supply the markets of Zanzibar and the coast with the staples of the interior trade, ivory and slaves. Among the many African peoples participating in this commercial system as independent traders and as porters in Arab-led caravans were the Nyamwezi of what is now called central Tanzania. Their importance derived from the strategic position of their homeland, which dominated the central portion of the trade route. By the 1820's the Arabs had felt the need of a center among the Nyamwezi, and after some years they decided to establish it in the Unyanyembe chiefdom.

A biographical sketch of Isike, ruler of Unyanyembe from about 1877 to 1893, is presented here, based on German, British, French, and Belgian private and governmental sources, both published and unpublished. Some oral information is included in these sources, but most of it is not the product of modern methods of collecting oral data. Thus, despite the large body of historical material on the central Tanzanian region for the middle and later periods of the nineteenth century, any biographical effort must suffer from the lack of African sources so vital for giving perspective to European-derived information. On the other hand, African and other researchers now engaged in the collecting of oral data do not always have available to them the full range of written sources. Where possible, a useful collaboration can result from the two methods of research. A recent example of this is a study by an East African scholar of another nineteenth-century Nyamwezi leader, Mirambo, which incorporates earlier written efforts along with new insights derived from interviews.[1]

The Emergence of Isike

The ruler of the Nyamwezi chiefdom of Unyanyembe, located near present-day Tabora, was inextricably tied into the Arab trading structure of eastern Africa. His state had become the principal base for Arab settlement of the interior, and a working relationship between Arab and African was necessary to keep commerce flowing. But the relationship was unstable as tensions arose between Nyamwezi rulers and Arab traders over the distribution of the profits of trade and over the extent of Arab power and influence within the Nyamwezi chiefdom. Thus, to understand and depict the life of Isike, one must be aware of the competition for power among Nyamwezi claimants for the chiefdomship, the impact of the Arabs on these quarrels, and the relationship of the later German rulers to the two groups.

The system of succession to the office of chief, or *ntemi,* among the Nyamwezi invited rivalry among many possible successors and often led to civil strife.[2] In Unyanyembe, the Arab presence further contributed to the instability. Prior to the death of *ntemi* Fundikira I in 1858 or 1859,[3] an agreement was apparently reached between the

1. See J. B. Kabeya, *Ntemi Mirambo* (Nairobi, Dar es Salaam, and Kampala: East African Literature Bureau, 1966).

2. R. G. Abrahams, "Succession to the Chiefship in Northern Unyamwezi," in *Succession to High Office,* ed. Jack Goody (Cambridge: Cambridge University Press, 1966), pp. 127–41, examines this with specific reference to some of the Kamba chiefdoms of Unyamwezi. There is also a valuable general discussion in Audrey I. Richards, "African Kings and Their Royal Relatives," *Journal of the Anthropological Institute of Great Britain and Ireland* 91 (1961): 135–50.

3. Speke to Rigby, 10 March 1861, in *General Rigby, Zanzibar and the Slave Trade,* ed. Mrs. Charles E. B. Russell (London: G. Allen and Unwin, 1935), p. 238; Richard F. Burton, "The Lake Regions of Central Equatorial Africa . . . ," *Journal of the Royal Geographical Society* 29 (1859): 204; James Augustus Grant, *A Walk Across Africa* (London and Edinburgh, 1864), p. 52.

Arabs and the Nyamwezi setting the terms for cooperation in trade: the Arabs were exempted from paying taxes on merchandise brought into Unyanyembe, while the Nyamwezi reaped the material benefits of the Arabs settling in their territory rather than in that of some rival Nyamwezi state.[4] Fundikira was succeeded by Mnywa Sere. With the aid of Muhammed bin Juma, an Arab who had married one of Fundikira's daughters, Mnywa Sere defeated the bid of another claimant, Mkasiwa. Once in power, however, Mnywa Sere attempted to gain an increased share of the profits of the trade flowing through Unyanyembe. His exactions were borne for a time, but when he moved against the family of Muhammed bin Juma, the Arabs joined together to drive Mnywa Sere out of the chiefdom.[5]

Mkasiwa then became *ntemi* with the support of the Arabs. He was generally considered a weak man and an Arab puppet.[6] There can be little doubt that he badly needed Arab support. Mnywa Sere actively opposed him until his death in 1865; two other Nyamwezi leaders, Mirambo and Nyungu-ya-Mawe, seriously threatened Unyanyembe in the 1870's.[7] When Mkasiwa died in 1876, he was succeeded by his son Isike. No less than his father, Isike needed Arab support to maintain himself in the face of Mirambo's and Nyungu's opposition.[8]

Without adequate African sources, and these are lacking, a wholly satisfactory description of Isike is difficult to gather. He may have had some knowledge of the world outside of Unyamwezi. There is record of a visit to Zanzibar in 1865 by two sons of Mkasiwa; only one, Swetu, is named, but perhaps the other was Isike.[9] European characterizations of Isike abound. They portray him as an Arab puppet

4. Alison Smith, "The Southern Section of the Interior, 1840–84," in *History of East Africa*, eds. Roland Oliver and Gervase Mathew (Oxford: Oxford University Press, 1963), vol. 1, p. 279. See also Burgess's letter of 11 September 1839, in *The Missionary Herald* 36 (1840): 119; Charles Pickering, *The Races of Man and Their Geographical Distribution* (London, 1849), p. 195.

5. *Maisha ya Hamed bin Muhammed el Murjebi yaani Tippu Tip*, Supplement to the East African Swahili Committee Journals No. 28/2, July 1958, and No. 29/1, January 1959, pp. 39–43. For a genealogical table of the Unyanyembe dynasty, see Aylward Shorter, "Nyungu-ya-Mawe and the 'Empire of the Ruga-Rugas,'" *Journal of African History* 9 (1968): 240.

6. For example, Grant, *Walk Across Africa*, pp. 52–53. A recent scholar affirms that Mnywa Sere was replaced by the Arabs with "a series of more compliant puppets." The "series," however, includes only two rulers, Mkasiwa and Isike—and the description does not justly describe Isike. Smith, "Southern Interior," p. 279.

7. Shorter, "Nyungu-ya-Mawe," pp. 239–43.

8. Ibid., pp. 243–53; C. Velten, *Schilderungen der Suaheli* (Göttingen, 1901), p. 10.

9. Steere's diary, entry of 13 December 1865, A.1.II, Universities' Mission to Central Africa Archives, London.

(as his father had been), a drunkard, and a generally worthless character in his early years, who later on became a fierce and resolute enemy of the Arabs and an even more determined foe of the new German rulers of East Africa. His early subservience to the Arabs was probably due to expediency: when he no longer felt the need for Arab support he quickly changed his attitude.[10]

The circumstances of life at Isike's center, his *ikulu,* made it relatively easy for him to maintain his position toward the Arabs, who lived in their own centers in Unyanyembe apart from the Nyamwezi. Isike did not generally leave his *ikulu;*[11] unlike Mirambo, Nyungu, and Mtinginya of Usongo, he was not a renowned leader of warriors.[12] Apart from having to meet specific Arab demands, he remained supreme in his own sphere as the ruler of his people. At the same time he profited from the Arab presence through trade revenues and the general prosperity of his state.[13] His early subservience to the Arabs is best explained as an adaptation to the realities of Arab power, since an alliance between the Arabs and his rivals would have presented an irresistible threat to his position in Unyanyembe.[14]

Early Relations with Arabs

When Isike took office in 1877, the official head of the Arab community was Said bin Salim, who had served as governor for about fif-

10. For some characterizations of Isike, see Jerome Becker, *La Troisième Expédition Belge* (Brussels, n.d.), pp. 91, 152, 284; Adolph Burdo, *Les Belges dans l'Afrique Centrale. De Zanzibar au Lac Tanganika* (Brussels, 1886), p. 51; *A l'Assaut des Pays Nègres. Journal des Missionnaires d'Alger dans l'Afrique Equatoriale* (Paris, 1884), p. 164.

11. Wilhelm Blohm, *Die Nyamwezi: Land und Wirtschaft* (Hamburg, 1931), p. 175; idem., *Die Nyamwezi: Gesellschaft und Weltbild* (Hamburg, 1933), p. 68. For a recent illuminating discussion about the office of *ntemi* see R. G. Abrahams, *The Political Organization of Unyamwezi* (Cambridge: Cambridge University Press, 1967), pp. 33–39.

12. Fritz Spellig, "Die Wanjamwesi," *Zeitschrift für Ethnologie* 59 (1927): 204; Charles Hespers, ed., *A Travers l'Afrique avec Stanley & Emin-Pacha. Journal de Voyage du Père Schynse* (Paris, 1890), pp. 114–15.

13. Burdo, *Les Belges,* pp. 302, 305.

14. Such an interpretation leads to reconsideration of statements by a recent scholar that the Arabs of the interior existed on the "suffrance" of the local African population and that the Arabs feared involvement in local quarrels since it would stop trade. The Arabs of Unyanyembe preferred to avoid involvements, but they first tried to create a situation that would make involvement unnecessary. Given the unstable Nyamwezi political system, the one existing on sufferance was really

teen years.[15] Said bin Salim owed his position more to the powerful Indian customs master of Zanzibar than to that island's ruler, Barghash bin Said,[16] who had no real power to intervene in the affairs of Unyanyembe.[17] Eventually inter-Arab rivalry in Unyanyembe led to the deposition of Said bin Salim. He was accused by his rivals of cooperating with Mirambo during the Arab-Mirambo hostilities of the early 1870's.[18] Expelled by Isike,[19] he went over to Mirambo, who gave him shelter.[20]

Isike acted at the instigation of Abdallah bin Nasibu, a very popular member of the Unyanyembe Arab community. Abdallah bin Nasibu was a successful trader and raider known for his generosity in the distribution of booty won in battle.[21] With the elimination of Said bin Salim he became the uncontested leader of the Arabs of Unyanyembe, making Isike's apparent subservience to him all the more necessary as Mirambo, Nyungu, and other Nyamwezi rivals all remained active in their opposition to the *ntemi* of Unyanyembe.[22]

Isike. Cf. J. Spencer Trimingham, *Islam in East Africa* (Oxford: Clarendon Press, 1964), p. 24; P. Ceulemans, *La Question Arabe et Le Congo (1883–1892)*, Académie Royale des Sciences Coloniales, Classe des Sciences Morales et Politiques, Mémoires, n.s., t.22, fasc.1 (Brussels, 1959), p. 27. This point is recognized regarding Unyanyembe in R. G. Abrahams, *The Peoples of Greater Unyamwezi, Tanzania* (London: International African Institute, 1967), p. 26.

15. Smith to Wright, 1 January 1877, with addenda of 16 January, C.A6/022, Church Missionary Society Archives, London [CMS].

16. See Velten, *Schilderungen,* p. 10; Livingstone to Granville, 14 November 1871, in *Life & Findings of Dr. Livingstone* (London, 1874), p. 275; note in E-67, Zanzibar Archives [ZA].

17. Kirk to Secretary of State for India, 2 September 1872, Secret Letters Received (various) p. 49, India Office Archives, London; Kirk to F.O., 25 January 1872, E-62, ZA.

18. Hore to Kirk, 15 April 1879, in Kirk to F.O., 7 November 1879, Q-22, ZA. Barghash of Zanzibar might have favored the deposition. See Horace Waller, ed., *The Last Journals of David Livingstone* (London, 1874), vol. 2, p. 183; Mackay's journal, entry of 13 May 1878, C. A6/016(b), CMS; note in E-67, ZA.

19. Kirk to Derby, 4 April 1878, F.O. 84/1514, Public Record Office, London [PRO]; Mackay'to Wright, 25 May 1878, C. A6/016, CMS.

20. For Mirambo's views see Thomson to Mullens, 4 August 1878, London Missionary Society Archives, London [LMS]; Henry M. Stanley, *How I Found Livingstone* (London, 1872), p. 268.

21. Richard F. Burton, *The Lake Regions of Central Africa* (London, 1860), vol. 1, p. 233; Becker, *La Troisième,* p. 89.

22. Southon to Kirk, 9 September 1879, K-1, ZA; Dutrieux' letter of 30 January 1879, in Association Internationale Africaine, *Rapports sur les Marches de la Première Expédition* (Brussels, 1879), p. 6; Becker, *La Troisième,* p. 100; Jerome Becker, *La Vie en Afrique* (Brussels, 1887), vol. 1, p. 245, and vol. 2, p. 86; Southon to L.M.S., 21 June 1880, LMS; Wookey to L.M.S., 26 January 1881, LMS.

In 1881 a French trader, E. Sergère, established a trading center in Unyanyembe with the approval of Sultan Barghash. The center was designed to supply goods to passing caravans and to allow Sergère to purchase ivory for export to Zanzibar. Sergère not only thus challenged Arab control of the local ivory market but also roused the ire of Isike. He sent, or had plans to send, gunpowder to Mirambo. He also became close to Swetu, Isike's brother, thus stimulating the latent dynastic fears of the Nyamwezi ruler—there were rumors circulating at the time that Swetu, with Sergère's aid, would poison Isike. The result was that Abdallah bin Nasibu and other Arabs made every effort to stop all individuals from trading with the Frenchman and that Isike followed with threats that caused Sergère to flee Unyanyembe.[23] Both the Arabs and Isike had thus good reasons for expelling the trader, but contemporary reporters, convinced of the dominant influence of the Arabs, believed that Isike had been forced to act by Abdallah bin Nasibu's assertions of a plot among Sergère, Swetu, and Mirambo to murder Isike and divide Unyanyembe. Abdallah bin Nasibu did indeed bring forward the idea of a plot, but the implication that Isike was simply following orders is unlikely. There was an element of plausibility in such a plot given the political conditions of Unyanyembe, especially since it was known that Sergère had made overtures to trade with Mirambo. Self-interest made Isike's action necessary, and there was little need of any pressure from the Arabs.

The aftermath of the Sergère affair seriously affected Isike's future. On his return to Zanzibar, Sergère protested against his treatment in Unyanyembe to both the French consul and Sultan Barghash. The end result was that the Sultan recalled Abdallah bin Nasibu from Unyanyembe during the latter part of 1881. It remains unclear why the Arab leader obeyed the Sultan's order in view of the Sultan's limited authority in the interior. There is also doubt as to Barghash's reasons for issuing the recall, though it appears that Abdallah bin Nasibu was heavily in debt to Indian merchants in Zanzibar and that he was connected wth an Arab faction hostile to the Sultan. In any case, the Arab leader returned to Zanzibar, where he was imprisoned and where he later died, allegedly from poison administered on Barghash's orders. Abdallah bin Nasibu's brother, Shaykh bin Nasibu,

23. Copplestone's journal, entries of 18, 19, 20, and 28 March 1881, G3. A6/01, CMS; Stokes to Wigram, 14 June 1881, CMS; Kirk to F.O., May 5, 1881, Q-25, ZA; Becker, *La Troisième,* pp. 152–53; Lucien Heudebert, ed., *Vers les Grands Lacs de l'Afrique Orientale d'après les Notes de l'Explorateur Georges Révoil* (Paris, 1900), p. 379; Southon to L.M.S., 23 February 1881, LMS.

carried on as head of the Arab community in Unyanyembe during his brother's absence, but he too died in 1882, allegedly from poison administered by an agent of Barghash.[24]

The Unyanyembe community of Arabs never fully recovered from the loss of the Nasibu brothers. No replacement was sent from Zanzibar to succeed Abdallah bin Nasibu.[25] Factional quarrels kept the remaining resident Arabs divided,[26] and Unyanyembe became known as "a veritable hot bed of intrigue."[27] Reports began to circulate that the Unyanyembe Arabs would throw their support to Mirambo instead of Isike because of fears that without Abdallah bin Nasibu's leadership Mirambo would soon defeat the Unyanyembe *ntemi*.[28] The only reported efforts to bring the Arabs of Unyanyembe under some form of control from Zanzibar were the offer of a governorship to Tippu Tip and later to his brother Muhammed bin Masud by Sultan Barghash. Either appointment could have posed a serious threat to Isike, since Nyaso, one of the Nyamwezi rivals for the rule of Unyanyembe, had been the wife of Tippu Tip's father, Muhammed bin Juma. Isike considered the threat serious enough to ask the White Fathers in Unyanyembe to aid him in gaining French protection. But neither Tippu Tip nor Muhammed bin Masud ever came to Unyanyembe as governor, and Isike soon dropped his quest for outside aid.[29]

In these circumstances, had the European characterizations of

24. Heudebert, *Vers les Grands Lacs*, p. 380; Guillet's letter of September 1881, in *A l'Assaut*, pp. 334–335; Paul Reichard, "Die Unruhen in Unjanjembe," *Deutsche Kolonialzeitung*, 5 (1892): 103; Blanc's letter of 8 June 1882, with addenda of 25 June, *Bulletin des Missions d'Afrique (d'Alger)* (1882–1886), p. 27; Copplestone to Lang, 17 January 1883, G3. A6/01, CMS; Becker, *La Vie en Afrique*, vol. 2, p. 448; Last to Wigram, 5 March 1879, C. A6/014, CMS; Mackay to Wigram, 2 November 1879, C. A6/016, CMS. See also Paul Reichard, *Dr. Emin Pascha* (Leipzig, 1891), p. 76.

25. Barghash once said that he did not send a new representative because he feared "misrepresentation" in the interior. Holmwood to F.O., 10 July 1887, E-99, ZA.

26. For example, Hore to L.M.S., 11 February 1887, LMS; Stokes to Kirk, 11 February 1887, E-97, ZA.

27. Mackay to Kirk, 24 August 1886, in Holmwood to F.O., 18 October 1886, F.O. 84/1775, PRO.

28. Hauttecoeur's letter of 2 March 1884, in *Bulletin des Missions d'Afrique (d'Alger)* (1883–1886), p. 215.

29. Ibid.; Faure's letter of 16 May 1883, ibid., pp. 115–117; *Maisha ya Tippu Tip*, pp. 139, 141; Becker, *La Vie en Afrique*, vol. 2, p. 448. There are some later references to one of the influential Arabs of Unyanyembe, Zid bin Juma, serving as governor, but he does not seem to have been appointed or recognized by the ruler of Zanzibar. See Kirk to F.O., 3 June 1886, E-93, ZA; Michahelles to Macdonald, 20 September 1887, E-98, ZA.

Isike been accurate, he no doubt would have soon lost control of the situation and been driven from power. But Isike reacted to the new challenges so successfully as to make himself the undisputed ruler of Unyanyembe and at the same time extend his influence over many of the neighboring Nyamwezi states. The death of Isike's most important opponents, Mirambo and Nyungu, in 1884 helped to improve Isike's position considerably. There are conflicting reports concerning the cause of Mirambo's death. An African source claims that Isike had him poisoned, while contemporary European witnesses assert that Mirambo died a natural death. Whatever the cause, Mirambo's state went into decline after his death. As for Nyungu's death, his state survived his loss, but his successors posed no important challenge to the Unyanyembe *ntemi*.[30]

Relations with Europeans

Secure in his own state, Isike now had to deal with the ever-increasing numbers of Europeans arriving in central Tanzania. Roman Catholic White Fathers had been active in Unyanyembe since 1881; their main concern was an orphanage for African boys, not local proselytizing. Isike tolerated their presence at first, extracting frequent gifts from them—too frequent in their view—but otherwise leaving them alone.[31] But if Europeans could engage in missionary activities in relative security, they could not seek ivory with equal ease. The German firm of H. A. Meyer, a major exporter of East Africa ivory, sent agents to Unyanyembe beginning in 1884. They met with hostility not only from members of the Arab community but also from Isike, who had by then become the dominant trader of Unyanyembe—he even sent his own caravans to the coast. The Germans were nevertheless allowed to settle in Unyanyembe after completion of various payments to Isike and to the then leading Arab, Zid bin Juma. Their trading efforts were, however, frustrated, and one German merchant was

30. Shorter, "Nyungu-ya-Mawe," pp. 256–258; Norman R. Bennett, *Studies in East African History* (Boston: Boston University Press, 1963), p. 29. The statement that Isike was Mirambo's successor, given in G. S. P. Freeman-Grenville, "The German Sphere, 1884–98," in *History of East Africa*, eds. Oliver and Mathew, vol. 1, p. 442, is obviously in error.

31. For example, Faure's letter of 4 April 1885, in *Bulletin des Missions d'Afrique (d'Alger)* (1883–1886), pp. 374–375; Raffray to M.A.E., 21 May 1886, Politique, Zanzibar, t. 2, Archives des Affaires Etrangères, Paris.

murdered by an Arab, Muhammed bin Kasum. Isike's role in the murder is unclear, but he did share in the booty taken from the dead German's stores. All this passed without serious repercussions since the real authority of the German colonial establishment in East Africa did not yet reach beyond the coastal regions.[32]

A new figure appeared at this point on Unyanyembe's political scene. Isike, while retaining his traditional role at his court, delegated authority to deal with outsiders to a man from the coast, Fundi Sugu, who had the experience required by the intricacies of commerce that Isike lacked. Fundi Sugu kept the Arabs under control. He made them pay heavily for the recruiting of porters, and he imposed several indirect taxes on them. The Arabs had no choice but to submit, since without Nyamwezi cooperation all trade was bound to stop; they knew that Isike could, for example, dispatch raiders to destroy the caravan of any recalcitrant Arab trader. Isike demonstrated his power in 1887 when he detained all ivory caravans for the coast for about three months. As a consequence of this and similar acts, some Arab traders left Unyanyembe, though their number was not significant enough to reduce the importance of the local Arab community.[33]

The German colonial establishment in East Africa eventually reached Unyanyembe, the focal point of the interior trade routes. German mismanagement provoked the coastal populations into an armed uprising during 1888–90, and the conflict had its repercussions in the interior. Isike, however, kept aloof from matters which, after all, did not directly affect Unyanyembe. London Missionary Society agents at nearby Urambo were told by some Arabs that it would be dangerous for them to visit Unyanyembe,[34] but it is not certain whether such danger really existed, as Isike had earlier informed British visitors that he wanted good relations with their country.[35] It is true that the White Fathers, however, did not fare too well. The Catholic order, which had decided to evacuate Unyanyembe in 1889, experienced considerable difficulties in doing this. Their reason for

32. Ibid.; Raffray to M.A.E., 17 November 1886, ibid.; Heudebert, *Vers les Grands Lacs*, p. 359 ff.; *Maisha ya Tippu Tip*, pp. 149, 151; Heinrich Brode, *Tipoo Tib* (London, 1907), p. 175; Franz Stuhlmann, *Mit Emin Pascha ins Herz von Afrika* (Berlin, 1894), p. 65; Stokes to Kirk, 11 February 1887, E-97, ZA.

33. Heudebert, *Vers les Grands Lacs*, pp. 364, 368–369, 392; Stokes to Holmwood, 5 November 1886, E-90, ZA; Stokes to Kirk, 11 February 1887, E-97, ZA; Boustead, Ridley and Co. to L.M.S., 1 August 1887, LMS.

34. Norman R. Bennett, "The London Missionary Society at Urambo, 1878–1898," *Tanzania Notes and Records*, 65 (1966): 49.

35. Hooper to Lang, 9 December 1886, G3. A5/04, CMS.

departure was Isike's continued demands upon the mission, but it does not appear that any special effort was made to force the missionaries to leave or to threaten their lives when they decided to leave.[36] The incident nevertheless embittered the White Fathers and added to the impression of German officials that Isike was a determined enemy of their colonial policies.

The government of German East Africa established a presence in Unyanyembe in a manner destined to create a highly unstable situation. Hermann von Wissmann, the German commander, had originally opposed occupation of Isike's center until sufficient German forces would become available to ensure obedience to government policy—a wise decision, since Isike reportedly had well over 1,000 firearms for his followers. Wissmann contented himself with sending a Muslim agent, Ismail Bilach, to Unyanyembe in 1890. Bilach succeeded in persuading the Arabs, still smarting under Isike's authority and also cognizant of German victories on the coast, to hoist the German flag, but Isike promptly made them lower it. Meanwhile, the well-know Emin Pasha, who had entered German service to lead an expedition to the Lake Victoria region, violated his instructions and proceeded to Unyanyembe. Emin did this largely on the advice of the equally well-known Carl Peters, who was then returning from his abortive Emin Pasha rescue mission and thought it dangerous for the German administration to leave the important Nyamwezi trade center in hostile hands. The Arab residents, already influenced by Wissmann's agent, quickly came to terms. Isike proved more difficult, but he finally decided it best not to expose his forces to an attack by Emin's well-equipped expedition and to conclude an agreement with the Germans. For their part, the Germans still feared an attack even after the agreement in view of Arab-reported rumors of an Isike-Angoni plot against them. All passed peacefully, however. How well founded the charges of a plot were remains unclear; they may have been the product of an Arab attempt to embroil Emin and Isike in a quarrel that would punish Isike for his acts against the local Arab community.[37]

36. Hespers, *Journal du Père Schynse*, p. 16 ff.; Hauttecoeur to Deguerry, 25 May 1889, in *Bulletin de la Société Antiesclavagiste de France* (1888–1889), p. 624; Bridoux to Lavigerie, 6 July 1890, in *ibid.* (1890), p. 361; Hauttecoeur to Bresson, 7 July 1889, in *Bulletin des Missions d'Afrique (d'Alger)* (1888–1889), p. 616.

37. Wilhelm Langheld, *Zwanzig Jahre in deutschen Kolonien* (Berlin, 1909), pp. 39, 46–51; Stuhlmann, *Mit Emin Pascha*, pp. 44, 57–69; Georg Schweitzer, ed., *Emin Pasha: His Life and Work* (Westminster, 1898), vol. 2, p. 41 ff.

It is hard to assess precisely Isike's role from that time on. He stayed secluded in his court and dealt with Germans and other outsiders through intermediaries, who were not always trustworthy agents and may at times have misrepresented his wishes. One indication that Isike's real policy was a passive one designed to ride out potential dangers is seen in his contacting the White Fathers returning with the Germans in an attempt to persuade them that the Unyanyembe Arabs and not he were to blame for their earlier withdrawal and to assure them that none of their abandoned property had been harmed.[38]

In any case, Isike remained quiet. The German authorities on the East African coast initially censured Emin Pasha for his actions in Unyanyembe. They informed him that he had exceeded his orders and that there were no German forces available to provide an adequate garrison to ensure fulfillment of his treaty arrangements with Isike and the Arabs.[39] But the step had been taken, and the German government was committed to action, though Wissmann's original fears of a precipitate German occupation by a garrison unable to carry out government policy were eventually to be proved all too correct. A German officer, Lieutenant Sigl, with only about seventy African troops, many of them poorly trained, occupied Isike's center in February 1891. Sigl was content to follow his instructions: as long as outward forms of submission were given to German authority, he was not to interfere in local problems. Sigl had a useful ally in the German-appointed head of the Arab community, Sef bin Said, who gave unreserved support to the new European administration.[40] Though unhappy with his precarious position and at what he considered lack of support from his superiors,[41] Sigl managed to keep Unyanyembe peaceful. Isike acted similarly, but his dissatisfaction with the Germans appeared in a letter sent to the British in Zanzibar asking British protection for his state.[42] To him an absent imperial power apparently looked better

38. Bridoux' letter of 6 July 1890, given in fn. 36. For Tippu Tip's role in later settling the issue of the White Fathers' property losses, see van Oost's journal, entry of 20 November 1890, *Bulletin des Missions d'Afrique (d'Alger)* (1891–1892), pp. 211–212.

39. Schweitzer, *Emin Pasha*, vol. 2, p. 90.

40. H. Hermann Graf von Schweinitz, *Deutsch-Ost-Afrika in Krieg und Frieden* (Berlin, 1894), pp. 57–58; Jacques' journal, extract in *Le Mouvement Antiesclavagiste* 4 (1891–92): 96–97; Joseph A. Moloney, *With Captain Stairs to Katanga* (London, 1893), pp. 70–75.

41. A.—M. de Saint-Berthuin, *Alexis Vrithoff* (Lille, 1893), p. 104.

42. Isike to the British Consul General, Zanzibar, 19 March 1891, E-131, ZA; Smith to Salisbury, 30 April 1891, F.O. 84/2147, PRO.

than a present one. The British, of course, took no notice of such a request from a German subject.

The Germans continued to show their disinclination to strengthen their tenuous control of Unyanyembe. The Hehe victory at Lugalo over a German expedition in August 1891[43] diverted the limited German manpower to more immediately pressing requirements.[44] When Sigl was replaced by Dr. Schwesinger as local commander in March 1892, the new officer brought an equally small garrison. His instructions were to concentrate on diplomacy to keep order and to avoid hostilities.[45] Isike left the Germans alone, however, and he even sent them gifts.[46]

The Fall of Isike

But a peace based upon mutual tolerance between often aggressive German officers and an equally determined African ruler could not last. The arrival of large troop contingents belonging to the German Anti-Slavery Society heralded new difficulties. Their destination was Lake Victoria, but they made it a practice to stop in Unyanyembe. In April 1892, the leader of such a group, Lieutenant Hermann, precipitated a crisis. Some of his African troops quarreled with the inhabitants of a village controlled by a son of Isike. The responsibility for the episode was unclear, but Hermann accepted the version of his men and stormed the village.[47] Unyanyembe was immediately filled with rumors. Some of them led to the belief that Isike, who had had no part in the original quarrel, would begin war. In the confusion, Africans in the service of the Arabs, who had aided the Germans, attacked a party of Isike's men sent under cover of a white flag to present the Nyamwezi ruler's version of the episode.[48]

43. Alison Redmayne, "Mkwawa and the Hehe Wars," *Journal of African History* 9 (1968): 418–20.

44. Wissmann had planned to lead an expedition inland for the German Anti-Slavery Society, but the Hehe victory prevented his leaving. See the reports in d'Avricourt to Ribot, 18 June 1891, 4 November 1891, Allemagne, Hambourg, t. 18, Archives des Affaires Etrangères, Paris.

45. Von Soden to Schwesinger, 6 December 1891, in *Deutsches Kolonialblatt,* 3 (1892): 74; Shaw to L.M.S., 16 April 1892, LMS.

46. "Von der Expedition des Lieutenants Hermann," *Deutsches Kolonialblatt* 3 (1892): 358.

47. Ibid., pp. 358–359; Schweinitz, *Deutsch-Ost-Afrika,* pp. 60–62; Shaw to L.M.S., 16 April 1892, LMS.

48. Schweinitz, *Deutsch-Ost-Afrika,* p. 62.

A major crisis was nevertheless averted. Isike refrained from making any hostile moves. Some of the Arabs of Unyanyembe who wished to avoid hostilities came forward as intermediaries in negotiations between the Germans and Isike. The Germans, who had decided Isike was to blame for the affair, wanted the Nyamwezi chief to come to their station and pay an indemnity. Isike did not appear, but his men brought an indemnity, which the Germans accepted. It was learned later that the Arabs had paid the indemnity, possibly without Isike's knowledge; no one knew what the Arabs had told him of the course of the negotiations. Hermann's forces then left Schwesinger in his weak position in Unyanyembe and proceeded on to Lake Victoria. Isike now had reason to believe that the Germans were hostile to his continued rule of Unyanyembe. He stopped sending gifts to the German authorities and began to build up his forces. German efforts to placate him, as, for example, when they persuaded a recalcitrant Nyamwezi chief to pay Isike tribute, had no effect.[49]

Hostilities began in June 1892. Isike had closed the Unyanyembe market to Europeans, and there were reports that Isike had asked other Nyamwezi leaders to join him in an attack on Europeans as soon as the remaining Anti-Slavery Society forces left. Schwesinger decided to mount, with some Arab support, a surprise attack against Isike's capital, but the attack was checked. Isike's position was weakened, but his fortress remained intact.[50]

Nevertheless, the Germans continued to maintain the offensive. They raided Isike's allies successfully, inducing many of his Nyamwezi enemies to come over to them. The Nyamwezi of Urambo, Mirambo's former center, were one such group. An increasing number of dissatisfied Nyamwezi gave their support to Isike's rival, Nyaso, whom the Germans now recognized as *ntemi* of Unyanyembe. By August 1892 Isike held only his *ikulu,* and the Germans prepared for another assault. The German attack, with considerable Nyamwezi and Angoni support, did much damage to Isike's fortress—Isike himself was wounded—but the fortress was not taken. The Arabs, some of whom

49. Ibid., pp. 62–64.
50. Ibid., pp. 64–65; "Vorgänge in Tabora," *Deutsches Kolonialblatt* 3 (1892): 444–46; "Bericht des Dr. Schwesinger, betr. des Vorgehen gegen den Sultan Sikki (Tabora)," ibid., pp. 608–609; "Die Kämpfe bei Tabora. Bericht des Herrn Josef Rindermann," *Deutsche Kolonialzeitung* 5 (1892): 126–127; Kapitan Spring, *Selbsterlebtes in Ostafrika* (Dresden-Leipzig, n.d.), pp. 70–75. Not all the Arabs supported the Germans. See Karl Hespers, ed., *P. Schynse's letzte Reisen-Briefe und Tagebuchblätter* (Köln, 1892), p. 6, for information on the Arab factions.

always supported Isike and whose trade was suffering from these hostilities, tried to arrange peace, but Isike, as before, did not appear for any negotiations. Since the Germans had failed to take his *ikulu*, he no doubt considered himself the winner.[51] Another German attack in September proved equally fruitless.[52]

By this time, however, Isike had suffered enough to seek an arrangement with the Germans. On October 30, 1892, the Nyamwezi ruler formally accepted German protection, agreed to leave decisions regarding peace and war in German hands, promised to end his raiding and to punish those of his subjects who continued, agreed to aid the Germans in keeping trade flowing, and promised not to exact any duties upon that trade.[53] The agreement was clearly intended to provide no more than a temporary halt to hostilities. The Germans had already extended their support to Isike's rival, Nyaso, and had even proclaimed her ruler of Unyanyembe. An increasing number of Nyamwezi leaders, anticipating Isike's final defeat, rallied around Nyaso.[54] Isike became upset; in November he asked for Nyaso's surrender, though, of course, he met with no response.[55]

A strong German force arrived in December under the command of the able Tom von Prince. He reported that Isike was in contact with another enemy of German rule, Mkwawa of the Hehe, and that further negotiations would serve no useful purpose. In January 1893 a combined German-Arab-African force successfully attacked Isike's stronghold. Isike attempted to blow up the powder magazine, and himself, in the last stages of the attack, but he survived the explosion. His mangled but still living remains were hanged from a tree by the victors.[56]

51. Schweinitz, *Deutsch-Ost-Afrika,* pp. 65–88, 184; Spring, *Ostafrika,* pp. 77–96; "Tagebuch des Leutnant Meyer aus Tabora," *Deutsche Kolonialzeitung* 5 (1892): 154–55; "Bericht des Leutnants Meyer," ibid., pp. 155–56.

52. "Bericht des Lieutenants Prince über die Niederwerfung und Vernichtung des Häuptlings Sike von Tabora," *Deutsches Kolonialblatt* 4 (1893): 199; Long's journal, entries of 30 August–19 September 1892, *Le Mouvement Antiesclavagiste* 5 (1892–93): 148–151.

53. "Ein Vertrag mit dem Sultan Sike von Unyanyembe," *Deutsches Kolonialblatt* 4 (1893): 20.

54. "Fortsetzung des Tagebuches des Leutnant Meyer von 15. Juli," *Deutsche Kolonialzeitung* 5 (1892): 177; Spring, *Ostafrika,* pp. 67, 89.

55. "Bericht des Lieutenants Prince," p. 199.

56. Ibid., pp. 200–204; "Bericht des Lieutenants Prince über den Rückmarsch der Tabora-Expedition vom 5. Februar bis 18. April. d. Js.," *Deutsches Kolonialblatt* 4 (1893): 267. Tom v. Prince, *Gegen Araber und Wahehe* (Berlin, 1914), pp. 187 ff.; Rodd to Rosebery, 15 May 1895, F.O. 107/4, PRO; Redmayne, "Mkwawa," p. 421;

With the demise of Isike, Unyanyembe lost its independence. It was not to be expected, of course, that Isike could, any more than any other African leader, defeat overwhelmingly superior European military forces, though he fought to the last to uphold the dignity of his traditional office. But before he was forced into a hopeless military confrontation with the Germans, Isike's long career showed him to be a most adroit and dynamic political figure. He steadily progressed from an early position of weakness in the face of the Arabs until he became the dominant force in Unyanyembe. He sought as far as possible to avoid armed conflicts and preferred diplomacy to achieve his aims. For many years he thus managed to frustrate Arab and European attempts to control his state for their own purposes and at the same time to keep many potential African rivals from allying themselves with outsiders to drive him from power.

Shorter, "Nyungu-ya-Mawe," p. 257. Nyaso was installed as ruler of Unyanyembe after Isike's defeat. See Prince's letter of 28 January 1893 in *Deutsche Kolonial-zeitung* 61 (1893): 65.

Goree and the Cape Verde Rivers

by George E. Brooks, Jr.

Few contemporary maps of West Africa show the island of Goree. Yet, for four centuries this tiny speck of volcanic rock and sand, measuring only half a mile in length and a few hundred yards in width, was strategically the most important trading center between the Senegal and Sierra Leone rivers. Goree's participation in the slave trade of the seventeenth and eighteenth centuries is well known, even exaggerated, but its importance in the legitimate trade of the nineteenth century and its role as the springboard for French commercial and political expansion on the Windward Coast have never received the attention they deserve. The islanders—Africans, mulattoes, and Europeans—served as catalysts in a process of economic, social, and political change that revolutionized the lives of the African populations inhabiting the coast between Senegal and Sierra Leone. An attempt will be made here to shed some light on the economic relations between Goree and the rivers south of Cape Verde, which nineteenth-century French traders called Rivières du Sud and English traders of that period referred to as Northern Rivers.

Goree's Geographical Advantages

Initially, the importance of these rivers derived from their serving as ports of entry for commerce with the Futa Jalon. Around the middle of the nineteenth century many of the areas along these rivers became important centers of peanut cultivation. Traders from Goree and Saint-Louis, as well as from Marseille and Bordeaux, followed the expansion of peanut cultivation southward along the coast; the economic and political influence they gradually acquired at the expense of their British and Sierra Leonean rivals generally determined the areas of France's territorial annexation in the 1870's and 1880's. Goree derived its maritime and commercial importance from its salubrity, its dominant position on the roadstead formed by the cradling arm of the Cape Verde Peninsula, and the natural protection an island offered European traders and their goods.

Goree served the interests of several European nations, Portugal, Holland, France, and Britain. It provided them with a fortress, a point of rendezvous for shipping, and an entrepôt for commerce along the coast between the Cape Verde Peninsula and the Gambia River. Vessels from Europe bartered their goods with local traders or rode safely at anchor while their boats and the cutters and schooners from the island visited the seasonal bazaars along the Petite-Côte, at places such as Rufisque, Joal, and Portugal and in the Gambia.

By the close of the eighteenth century a natural symbiosis had evolved between the island's inhabitants and the Lebous, who occupied the Cape Verde Peninsula. The thousand-odd Goreens came to depend on the mainlanders for water, fresh meat, vegetables, fruits, firewood, and construction materials. In turn, the Lebous, who in the 1790's had revolted against the overlordship of the *damel* (king) of Cayor, the Wolof state which dominated their hinterland, came to depend on the Goreens for military supplies and millet brought in from the Petite-Côte. There was some friction resulting from numerous exactions imposed by the Lebous on the Goreens until 1830, when the French commandant of the island succeeded in putting an end to them. The Lebous also used to pillage shipwrecks. Like many others in West Africa, the inhabitants of the mainland opposite Goree subscribed to the notion that while the sea might belong to white men, the land belonged to Africans, and shipwrecks were windfalls to which they were entitled. The pillaging of shipwrecks continued until 1857, when the French occupied the Cape Verde Peninsula.[1]

British dominance of the trade along the Gambia considerably restricted Goree's commercial potential. Britain did not allow French and Goreen traders to travel farther upstream than their post at Albreda, some twenty miles above the Gambia's mouth. Goreen mulattoes often took advantage of family connections and business alliances with "Portuguese" mulatto traders operating the length of the river to circumvent British restrictions; even so, they were only able to bring small lots of slaves, gold dust, ivory, gum, and wax overland to the Petite-Côte.

Socioeconomic Factors

At the close of the eighteenth century, according to an estimate by Goldberry, Goree had a population of about 2,000. The population was made up of 166 mulatto and free African property holders, 522 free Africans without property, 1,044 *captifs de case* (domestic slaves), about 200 slaves held for trade, and about 80 European officers, soldiers, and employees of the Senegal Company.[2] This was already a rather sizable population for an island of such small dimensions, especially if one considers that one-third of the space was taken up by the *castel*, the fortified volcanic ramparts at the southern end of the island. The *castel* was reserved for military functions, though it also served as the home of Mam Koumba Castel, Goree's resident genie and protectoress. Yet during the nineteenth century the population grew even more. A census taken in 1842 recorded 4,983 inhabitants: 1,070 mulattos and free Africans, 3,713 *captifs de case*, 152 temporary workers, and 48 Europeans.[3] Three years later the total population topped 5,000, and in 1848 it reached 5,370—about seven times the island's present population.[4] Several large trading firms—Malfilâtre, Gaspard Dèves, Maurel et Prom, Maurel Frères, and others—had their

1. Claude Faure, *Histoire de la presqu'île du Cap Vert et des origines de Dakar* (Paris, 1914), pp. 53 ff. See also Armand-Pierre Angrand, *Les Lébous de la presqu'île du Cap Vert* (Dakar, 1946?), pp. 50–53; 69 ff.
2. S. M. X. Goldberry, *Fragments d'un voyage en Afrique, fait pendant les années 1785, 1786 et 1787* (Paris, 1802), vol. 1, pp. 60–61.
3. Faure, *Origines de Dakar*, p. 109.
4. Pierre Cariou, "Promenade à Gorée," unpublished manuscript, p. 30.

main office or a branch office in Goree. Some firms had agents, often mulattoes from Goree and Saint-Louis, scattered along the coast to the south as far as Sierra Leone. With the elimination of restrictions on foreigners trading in Senegal in the 1850's, merchant consuls from a number of countries also established themselves on the island.

The mulattoes formed the most important social group in Goree. They owned many of the island's vessels and small craft, as well as the *captifs de case* who manned them. In 1778 one of them was named mayor. Many of the rich mulatto traders and owners of some of the finest residences on the island were women, the redoubtable *signares*. As the wives and mistresses of the resident French traders and officers of the garrison, they lost few opportunities to further their own interests and those of their families.

In 1816–17, when the British traders and military who had occupied Senegal during the Napoleonic Wars removed to the Gambia in anticipation of the restitution of the colony to France, a number of *signares* from the island and some from Saint-Louis went along with the British. Through their commercial role, which was facilitated by their family and business connections in Goree and Saint-Louis,[5] the *signares* made an important contribution to the founding of Bathurst, which soon became Goree's rival as an entrepôt for the trade of the Petite-Côte and the rivers.

The French reoccupation of Goree in 1817 found the island's population declining and the remaining traders impoverished and dispirited. Their most lucrative commerce, the slave trade, had ended, the Gambia was closed to them, and they were hard pressed to compete with their Gambian rivals in the Petite-Côte. To add to their hardships, France imposed the Exclusif, a set of mercantile regulations reserving Senegal's commerce solely to French vessels and merchants —this at the very time when France's war-depleted merchant marine was incapable of adequately provisioning her far-flung possessions. Deprived of essential trade goods, Goreen coastal traders resorted to smuggling; they obtained trade goods surreptitiously in the Gambia and in clandestine rendezvous with American vessels trading along the coast. Alarmed at the plight of the islanders and increasingly resentful of British encroachments on the Petite-Côte, French administrators in Senegal addressed their superiors in France with eloquent pleas for changes in the oppressive mercantile regulations. The result was

5. See Florence K. Omolara Mahoney, "Government and Opinion in the Gambia 1816–1901" (Ph.D. diss., University of London, 1963).

the Decision Royale of 1822, which made Goree an entrepôt for certain non-European products, particularly American tobacco and rum. With ample supplies again at their disposal, Goreen traders quickly regained their previous position in the Petite-Côte and even put traders in the Gambia on the defensive by smuggling large quantities of rum and tobacco into their area. The resident traders in the Gambia appealed to the British commander to take measures against the Goreen intruders, but under existing Anglo-French treaties, French and Goreen vessels could not be denied access to Albreda, and the presence of numerous "relatives" of the Goreens in Bathurst and upriver made smuggling impossible to prevent. Eventually the British Navigation Acts were set aside, so that American vessels could trade at Bathurst as well as at Goree. But since Goree's customs duties were substantially lower than those of the Gambia, it paid French and Goreen traders to continue smuggling large quantities of goods into the Gambia. This they often did with the connivance of British businessmen who had established factories close to the French trading post at Albreda.[6]

Goreen trade with the Casamance River area on a sustained basis dates back to 1828, when a trading post was founded in the river's mouth, on Mosquito Island. French authorities actively encouraged Senegalese coastal traders to enter the river and challenge the Portuguese, who until then had considered the Casamance their exclusive trading area. In order to give greater thrust to the Goreen's rather timid ventures, the Compagnie de Galam was recognized in 1836 as the Compagnie de Galam et de Casamance, and some of its resources were directed to establishing the new commerce on a permanent basis. In 1838 a trading post with a small garrison of soldiers was established at Sedhiou, about 100 miles upstream. Sedhiou lay on a caravan route connecting the Futa Jalon and the upper Gambia; by establishing a post there the French were able to siphon off much of the commerce that previously had passed downriver to Ziguinchor, the principal Portuguese center in the Casamance. The Portuguese tried to deter the French in their purpose with diplomatic protests and by harassing Senegalese traders; after these efforts failed, Portuguese businessmen in the area reconciled themselves to the new situation and entered into profitable commercial relations with French and Goreen traders. British

6. George E. Brooks, Jr., "American Trade as a Factor in West African History in the Nineteenth Century: Senegal and the Gambia, 1815–1835," *Boston University Papers on Africa*, vol. 4.

and Gambian interests also entered the area and set up factories near the Sedhiou post.[7]

The Peanut Revolution

The period 1835–45 marked the initial stage of the economic revolution in the Senegambia engendered by the cultivation of peanuts for export. In the 1840's, possibly earlier, peanuts were cultivated along the rivers south of the Gambia. During the 1850's and 1860's peanut cultivation spread to areas south of the Nunez. The first commercial shipment from the Gambia took place in 1834 on the initiative of Forster and Smith, the most enterprising British firm to trade with West Africa during the first half of the nineteenth century.[8] Once the industrial uses of peanut oil, especially in the manufacture of soap and candles, came to be appreciated in the Western world, peanut exports from the Gambia rose dramatically: 213 baskets in 1834, 47 tons in 1835, 129 tons in 1836, and 671 in 1837. By the 1840's, annual exports were counted in thousands of tons.[9]

Though samples of peanuts and peanut oil were first sent to France in the 1830's, substantial exports from Senegal date from the early 1840's.[10] Still, the Senegalese crop was too small to meet French demands and French merchants bought increasingly larger quantities of Gambian nuts. By the 1850's virtually the entire Gambian crop was shipped to France and in French bottoms, to avoid surtaxes levied on foreign vessels unloading in French ports. Economically, the Gambia became something of a French colony, with the French *bourdeau* (eight bushels) recognized as a standard measure and the five-franc piece as legal tender.[11]

7. Georges Hardy, *La mise en valeur du Sénégal de 1817 à 1854* (Paris, 1921), pp. 297–9.

8. R. Montgomery Martin, "Possessions in Africa and Austral-Asia," *History of the British Colonies* (London, 1835), 4: 560. One hundred baskets of peanuts worth a half dollar per basket were exported in 1830, presumably an experimental shipment. Captain Belcher, "Extracts from Observations on Various Points of the West Coast of Africa," *Journal of the Royal Geographical Society,* vol. 2 (1831), p. 297.

9. J. M. Gray, *A History of the Gambia* (Cambridge, 1940), pp. 379–80.

10. E. Bouet-Willaumez, *Commerce et traite des noirs aux côtes occidentales d'Afrique* (Paris, 1848), p. 52. Jaubert, a French trader established on Gorée, sent a sample of peanut oil to Marseille in 1833, but there was no immediate follow-up. Paul Masson, *Marseille et la colonisation française* (Marseille, 1906), p. 470. There is conflicting evidence about the date of the first shipment and by whom.

11. Gray, *Gambia,* p. 384. Bernard Schnapper, *La politique et le commerce français dans le Golfe de Guinée de 1838 à 1871* (Mouton: Paris, 1961), pp. 229–31.

Peanut oil was sought in France not only because of its industrial uses but also as a consumer item, since French housewives found peanut oil an inexpensive substitute for olive oil in cooking. To meet this demand for vegetable oils, French businessmen found it advantageous to exploit their long-standing commercial ties with the Senegambia and concentrated on peanut imports from the dry savanna areas of West Africa, while British businessmen relied mainly on palm oil imported from the forest regions of the Leeward, or Guinea, Coast. This early differentiation of areas of economic interest had a striking influence on the patterns of colonial acquisition in the latter half of the nineteenth century.

The peanut commerce of the 1840's reinforced an earlier phase of Goreen expansion southward to the rivers providing access to the trade of the Futa Jalon, principally the Nunez and the Pongo. The movement of Senegalese coastal traders to the south of the Gambia River has yet to be fully charted. The evidence examined to date is still too inconclusive to determine whether the movement was the result of a steady progression of trading down the coast or a striking out for the Nunez and the Pongo, bypassing what is now Portuguese Guinea. The second alternative is suggested by the fact that the Nunez area was commercially attractive, while the attempt to trade in territories under Portuguese influence always met with difficulties.

The Portuguese, Cape Verdian, and indigenous mulatto (filhos da terra) traders who frequented the area from the Casamance to the Rio Cacine jealously guarded their prerogatives of exclusive commerce along the two principal rivers, the Cacheu and Grande, at the cost of considerable conflict with the African peoples residing there. Although a few Goreen traders, and perhaps some from Saint-Louis and the Gambia, dealt with the Portuguese entrepôts at Cacheu and Bissau, as well as with those in the Cape Verde Islands, even before 1820, there does not seem to have been any significant amount of commerce until the 1840's and 1850's, when legitimate trade began replacing the slave trade.

The first peanut exports from Bissau were recorded in 1846, probably a later date than in the Nunez River area to the south.[12] Legitimate commerce with Portuguese Guinea thereafter expanded rapidly,

12. A. Teixeira Da Mota, Guiné Portuguesa (Lisboa, 1954), vol. 2, p. 31, and Da Mota and João Barreto, História da Guiné 1418–1918 (Lisboa, 1938), are the most useful sources for the history of Portuguese Guinea in the nineteenth century. However, neither provides a satisfactory treatment of commerce.

and foreign traders flocked in. Reportedly, thirty or more sloops and schooners from Goree and the Gambia were trading with Cacheu and Bissau in the early 1850's, each making two or three voyages every year.[13] In 1855 a French naval officer reported that half of Bissau's foreign trade was controlled by French and Goreen traders, with most of the rest being in the hands of Englishmen and Americans.[14] A decade later a French merchant residing at Bissau described it as one of the most important commercial centers between Saint-Louis and Sierra Leone. He reported that French and Goreen traders accounted for two-thirds of the commerce in peanuts from Bissau and the Rio Grande.[15]

The slave trade long continued in the Nunez and Pongo areas, particularly in the latter. Only gradually, perhaps beginning in the 1830's, was legitimate trade disassociated from it. Of the two rivers, the Nunez was commercially the more important, and vessels from both Goree and Saint-Louis were trading there by the 1830's.[16] The principal factories were at the head of navigation, forty-odd serpentine miles from the river's mouth.[17] Here Fulbe and Mandingo traders from the neighboring highlands of the Futa Jalon came to barter gold (worked into rings), ivory, and hides for salt, guns, powder, cloth, tobacco, and other European and American goods brought by Englishmen, Sierra Leoneans, Goreens, Frenchmen, Americans, and others.

The slave and legitimate trades existed in a sort of symbiotic relationship, each sustaining the other. The caravans were composed of both free men and slaves, and some slaves were sold in the Nunez or, more often, in the Pongo area. Similarly, merchandise brought there by legitimate traders and bartered for hides, coffee, etc., was subsequently used to purchase slaves in the interior. The principal middlemen in

13. Francisco Travassos Valdez, *Six Years of a Traveller's Life in Western Africa* (London, 1861), vol. 1, p. 260. Travassos Valdez visited Portuguese Guinea in 1852.

14. Extrait du rapport du commandant du brick *le Victor*, December 19, 1855, Gorée et dépendances XIII, la, Archives Nationales, Section d'Outre-Mer (Paris).

15. Rapport de Adolphe Demay, August 1864, Folder J-e-24, 2F3, Archives, former French West Africa (Dakar). Hereafter cited as A.A.O.F.

16. The progression of traders from Gorée and Saint-Louis has yet to be worked out. A French naval officer visiting the Nunez area in 1837 mentions several traders from Saint-Louis (the brothers D'Erneville, René Valentin), one Goreen (Robert Heddle), and one Frenchman (M. La Porte). Heddle was described as "settled" in the Nunez area. Lt. Guerret to commander of *la Triomphate*, April 16, 1837, 7 G6, A.A.O.F.

17. The region at the head of navigation was termed Kakundy, reputedly from a sacred grove of Pullman, or "Cotton," trees found there. Extract from the Journal of Dr. D. G. Miller, Surgeon of H.M.S. *Aetna* (1831), 7 G6, A.A.O.F.

the exchanges were mulatto families indigenous to the rivers, descendants of European slavers and female relatives of their "landlords," the African chiefs who controlled commerce. The long-established families, the Proctors and Skeltons on the Nunez, the Lightbourns, Curtises, and Fabers on the Pongo, wielded enormous influence. Their commercial ties and family relationships with European and mulatto traders extended from Saint-Louis to Freetown.[18]

Trade in the rivers was generally confined to the dry season from December to April, when the paths were open and goods could be safely transported. The customary method of trade was for the seasonal visitors to pay stipulated customs to the chiefs, after which they advanced goods to the resident middlemen who promised returns later in the trading season. "Advances" were disliked by the visiting traders, but giving credit was unavoidable, for few of the resident middlemen had sufficient capital to operate without it. The creditor lived in constant fear that trade stoppage, warfare, the death of the resident trader, or his cupidity might prevent completion of the bargain. There was no recourse to legal means or to European men-of-war, for until the 1850's naval vessels infrequently visited the rivers, even in the dry season, knowing from experience the dangers to their crews.

The lucrative caravan commerce in the Nunez area was frequently interrupted by disputes between the Nalou and Landouman peoples who lived upstream and the *alimami* who ruled the Fulbe state in the Futa Jalon and held an insecure suzerainty over them. The *alimami's* demands for tribute or for redress of grievances involving Fulbe traders sometimes halted trade for months, though the resident mulatto and European traders did their best to mediate for the benefit of all concerned. The halting of trade, for whatever reason, was an endless source of frustration for the seasonal visitors, venturing hundreds or thousands of miles as they did only to find that their hopes for the season had miscarried.[19]

Senegalese and French traders steadily grew in number and influence

18. The author and his wife are compiling file cards on African, European, and mulatto traders who lived on the Windward Coast from Senegal to Sierra Leone c. 1780-c. 1860. Preliminary findings show a remarkable number of family links.

19. André Arcin, *Histoire de la Guinée française* (Paris, 1911); A. Demougeot, "Histoire du Nunez," *Bulletin*, Comité d'Etudes Historique et Scientifiques de l'Afrique Occidentale Française, Vol. 21 (1938); Christopher Fyfe, *A History of Sierra Leone* (Longmans: London, 1962), passim. See also Norman R. Bennett and George E. Brooks, eds., *New England Merchants in Africa; A History Through Documents, 1802 to 1865* (Boston: Boston University Press, 1965), pp. 283–339.

in the two riverine areas, and gradually they began to replace the Sierra
Leonean and British traders who had preceded them. In the 1840's
some became more or less permanent residents. One of the first to do
so was Auguste Santon, a Frenchman who established a plantation at
Katekouma (Bel-Air) and raised peanuts and coffee. By the 1840's
mulattoes from Senegal were joined by Moslem Wolof traders, notably
Ishmael Tai, who became one of the more important traders in the
Nunez area.

In the 1840's and 1850's agricultural exports—coffee and indigo, as
well as peanuts—greatly increased the value of Nunez trade. Peanut
exports were soon worth several times the value of caravan commerce.
Existing import regulations on coffee in France and Britain militated
against the introduction of Nunez coffee, since it was not produced
within the boundaries of a recognized colony and was therefore subject
to high tariffs. The French Minister of Marine suggested in 1840
that Nunez coffee be shipped overland to the Casamance, from where it
might be imported as "colonial produce," but the suggestion was not
followed up. Finally, in 1846 a French trader in the Nunez area was
designated to provide certificates of origin for coffee grown there, and
thereafter it was exported to France via Goree as originating from a
French establishment.[20]

Competition and conflicts of interest increasingly disturbed the
Nunez trade in the 1850's and 1860's. Trade, politics, warfare, and
treaty-making became more and more complicated with so many conflicting interests involved: those of the Landouman and Nalou chiefs,
the *alimami* of Futa Jalon, the old resident families, the seasonal residents, and European warships come to intervene on behalf of their
nationals. The events of those years are so far only imperfectly described by historians.[21]

Goree was not only the springboard for French commercial thrusts
southward—which included after 1843 trading posts on the Ivory
Coast and in Gabon—but also served as the principal base for the
French naval squadron in West Africa. In 1845 the senior naval officer
in West Africa was named *inspecteur général des comptoirs,* with
headquarters at Goree. From 1855 to 1859 Goree was separated from
Senegal and made the headquarters of a new colony, Gorée et dépen-

20. Demougeot, "Nunez," pp. 206–7; Hardy, *Mise en valeur,* pp. 306–8. See also
Fyfe, *Sierra Leone,* pp. 226–27.
21. Arcin and Demougeot so far provide the fullest coverage, but they use a
limited selection of sources and omit or misconstrue certain aspects.

dances, which included all French possessions and interests as far south as Gabon.[22] In 1859 Goree was reattached to Senegal but continued in its role as the main naval base for France's West African squadron. The island's prosperity continued undiminished, as a number of residences and public buildings still in existence attest.

In 1857 an Anglo-French convention arranged for the exchange of the French post at Albreda in the Gambia for British trading rights at Portendic in Mauritania. The political settlement, however, had little influence on trading patterns: the Gambia's peanuts continued to be shipped to French markets. The governor of the Gambia, Colonel D'Arcy, wrote in May 1860 that "the fact is isolated in colonial history, but, while I write, I count thirty tricolours, six stars and stripes and but one union jack flying in the port of Bathurst."[23] French interests indeed dominated the commerce of the coast from Senegal to Sierra Leone. On virtually the same date that Colonel D'Arcy deplored the state of affairs in the Gambia, Governor Faidherbe of Senegal exultantly reported his findings after a tour of the coast:

> One fact is immediately apparent. It is that French commerce is entirely predominant in this part of Africa; even at the Portuguese establishments and the English establishments in the Gambia the French flag is almost the only one seen. The same statement may be made for as far as Sierra Leone.[24]

Faidherbe's successor, Pinet-Laprade, fostered an activist expansion policy. In 1865 and 1866 treaties of protection were signed with a number of African rulers in the Nunez, Pongo, and Mellacourie areas, and French authority was asserted by the construction of military posts. The formal annexation of territory and concomitant Anglo-French competition and negotiation over demarcations dragged on for several decades.[25] It was a classic instance of the flag following trade: where Goreen and French traders had pioneered and successfully established close commercial and political ties with African rulers, there the *tricolore* was implanted from the 1860's onward.

---

22. Schnapper, *La politique*, ably relates Goree's role to the larger picture of French expansion in West Africa. See also Schnapper, "La fin du régime de l'exclusif: le commerce étranger dans les possessions" (Paris); Francois Zuccarelli, "L'Entrepôt fictif de Gorée entre 1822 et 1852," ibid.

23. Gray, *Gambia*, p. 384.

24. Voyage de Gouverneur Faidherbe à la Côte Occidentale d'Afrique, June 1860, 1G26, A.A.O.F.

25. John D. Hargreaves, *Prelude to the Partition of West Africa* (London: Macmillan, 1963).

French commerce and influence on the Windward Coast had been destroyed during the Napoleonic Wars; renewed and spearheaded by the traders of Goree, within a half century it dominated the 500 miles of coastline between Senegal and Sierra Leone. Goree, its historical function seemingly now served, became absorbed by the rising seat of empire to which it had given birth. Goree's rivals are no better served by history: Bathurst presides over a commercial *cul-de-sac;* so too does Freetown, lacking a hinterland for its magnificent harbor. All three entrepôts live in the past, in the reflected glories of what was—or might have been.

Rebels and Rebellions in Angola, 1672-1892

by Douglas L. Wheeler

The history of Portuguese Africa seems to be little more than a solemn parade of petty trading and bush warfare. Fage and Oliver convey such an impression in referring to old Angola and Mozambique as "ill-defined trading preserves."[1] So also does Duffy in summing up the first three centuries of Angola's history as "a chronology of small wars, expeditions to the interior, and of a dedicated commerce in black humanity."[2] But first impressions can be deceptive. Progress is now being made in original research in Portuguese archives and libraries, and one may confidently predict that the history of Angola will eventually reveal useful parallels with other African territories and help to illuminate current developments.[3]

1. J. D. Fage and R. Oliver, *A Short History of Africa* (Baltimore: Penguin, 1962), p. 181.
2. James Duffy, *Portugal in Africa* (Cambridge, Mass.: Harvard University Press, 1962), p. 47.
3. Since 1966 several detailed, valuable historical studies on Portuguese Africa have appeared: R. J. Hammond, *Portugal and Africa 1815–1910* (Stanford, Cal.: Stanford University Press, 1966); David Birmingham, *Trade and Conflict in Angola*

There is a marvelous unity about the history of Angola. Many recent events look like replicas of the past, particularly when it comes to rebels and rebellions. The struggle for paramountcy of European settler interests against Africans or against faraway Lisbon has been going on since the sixteenth century. The African desire for independence from Portuguese rule was never entirely suppressed even in the territory known as the kingdom of silence. Events in 1672, 1790 and 1860 have their echoes in the insurgency of 1961 in northern Angola. It is a political wonder of the modern world that Angola is still a Portuguese territory.

Some rebellions are lost to African history, forever obscured by artifice or by accident, like

> Some village-Hampden, that with dauntless breast
> The little tyrant of his fields withstood, . . .
> Some village Cromwell, guiltless of his country's blood.[4]

Still, the reports of Portuguese officials in Angola contain much material on local rebellions. The picture they often paint is one of woe and helplessness. About 1790, for example, a Brazilian-born soldier and historian with extensive personal experience in Angola commented:

> In no other part of the Portuguese world is the militia more necessary than in Angola. . . . No other continent will be more subject to revolutions, uprisings, murders by the natives and robberies on the roads. None more liable to the disobediences of National Chiefs who, shackled to the chain of vassalage,[5] make their lot even sadder and more afflicted [by revolting].

This passage from Elias Silva Correia's *História de Angola* reflects the precarious nature of Portuguese power in eighteenth-century Angola. The most important African rebellion of the eighteenth century occurred when the chief, or king, of Mossul, in northwest Angola, reacted to Portuguese attempts to monopolize trade in his area and invaded Portuguese-controlled territory. African forces reached to within a few miles of Luanda, the capital of Angola, killing

---

(Oxford: Clarendon Press, 1966); Eric Axelson, *Portugal and the Scramble for Africa 1875–1891* (Johannesburg: Witwatersrand University Press, 1967).

4. Thomas Gray, "Elegy Written in a Country Church Yard" (1750).

5. "Vassalage" was the Portuguese term for the quasi-feudal arrangement in Angola where the Portuguese supported certain chiefs in return for their support in trade, war, and slaving.

European settlers and Africans alike, capturing Portuguese slaves, and selling them to French and British traders at the port of Ambriz, outside of Portuguese control. The governor reported to Lisbon that this was the most serious invasion the Portuguese had had to face in Africa since 1641, when a Dutch expedition captured Luanda.

The Mossul rebellion of 1790–91 established a pattern that continued into the twentieth century. The country to the north of Luanda up to the Congo River contained many pockets of active resistance to Portuguese rule. Unhealthy climate, broken and hilly terrain, and scanty European settlement made it difficult to administer the Congo district and Dembos. The Portuguese did not control that coast until after the 1880's. The names of rebel nests in the eighteenth and nineteenth centuries have been reproduced on combat reports since March 1961. For example, the town of Nambuangongo, one of the first areas to be hit by insurgency in 1961, was the most persistent obstacle to Portuguese trade and communications with the interior before partition and the so-called pacification campaigns of 1890–1920.

Major African Rebellions

Since the seventeenth century Portuguese interests in Angola gradually shifted from the Kongo Kingdom in the north to southern regions. Originally, the Portuguese founded a trading empire supported by a military caste of Europeans and their African auxiliaries and ministered to by Jesuits and Capuchins. Their small numbers and the commercial nature of their interests impelled the Portuguese to work out a system of "vassalage" among friendly African sobas (chiefs) . The frontier of Angola was marked by the limits of sovereignty of "vassal chiefs"; beyond the frontier were the non-vassals, often called gentio, literally "heathen." This crude political arrangement was fed largely by a continuing slave trade and concomitant activities, and it did not alter very much over three centuries. As long as the number of Portuguese was small and as long as African sobas were willing to trade and contribute porters and levies of warriors in exchange for Portuguese gifts and privileges, there seemed to be no reason for changing this arrangement.

Luanda was founded as a settlement in 1576, and it soon became the major port of a trading empire that lived on the export of African slaves to the Americas and of wax and ivory to Europe and Brazil.

Within a century the Portuguese had conquered the three major African kingdoms north of the Kwanza River: Kongo, Ndongo, and Matamba. Some African kings contributed men to the Portuguese army, and these groups made up the famous *guerra preta* ("black war"), an auxiliary corps that was sometimes used as a reserve of irregulars to snuff out African rebellions. Just as often, however, its members fomented petty warfare, rapine, and unrest without Portuguese prompting. In his *História Geral das Guerras Angolanas,* the Portuguese chronicler-settler-soldier António de Oliveira Cadornega tells us that the Angolan history of his day was mainly a history of "civil war" among thousands of Africans presided over by handfuls of Portuguese.

A considerable mulatto (called *mestiço* or *pardo*) class grew up in Angola. By the end of the eighteenth century and in the early nineteenth mulattoes were perhaps more numerous in Angola than at any other time in history. The ratio of mulattoes to Portuguese was then about 5 to 1, whereas today that ratio is about 1 to 3. Though there were numerous African rebellions against Portuguese rule earlier, the first important insurrection in the seventeenth century was one led by *mestiços* in the Portuguese service. It reportedly occurred around 1672 or 1673 in the fortress town of Massangano.

There is some controversy as to whether such an uprising did take place. Ralph Delgado, a distinguished Portuguese historian, claims that he could not find any documents mentioning the revolt and that other historians may have mistaken a local European revolt for a *mestiço* insurrection at Massangano. He could not see why *mestiços* would revolt, as they enjoyed privileges denied to Africans.[6] But the *mestiços* appear to have been the most discontented class in Angolan history. And all major chronicles and histories of the pre-twentieth-century period, including the one by the usually reliable Silva Correia (whom Delgado does not cite), describe the Massangano insurrection as one led by *mestiços.*

Apparently, then, the *mestiço* rebels laid siege to the fort, gathered African forces, and pledged themselves to kill as many whites as they could and drive the remainder into the sea. Though the revolt did not succeed—for it was quickly suppressed by the captain-general of Angola—the Massangano rebels had some reasons for believing that it might. Shortly before, in 1670, the Portuguese army had sustained a severe defeat in the Kongo Kingdom, and much of northern Angola

6. Ralph Delgado, *História de Angola,* vol. 3, pp. 384–87.

was up in arms. The prevailing atmosphere was one of upheaval, and, as Livingstone noted later while traveling through northern Angola in 1855, a small success of an African rebel force could easily trigger a general revolt in the country.[7]

To what causes may we attribute this and other African rebellions? The works of Silva Correia paint a picture of poverty, sloth, misery, and desperation in old Angola. A writer for a Lisbon newspaper claimed in 1864 that Portuguese officialdom was largely responsible for destroying the goodwill created among Africans by the few missionaries who had dared enter the Angolan interior before 1900. He accused Portuguese judges, officers, district officials, and tax collectors of behaving like "little tyrants" and thus provoking Africans into open rebellion.[8]

Another major cause for widespread violence in Angola during the nineteenth century was the abolition of the trans-Atlantic slave trade. Traffic-minded *sobas* near the coast and as far east as Lunda were baffled by the news that the Europeans had decided to abolish the slave trade. A number of chiefs openly opposed abolition, and some of them showed their resentment by attacking Portuguese settlements in the 1830's.

Some Portuguese statesmen—such as, for example, the liberal patriot Marquis Sá da Bandeira—feared the loss of African territories through interference by foreign powers as well as African uprisings, and they tried to enter into secret treaties with their ancient ally Britain to guarantee the territorial integrity of Angola and Mozambique. It is not clear whether such treaties were actually concluded, but as the text of a treaty proposed in 1838 shows, Portuguese anxieties were real enough. The draft treaty of 1838 asked Britain for an

> explicit guarantee of the above Dominions [Angola and Mozambique] for the Crown of Portugal against any uprising, which could occur in those Provinces, as well as against any attempts by foreign powers to try to foment rebellion, or to try to possess these Dominions.[9]

It should be added, however, that later in the nineteenth century, on the basis of more subtle arrangements, Britain did help Portugal to

7. David Livingstone, *Missionary Travels and Researches in South Africa* (New York, 1858), p. 483.
8. *Jornal do Commercio*, March 1864.
9. *Documentos Officiaes Relativos a Negociacão do Tractado entre Portugal e a Gram Bretanha Para a Suppressão do Trafico da Escravatura* (Lisbon, 1839), Doc. no. 5, p. 29.

foil the aggressive designs of Germany and Cecil Rhodes against Portuguese possessions in Africa.

After the slave trade was doomed, Africa-related unrest subsided. Later, however, Portuguese tax policy spawned another wave of rebellions. In 1841 the Dembos people revolted under the leadership of an educated prince, Dom Aleixo (Alexus), brother of King Henry II of Kongo. Captured by the Portuguese, Alexus was incarcerated in a Luanda fortress from 1841 to 1856. The Portuguese did not dare to execute the prince, fearing the reaction of various African groups. Instead, they imprisoned him and every month paraded him in a Portuguese general's uniform to a reception at the governor's palace in a mock ceremony designed to impress the African population. Georg Tams, a German traveler, visited Alexus in prison and was told by him in good Portuguese that:

> The Queen of Portugal [Maria II (1834–53)] was not his rightful Queen—
> that she had no direct right to rule his country—because this prerogative
> belonged only to him and his brother, the King of Congo. . . . His im-
> prisonment had been arbitrary, since he had committed no crime.[10]

Prince Alexus, who died shortly after his release from prison, was a member of the Agua Rosada e Sardonia, an African dynasty that dominated the throne of Kongo since the early eighteenth century. To the Kongo kings, the Portuguese rulers at Luanda were in a sense patrons, as the dynasty depended upon Portuguese support to maintain its power at São Salvador, the capital. A few of them were educated in Luanda, and some went to study in Lisbon. Many of them laid claim to the throne of Kongo and were inclined to rebel against the Portuguese if the latter supported their rivals. The Portuguese became involved in a similar succession crisis in the Congo District from 1955 to 1957, an affair that had serious political consequences and contributed to the founding of an African nationalist party.

Another noteworthy African rebel was the *assimilado* Prince Nicolas of Kongo, a son of King Henry II of Kongo.[11] Born about 1830, Nicolas received a Portuguese education and held minor posts in the Portuguese civil service in Angola. Although he planned to enter the clergy, he became involved in 1859 in a dispute over the succession

10. Georg Tams, *Visita as Possessões Portuguezas Na Costa Occidental d'Africa* (Oporto, 1850), vol. 2, pp. 17–19.

11. *Assimilado,* "an assimilated one," was an African with the education and culture of a Portuguese. In the 1920's the term took on a legal meaning, referring to Africans who had the rights of the Portuguese.

to the Kongo throne.[12] This happened in a period of expanding Portuguese influence in the Kongo Kingdom. Nicolas wrote a letter to a Lisbon newspaper in which he accused the Portuguese of having taken advantage of the Kongo king's (and his advisers') ignorance of Portuguese to place him in a position of subordination to Portugal. Nicolas claimed that his knowledge of Portuguese enabled him to act as protector of Kongo sovereignty. Before he could carry out a plan to escape from Angola and board an English vessel, he was murdered by a group of Africans who mistook him for a tool of the Portuguese and a traitor to the cause of the independent tribes. But Nicolas had dreamed of a Congo separate from the colony of Angola. Both he and his relative Alexus, obscure figures as they were, had sought to voice African aspirations.

By the middle of the nineteenth century conditions in Angola deteriorated even further. Editorials in Lisbon newspapers spoke in 1860 of the possibility, after numerous African rebellions, of Portugal losing her African territories. The chief cause of renewed unrest was a government plan aimed at territorial expansion, an increase in trade, the abolition of forced labor, and increased African taxation to make up for the loss of revenue that had resulted from the abolition of the slave trade. The Portuguese sent expeditions into the northern territory, built new garrisons, mined copper, and attempted to keep the roads open. Because of African hostility, the deadly climate, and poor resources, attempts to carry out the plan were eventually abandoned.

The Portuguese authorities tended to blame the unrest on foreign, especially British, interference. British merchants on the Congo coast did indeed sell arms and powder to Africans, but so did Portuguese traders. Still, the British acted as water-borne despots along the Angolan coasts and thus alienated the Portuguese. And the memory of the prominent role that Britain had played in the emancipation of Brazil from Portuguese rule certainly intensified Portugal's suspicions of British intentions regarding its African dominions.

Attempts to increase taxes caused the Dembos to rise once again in 1872–73. Lisbon again dispatched an army expedition, which did not succeed, however, in suppressing the revolt. Full Portuguese control was not established in Dembos territory until World War I, when an expedition finally conquered the region. Other rebellions broke out in several Angolan regions around 1890. The plateau saw

12. See Douglas L. Wheeler, "Nineteenth-Century African Protest in Angola: Prince Nicolas of Kongo (1830?–1860)," *African Historical Studies* 1 (1968): 40–59.

a series of military campaigns for another generation, with sporadic local revolts still erupting in the 1920's and even later. Portuguese occupation and colonization continued to be limited to the coastal hinterlands around the major towns of Luanda, Benguela, and Moçamedes. Even after the last tribal resistance was said to have been crushed, despite the confidence of the twentieth-century governments, the extent of effective Portuguese control of the country thus remained an open question.[13]

European Unrest in Old Angola

European society in Angola has been noticeably short on both quantity and quality. The original conquistador, Paulo Dias de Novais, who founded Luanda, was forced to recruit for his Angolan expedition by scouring the jails of Lisbon. Between 1575 and the 1920's at least half and often the majority of the Europeans in the colony was made up of *degredados*[14]—criminals, felons, or political prisoners transported from Portugal for punishment. Much of the Portuguese part of the army consisted of deserters, and until the twentieth century the colonial service was largely staffed by second-raters, trimmers, and disappointed individuals.

Until the early nineteenth century the African territories were subordinated to the economic interests of Portuguese America. Brazil was the heart of the Portuguese empire. Angola, the "Black Mother" of Brazil, provided slaves to American plantations in exchange for various goods. Angola became largely dependent upon Brazil for various food staples, building materials, and capital. This was true even as late as the middle of the nineteenth century. Thus, Brazil cast a shadow on Angola long after it had ceased to be a part of the Portuguese empire in 1822. When they talked about ways of improving conditions in Angola, Lisbon reformers often showed that they were thinking in terms of their Brazilian experience. Indeed, many of them hoped that Angola would become "a new Brazil" for Portugal.

Perhaps the earliest important European revolt occurred in 1694, when infantry in Luanda, led by Brazilian-born Portuguese—or "sons

13. See Douglas L. Wheeler, "Portuguese Expansion in Angola since 1836: A Re-Examination," Central Africa Historical Association, *Local Series Pamphlet*, no. 20 (1967).
14. *Degredado* means "one who is exiled."

of Brazil," as they were called—revolted against the captain general. This barracks coup was crushed by the government, but it set a pattern of settler hostility to Lisbon rule. As Boxer has observed, Portuguese pay in the tropics was bad, late, or never; health conditions were wretched; and the leadership of the colony was not well prepared to cope with problems. There was not much incentive for enlightened rule in a colony of transported criminals.

In the eighteenth century the draconian punishments meted out by governors who tried to rule with an iron hand provoked several convict revolts. In 1878 Governor Vasco Guedes spoke out sharply against the Portuguese policy of convict transportation to Angola and asserted his belief that a great "moral deficit" was piling up in the country.[15]

Few Portuguese settled permanently in Angola during the first three centuries. The European population did not exceed 9,000 until after 1900. In 1778 a reliable estimate gave a population of 1,700 Europeans. A century later there were about 3,000 Portuguese. Colonization schemes in the 1880's caused an increase in the European population, but the most significant increases came only after World War II.

The most notable European separatist movements came in the nineteenth century. Brazil declared its independence in September 1822. Within a few months Brazilians in Angola combined with dissident Angolans to form a Brazilian Confederation in order to maintain lucrative economic ties with Brazil and exclude monopolistic Portugal. Portuguese forces in Luanda prevented the success of this separatist plot. In the south coast town of Benguela, always a locale of autonomist ideas, a separatist junta survived a short while, only to fall to the Portuguese forces in 1823.

Brazilians were involved in other such plots in Angola in the following decades. Political changes in Portugal also influenced European movements in Angola. A Portuguese colonialist wrote in 1830 that "when the Metropolis suffers, then the colonies must also suffer; and the evils that afflict the colonies must affect the Metropolis."[16]

In the political activities surrounding the coming of a constitutional monarchy to Portugal absolutists opposed liberal constitutionalists. The heated struggle was echoed in Africa as political exiles of all

15. Francisco Castelbranco, *História de Angola* (Luanda, 1932), p. 244.
16. J. A. Das Neves, *Consideracões Politicas e Commerciaes sobre os Descobrimentos e Possessões Portuguezas na Africa* (Lisbon, 1830), pp. 349–50.

stripes were shipped out to Angola. In the 1830's and 1840's Portuguese governors had to adopt severely repressive measures to put down a number of revolts in Luanda and Benguela.

Discontent among Europeans brewed anew after 1854 when the first of the Portuguese emancipation laws leading toward an abolition of slavery was passed. Many settlers and plantation owners, some of them Brazilian, threatened to rebel against measures designed to bring about a gradual emancipation. About 1860, coincident with the Prince Nicolas affair, a European independence movement blossomed in Luanda. We have a brief account of it by a contemporary writer, Alfredo de Sarmento:

> At that time in Luanda, some utopian ideas of independence fermented so that some radical natives tried to liberate the *mother country*, as they called it, from Portuguese rule. They talked of a Republic, preferring Brazilian nationality, and there were even those who thought of making a present of the beloved country to the republic of the United States of America.[17]

The Portuguese government could not afford to compensate slave-owners for losses incurred in the transition from an economy based on slave labor to one based on free labor. Though liberal reforms were conceived in Lisbon, they were rarely implemented in Africa. Settlers like the *sertanejo*,[18] who traded and traveled in central Angola, dared statesmen to come to Angola to apply their principles. The example of Brazil—where slavery was not abolished, because of violent opposition, until 1888—of course had an impact on Angola. Angolan settlers felt that 1878 as the legal year for emancipation was an unreasonable deadline. Slavery and forced labor persisted there long after that year. Domestic slavery was not eliminated in some areas of interior Angola until 1924–25,[19] while various forms of forced labor apparently continued until 1961.

The slavery issue became confounded with political ideologies. In Europe the Portuguese monarchy was assailed by republican agitators until it finally fell in October 1910. Republican exiles, considered subversive in Lisbon, were shipped to Angola and Mozambique. These men established political circles in Angola, enjoyed relative freedom of movement, and published newspapers in which they attacked the gov-

17. Alfredo de Sarmento, *Os Sertões d'Africa* (Lisbon, 1880), p. 67.
18. *Sertanejo* was a "person of the backlands"; it came to mean a European trader-settler in plateau Angola in the nineteenth century.
19. Robert Davezies, *Les Angolais* (Paris: Minuit, 1965), p. 239.

ernment and urged Angolan autonomy. One such newspaper was the short-lived Luanda weekly *O Cruzeiro do Sul* (*Southern Cross*), which began its publication in 1873.

The prevailing atmosphere in Angola, however, was extremely conservative. Autocratic tendencies prevailed over republicanism and utopian reformism. Few governors in the nineteenth century or later could resist muzzling the press when the criticism became too effective or too heated. The military nature of the Lisbon-appointed administration (most of the governors were soldiers or sailors) discouraged freedom of the press. Even in Lisbon freedom of the press was ephemeral. Nevertheless, the short-lived settler newspapers and not a few African newspapers in the 1880–1930 era served a useful purpose in Angola. Some of the ideas they expressed on agriculture, investment, finance, and colonization later came to be recognized as having some value.

Lisbon's army expeditions to Angola could serve two purposes: to crush African rebellions and to keep unruly settlers in line. Those perennial "enemies within and without" seemed to be everywhere. Editorials in *O Cruzeiro do Sul* argued that political freedom should not vary with geographical latitude. But the authorities had their own view of what could be permitted in an era when it was uncertain whether or not Portugal had the strength to remain in Angola. Under the constitution, Angola could elect deputies to represent the colony in the national parliament in Lisbon. Elections for these deputies during the nineteenth century were little less corrupt than elections in Portugal, the difference being that in Angola the mass blocs of votes bought were among tribal Africans and not among Portuguese. Given the chaotic nature of European society in old Angola, the civil rights enjoyed in Europe could be periodically eliminated to suit the authorities. Censorship and military force were the means used to keep "order."[20]

A noteworthy separatist movement among Europeans in Angola came into being during the early 1890's. As before, crises in Brazil and Portugal inspired the movement. In 1888 republicanism won a triumph in Brazil, as the emperor went into exile in Europe and the country was declared a republic. Republicanism in Portugal and Angola was thereby encouraged. In addition, a crisis broke out in Portugal when the government, after being humiliated at the Berlin Conference (1884–85), yielded to a British ultimatum in a dispute

20. The most complete history of Angolan journalism is in Júlio de Castro Lopo, *Jornalismo de Angola* (Luanda, 1964).

over Nyasaland (now Malawi) in early 1890. The Portuguese monarchy
tottered and ministries fell. The Republican party of Portugal, which
had been gaining strength since the 1870's, took full advantage of the
government's embarrassments and portrayed the Portuguese retreat
before the British ultimatum in the Nyasaland affair as a betrayal of
national interests and a signal of the end of the monarchy. As one
fanatic Republican wrote of the day Portugal was forced to accept the
British ultimatum: "This day was worth centuries."[21] Portugal was
at that time in serious financial difficulties: European creditors were
pressuring her, and the colonies were treated as footballs by competing
political and economic interests. It was in this climate that republican
exiles in Angola renewed their agitation for autonomy.

The movement in Angola reached its zenith in 1891–92. The
American consul in Luanda, Heli Chatelain, left a detailed account
of it in his official reports to the State Department.[22] Convinced that
the Portuguese empire was about to collapse and favoring American
imperial expansion in Africa, Chatelain went so far as to suggest to
the State Department that the American government purchase the
Cape Verde and Azores islands, as well as Cabinda (an Angolan
enclave north of the Congo River). He was in close contact with the
exiled revolutionaries from Lisbon, who believed that a Republican
government in Lisbon would not oppose the idea of Angolan independence. So influenced was Chatelain by their views that in 1891 he
confidently predicted in a report that Portugal would not be afraid
of Angolan independence as long as "the Portuguese element remains
paramount."

Chatelain was, of course, mistaken. He overlooked Portuguese re-
silience in Africa. Outward signs of weakness were deceptive; to Portugal colonialism was an integral part of any national policy of home
revival, and vested European interests in Angola tied to Lisbon interests acted as the final arbiters of Angola's fate. Only a handful of
Europeans, often quarreling among themselves, favored annexation
by or association with the United States in 1892; the majority remained in the Portuguese tradition. The Portuguese government was
bound to prevail in these circumstances and to tighten its control of
Angola, though only to a degree, after a short period of *confusão*.[23]

21. Bazílio Telles, *Do Ultimatum ao 31 de Janeiro* (Oporto, 1905), p. 1.
22. *Despatches from United States Consuls in St. Paul de Loanda*, T-430, Roll 5,
National Archives, Washington, D.C.
23. *Confusão*, which literally means "tumult, chaos, pandemonium," was used in
1961–66 to describe the time of troubles in Angola.

As the result of a series of treaties between 1885 and 1926 the boundaries of Angola were delimited and Angola was legally made a Portuguese territory. But these acts never enabled the Portuguese to exercise full and effective control over the area, as unrest continued among Africans and Europeans.

In sum, though often isolated, veiled, and even obscured from outside view, Angola experienced many outside influences over the centuries. Dissatisfaction with various aspects of Portuguese rule is not a twentieth-century phenomenon. Angolan society has proven responsive to Brazilian influences, ambitions of educated Africans, foreign suggestions, Western political ideals, and, of course, Portuguese politics and culture. Relations between Angola and Portugal have never been easy. Indeed, Portugal's presence in Angola has been in jeopardy more often than present patriots in Lisbon would like to recall.

The Separatist Challenge to
White Domination
in South Africa

by Newell M. Stultz

This essay examines the activities of two organizations in South Africa, the South African Bureau of Racial Affairs (SABRA) and the Transkei National Independence Party (TNIP), and the effectiveness of the challenge that these two organizations have presented to white domination in that country. Though different in many respects, both of them advocate what for the sake of brevity will be referred to here as "separatism."

The essence of separatism is the belief that the 12.5 million or so Africans and the approximately 3.5 million whites of the Republic of South Africa—or, at any rate, a sizable majority of both groups—should be territorially separated from each other through the creation of two or more politically autonomous, if not independent, states. Separatists reject as undesirable not only the present domination over Africans by a white minority but also the prospect of future domi-

95

nation over whites by an African majority. The second of these alternatives, they are convinced, would be the inevitable end result of a
policy that accorded, however gradually, political equality to all persons in South Africa irrespective of race.

How realization of their goal would affect other ethnic groups is a
question to which separatists have no clear and uniform answer.
Although there are 2 million Coloreds (persons of mixed blood) and
half a million Asians in the republic, no important voices have been
heard calling for the establishment of separate Colored or Asian
"homelands." The truth is that most separatists are not particularly
interested in the fate of the Colored and Asian communities; the only
problem of real concern to them is that of relations between whites
and Africans, the solution to which they see in the creation of some
sort of a new political environment in South Africa that would in
effect result in alien status for non-Africans in African-inhabited territories and in alien status for non-whites in white-controlled areas.
Such a solution, if adopted, need not affect the present subordinate
position of Coloreds and Asians in relation to whites, and few
separatists, apparently, expect that it will, though some of them have
expressed the hope that once a substantial degree of separation between whites and Africans has been attained discrimination against all
non-whites might be significantly lessened.

Even in this imprecise form, the idea of an equitable partition of
the republic along racial lines exercises a strong hold on many minds
in South Africa. But this does not mean that the South African white
community can be expected to surrender overnight all the political
privileges and material comforts it has enjoyed for so many years by
virtue of its ability to discriminate against other races. To believe
otherwise would be to overrate the force of a mere idea. Separatism
calls for changes so drastic in the white South African structure of
social values that they could not be brought about without first overcoming the powerful forces of tradition, self-interest, fear, and
prejudice that operate to preserve the *status quo*.

If it is to have any chance of succeeding at all, separatism must meet
two requirements. First, it must be promoted through an organized
effort. It is for this reason that the activities of SABRA and TNIP, the
only organizations thus far formed in South Africa to advance the
separatist cause, have been singled out here for scrutiny. Second, a
separatist organization must be able to function without the support,
direct or indirect, of the South African government. This point is

crucially important. Though the South African government professes to favor racial separation, it remains committed to the preservation of existing laws and institutions. Sooner or later, therefore, any organization that genuinely wishes to promote separatism is bound to find that the basic interests of the South African government, official policy declarations notwithstanding, do not coincide with its own.

Historical Antecedents

The idea of separatism is not new. It appeared very early in the history of South Africa. At the end of the so-called Hottentot War (1658–60), Jan van Riebeeck delimited the newly founded Cape Colony's boundary, a line running from the mouth of the Salt River to the mountain slopes behind Wynberg, and directed that Europeans and Hottentots stay on its opposite sides.[1] Disregarding it, a group of Dutch farmers soon thereafter pushed eastward. In 1750 they reached the Keiskamma River; there they clashed with the Xhosa, who in the meantime had been moving with their herds southward in search of fresh grazing lands. Again the Cape government vainly tried to keep whites and blacks apart by demarcating a border. In 1743 it fixed the border at the Great Brak River, but in 1770 it had to shift it eastward to the Gamtoos River and in 1775 still farther east to the Fish River. By 1866 European control extended over all the tribes living south and west of the Kei River, in the area now called the Ciskei.

During the latter half of the nineteenth century, the Cape government, having abandoned the last vestige of hope of maintaining a political boundary between whites and Africans, proceeded to annex the 16,000 square miles of tribal lands between the Kei River and the Natal border. This area is now known as the Transkei. It was reserved for African occupation, but white magistrates supported by police forces were sent in to administer it. The same procedure was applied to all other tribal lands that were later brought within the confines of the present South African Republic.

In 1910 the Union of South Africa was formed as a self-governing member of the British Commonwealth. Three years later tribal territories were formally organized as Native Reserves under a new Land Act. The previous practice of restricting occupancy to Africans was reaffirmed. Government purchase of additional land was declared to

1. Eric A. Walker, *A History of Southern Africa* (London: Longmans, 1962).

be the only legal method of increasing the size of the reserves, which represented then—as they still do—about 13 percent of South Africa's total area. Inside the reserves African communal ownership was recognized as the sole form of land ownership; outside, Africans were forbidden to acquire land not already owned by other Africans.

The Land Act of 1913 thus established the principle of territorial segregation of Africans, though only in regard to land ownership. Subsequently, the distinction between principle and fact was blurred by the attempts of a succession of white political leaders throughout modern South African history to win support for the thesis that the Native Reserves were the only "national homes" of Africans and on that basis to justify their exclusion from ordinary citizenship rights in so-called "white South Africa." The thesis was so used, for example, by the Nationalist party during its successful 1948 electoral campaign. Since the reserves, the Nationalist party stated in its program, were "the true fatherland of the Native," he should be regarded "as a 'visitor' who can never be entitled to any political or equal social rights with Europeans in European areas."[2]

A century earlier most Africans did indeed live in geographically separate and self-contained communities that could be easily distinguished from those of South African whites. Racial discrimination existed even then, but it affected an insignificant number of Africans who for one reason or another had left the tribal lands. By 1911, however, half a million Africans, or 12 percent of the country's African population, were living in cities and accounted for about one-third of the total urban population. A census taken in 1960 showed that only about one-third of the total number of Africans inhabited the reserves and that nearly half of those outside lived in urban areas. This trend has continued, to the point where Africans now outnumber whites in the cities. The thesis that Africans constitute geographically separate communities in South Africa can thus find some support in the principle laid down in the Land Act of 1913 but not in the known facts concerning the present racial distribution of the country's population and the historical trends that led to it.

The principal reason for the steady exodus of Africans from the reserves is the extreme poverty of these areas. The sole economic activity of any importance there is subsistence farming, which is inefficient and incapable of supporting a growing population. Many Africans are therefore forced to seek wage employment, but few jobs

2. "The National Party's Colour Policy," 1948.

are to be had in the reserves. Of the nearly 1.5 million Africans living in the Transkei in 1962, for example, only 21,000, according to official statistics, worked for wages; another 145,000 migrated to other areas, seeking employment wherever they could find it—in mines, on white farms, or in industries.[3]

The basic reality is that today most of South Africa's Africans, and nearly all Coloreds and Asians, live outside the native reserves. They are in continuous daily contact with whites under a social system governed by the principle of white supremacy and sustained by an ever-more unreal belief that Africans have no permanent interests outside the reserves. But there is no escape from the fact that the reserves, barring a radical and extremely costly transformation of their economies, cannot support more than a small fraction of the African population.

The Rise and Decline of SABRA

The origins of SABRA can be traced to some of the economic and social trends that emerged during World War II. The war accelerated industrial development in South Africa, and this in turn provided a major stimulus for increased African migration into urban areas. Since municipal authorities could not, because of wartime restrictions, take adequate measures to accommodate the heavy flow of in-migrants, the material and social welfare of urban Africans deteriorated markedly. White public opinion became disturbed not only about some of the immediate social effects—such as, for example, a rising level of "native crime"—but also about the long-term implications of the new racial situation in the cities. Should Africans, many whites wondered, be treated as permanent city residents? If so, could equal rights be denied to them? If not, what was to be their future?

The white segment of South Africa's population became so restive over this problem in the immediate postwar years as to impel both major political parties, the United party and the Nationalist party, to search for a solution. Prime Minister Smuts tried to curb the African influx into the cities, but he was unable to build a consensus within his United party for a comprehensive racial policy and in 1946 he turned the matter over to a special commission of inquiry. The following year the Nationalist party appointed a commission of

3. House of Assembly Debates (Hansard), May 28, 1963, col. 6772; March 18, 1963, col. 2962.

its own and asked it to provide guidelines for a "native policy." The commission drew up a report which laid the basis for the *apartheid* (separate development) program of the alliance between the Reunited National and the Afrikaner parties that won the general election in 1948.[4]

The quest for a solution to the racial problem engaged not only the efforts of government experts and party politicians but also those of intellectuals. At a Rotary Club luncheon held in 1947 at Paarl, in the Western Cape Province, Professor N. J. J. Olivier of the University of Stellenbosch delivered a momentous address in which he expatiated on the idea of racial separation with justice for all groups. Though the idea was not new (Professor Hoernlé had explored it eighteen years earlier, in a public lecture at the University of Cape Town[5]), Olivier's Paarl address received nationwide publicity and aroused so much interest in Afrikaner circles that a group of Afrikaner academicians, mostly from the University of Stellenbosch, met soon thereafter in Johannesburg to consider the forming of an organization for the study of racial affairs. The outcome of the meeting was the creation of SABRA.[6]

This decision was reached in spite of the fact that there already existed in South Africa an organization, the South African Institute of Race Relations, with a record of experience in the field of racial studies going as far back as 1929. The group that met in Johannesburg wanted to set up a separate body because, for one thing, it objected to the dominant role of English-speaking South Africans in the institute's affairs; and, for another, it felt that the institute's more-or-less liberal views did not reflect the sentiments of most Afrikaners, indeed of most whites, in South Africa.

SABRA held its first formal meeting on September 23, 1948, at Cape Town. Several prominent Afrikaners, including three future Cabinet ministers, joined it on that occasion. Another who was allowed to join was Colonel Stallard, leader of the right-wing English Dominion party. His admission was essentially intended as a gesture to show that SABRA did not wish to be a purely Afrikaner organization. Yet this is

4. *Verslag van die Kleurvraagstuk-Kommissie van die Herenigde Party,* 1948.
5. See R. F. A. Hoernlé, *South African Native Policy and the Liberal Spirit* (Johannesburg: Witwatersrand University Press, 1945), pp. 168–78.
6. E. S. Munger, "Suid-Afrikaase Bure Vir Rasse-Aangeleenthede [South African Bureau of Racial Affairs]: An Intimate Account of SABRA's Origins, Leadership, Organization and Views, and Its Interaction with Afrikanerdom's Church, Press, Party and Public," American Universities Field Staff Newsletter, AFRICA ESM-6-'56.

precisely the image SABRA has earned for itself, partly because its initial funds came from the *Federasie van Afrikaanse Kultur-Vereeniging*, an Afrikaner cultural group; partly also because its membership since its inception has been predominantly Afrikaner; and, finally, because its conduct never gave cause to doubt its allegiance to the principles and institutions of Afrikaner nationalism.

During the first decade of its existence SABRA grew rapidly in strength. By 1956 it claimed an individual membership of more than 3,000 and the affiliation of some 230 municipalities, churches, and cultural groups. This rapid growth enabled SABRA to finance all its activities—including the organization of annual conferences, the circulation of a bimonthly newsletter, and the publication of a bilingual quarterly, the *Journal of Race Affairs*—out of members' subscriptions and private gifts. At no time did it either solicit or receive financial contributions from the government, the Nationalist party, or the universities.

The lack of a financial connection, however, did not prevent SABRA from becoming closely identified with the University of Stellenbosch during the 1950's. Several factors contributed to this result. One was that SABRA maintained its main office there until 1964. Another was the university's heavy representation in SABRA at the policy-making level. Though SABRA is formally governed by a council elected by the membership at large, the council's only substantive function is to elect a fifty-four member executive committee; the latter appoints a sixteen-man *dagbestuur,* or "day committee," which in practice makes most of the organization's policy decisions. In 1956, twelve members of the *dagbestuur* belonged to the Stellenbosch faculty. But the most important factor was the role of Professor Olivier, of Paarl-address fame. As national vice-chairman, a post he filled until 1961, he contributed more than any other single person to the building up of SABRA and was widely regarded during the 1950's as its leading spokesman.

The formulation of SABRA's separatist philosophy owed much to his views. Agreement on it was reached within the organization as early as 1952, and apparently with little debate. Its main features were spelled out in a thirty-five page pamphlet issued in the same year under the title *Integration or Separate Development?* Both the prevailing policy of white discrimination against Africans and the alternative of providing equal treatment for the two races within a common political framework were found wanting: the former because it was oppressive and bound to fail in the long run, the latter because it implied the eventual disappearance of the white community as a distinctive entity in South Africa. The only sensible course for the country, the pamphlet claimed, was to aim at "the free and separate development of the two racial groups." The services of African workers would continue to be assured to the white community through a system of migrant labor, since territorial separation was not meant to deny Africans access to the "European territory," only to prevent them from acquiring permanent interests there.[7] Effective separation demanded, however, that the white community assume the burdensome costs of financing the economic development of African territories. To SABRA, as we shall see later, this point was of decisive importance. As for the political consequences of territorial separation, the pamphlet did not venture beyond the view that African territories were likely to remain subject to white control "for a long time," apart from an obscure reference to the eventual emergence of independent "Bantu states."

The translation of this philosophy into an effective action program depended in the main for its success on the state of SABRA's relations with the ruling Nationalist party. At first these relations were extremely cordial; later, however, largely because of differences of opinion over the recommendations of the Tomlinson Commission, which the government had appointed in 1951 to look into measures for the socioeconomic development of Bantu areas, they became acutely strained.

The Tomlinson Commission was unable to complete its investigations and present its findings before 1956. Until then the racial policy advocated by the government in parliamentary debates found constant SABRA support. The Nationalist party had every reason to be pleased: its *apartheid* doctrine lacked intellectual respectability and SABRA's carefully articulated arguments provided at least a veneer of it. The Nationalist party felt so warmly disposed toward SABRA in those years that it came to look upon it as some sort of informal adjunct to the state machinery it controlled.

SABRA, of course, looked forward to the publication of the Tomlinson Commission's report with keen anticipation, since the commission was expected to recommend measures for the economic development of African areas, measures considered by SABRA as essential to the ful-

7. The idea that urban Africans should be considered temporary migrants was **not** new. A similar view had been put forward by the Transvaal Local Government Commission, the so-called Stallard Commission, as early as 1922.

fillment of its separatist aspirations. When the report finally appeared, SABRA, obviously impressed, decided to promote a general public discussion of it by sponsoring a *Volkskongres* (People's Congress) at Bloemfontein. The *Volkskongres* convened in June 1956, but the event was marred by the publication shortly before it took place of a white paper outlining the government's reaction to the commission's report. The government, the white paper indicated in broad language, basically sympathized with the commission's reasoning; nevertheless, and this was the main point, it could not go along with a proposal asking it to spend within ten years the equivalent of nearly $300 million on the African reserves.[8] An effort was made at the *Volkskongres* to maintain complete silence about this unexpected development. None of the formal papers read on that occasion mentioned it. It proved impossible, however, to prevent some of the participants from using the opportunity afforded by floor discussion of the various papers to voice their irritation at the government's reaction.[9] This was the first public indication that a rift was beginning to form between SABRA and the Nationalist party.

In the two years that followed the rift widened considerably. In 1958 SABRA held its annual conference at Stellenbosch in an atmosphere that reflected a widespread feeling of dissatisfaction with the government's stand on the racial question. According to one observer, the director of the University of Natal's Institute for Social Research, Dr. J. F. Holleman, most of the participants appeared to be convinced that the difference that had emerged earlier between the Tomlinson Commission's recommendations and the government's *apartheid* policy, far from being resolved, was actually growing sharper; that, meanwhile, the racial situation in South Africa was rapidly deteriorating; and that consequently not much time was left in which to find a suitable remedy.[10] A motion was presented asking the executive committee to organize a joint meeting with a number of prominent Africans. Its supporters argued that such a meeting might produce plans for separate development acceptable to both whites and Africans. The motion passed by an overwhelming margin. The Nationalist government, obviously stung, reacted swiftly. Shortly after the conference ended, a Cabinet minister publicly denounced "parlour in-

8. *White Paper*, F-'56.
9. M. Horrell, comp., *A Survey of Race Relations in South Africa, 1955–1956* (Johannesburg: South African Institute of Race Relations, n.d.), p. 152.
10. Ibid., *1957–1958*, pp. 15–16.

tellectuals, who venture to question the Nationalist policies."[11] The minister of native affairs, Dr. Verwoerd, resigned his membership in SABRA—an event that took on added significance with his elevation to the prime ministership four months later.

Despite the huge vote in support of it, the proposal to convene a joint conference never went beyond a preliminary stage in which a group of SABRA representatives headed by Professor Olivier met informally with African spokesmen. The South African press reported in early 1959 that Prime Minister Verwoerd had stubbornly insisted in several heated discussions with SABRA leaders that only government officials could properly enter into formal consultations with African leaders. Pressure to call off the proposed conference was also exerted within the ranks of SABRA. Reports circulated in late 1958 and early 1959 that several members, most of them from the Transvaal, had accused the Stellenbosch-dominated leadership of trying to embarrass the government through a public display of SABRA opposition to official policy. It may not be amiss to point out here that Dr. Verwoerd from 1958 to the time of his death was the leader of the Nationalist party in the Transvaal. Apparently the Stellenbosch group managed at that time to restore harmony within the organization, but only by agreeing to some sort of a compromise that resulted in the indefinite postponement of the proposed SABRA-African meeting.

Yet these efforts to find an accommodation between the Stellenbosch intellectuals and Dr. Verwoerd's Nationalist party were bound to fail ultimately, since they left a fundamental question unanswered. The question, simply stated, was whether SABRA was to be allowed to be anything but a subservient tool of government policy.

The answer came in 1961. A study group headed by Professor Olivier prepared a report on the future of the Coloreds, in the expectation that the report would serve as the main theme of SABRA's twelfth annual conference. The subject had a special appeal to Professor Olivier and the men around him, all of whom were Cape Nationalists; for the Coloreds form, in the main, a community of the Western Cape Province. There was a strong chance, however, that a conference centered on the Colored question would offend the Nationalist party, which clearly did not welcome efforts to draw public attention to a major flaw in the official ideology of *apartheid*. The party was all too conscious of the fact that by invoking, as it had so often done,

11. Ibid., pp. 16–17.

cultural and territorial differences as the basis of its doctrine of separate development, the doctrine could be made to apply to the Africans, but not to the Coloreds, who lacked a sufficiently differentiated culture or a territory of their own even remotely comparable to the African reserves.

How provocative the study group's report actually was it is impossible to say for certain, for the report was never made public. The executive committee at any rate evinced sufficient alarm over it to rule against its disclosure and in favor of a new and much more innocuous conference theme—"Relations between English- and Afrikaans-speaking South Africans." As a result the conference, which had been scheduled for April, was postponed until September. But that was not all. For a point had been reached where it was felt that the basic issue that had agitated SABRA since 1956—whether the organization was meant to operate as an independent body of scholars or, in Dr. Holleman's words, "within the prescribed limits of the unitary concept of Afrikaner Nationalism"—could no longer be sidestepped.[12] On the second day of the conference the executive committee met again, in private session, to tackle the issue. It is not known precisely what went on at that meeting, but, significantly, during the open balloting that followed for membership in the executive committee, Professor Olivier was heavily defeated in his bid for reelection, and his place as vice-chairman was taken by the director of the government-sponsored Africa Institute of Pretoria, Professor P. F. D. Weiss; whereupon Professor Olivier's disheartened supporters withdrew their own nominations.

One year later at Pretoria, the site of SABRA's thirteenth annual conference, the effects of these changes in leadership could already be felt. The theme of the conference—the coming of "self-government" to the Transkei—though timely, having been chosen in the wake of an announcement by Prime Minister Verwoerd that some sort of autonomy would be granted to the Transkei in 1963, attracted a relatively small audience. The papers presented at the conference's various sessions dealt mostly with such bland topics as the administrative history of the Transkei. A single attempt by an individual at one session to raise a controversial issue was neatly sidetracked by a motion to adjourn the session for "tea-time." The uneventful conference dragged on until, as a final gesture, the participants were asked to

12. J. F. Holleman, "Sabra 1961: The Great Purge," mimeographed (Durban: Institute for Social Research, University of Natal, 1962).

approve a motion of confidence in the government's policy—which they did, without debate and by a unanimous vote.[13]

In 1964 Professor Weiss became chairman of SABRA, and its main office was moved from Stellenbosch to Pretoria. These were not important events, except symbolically: they represented the final steps in the process of liquidating the old organization and what it had stood for. SABRA became a propaganda instrument of the government, though hardly a useful one. Its earlier posture as an authentic champion of separatism had enabled it to wield a certain amount of intellectual and moral authority; this posture it could not credibly maintain once it forfeited its independence, and in consequence it lost nearly all influence on the South African scene.

Matanzima and the TNIP

Though an advocate of separatism, the Transkei National Independence party (TNIP) contrasts sharply with SABRA in several important respects. First, unlike SABRA, TNIP is a political party, albeit one still going through an early formative stage. Second, it is an African organization. Third, notwithstanding its relative inexperience in the conduct of modern political affairs, its present control of the machinery of government in the Transkei gives it a measure of legislative and executive authority to which SABRA, as a mere study group, could not even aspire. Fourth, whereas SABRA made the future of race relations in all of South Africa its concern, TNIP's professed interest lies solely in the future of the Transkei's inhabitants. The two organizations, however, have one noteworthy feature in common. Each one bears the indelible imprint of a forceful personality — SABRA that of Professor Olivier, TNIP that of Paramount Chief Kaiser D. Matanzima.

The son of a chief and a native of Emigrant Tembuland, a peripheral region of the Transkei, Matanzima studied law at Fort Hare University College in the thirties and was eventually admitted to practice as an attorney in the Cape Province. He gained some prominence in 1958, when the South African government recognized his claim to authority as the senior tribal chief of Emigrant Tembuland. His stature was further enhanced in 1966, when his chieftaincy was

---

13. The writer attended the conference.

reconstituted as a paramount chieftaincy. But more than anything else it was his involvement in the drive for Transkeian self-government and his leadership of TNIP, which he founded, that contributed to his fame.

In 1961 a member of the Transkei Territorial Authority proposed at a meeting of that body that the South African government be asked to allow the Transkei to become a self-governing state "under the control of the Bantu people."[14] The only action the Territorial Authority could be persuaded to take was to appoint a twenty-seven-member committee under Matanzima's chairmanship to study the proposal's "implications." Working in close consultation with officials of the Department of Bantu Administration and Development, the committee prepared a report that included a draft constitution for a politically autonomous Transkei. Though the committee had thus clearly exceeded its mandate, the Territorial Authority accepted the report and in 1962 submitted the draft constitution for approval to the South African government. It was on this basis that Prime Minister Verwoerd was able to announce in the same year that the Transkei would shortly be accorded some form of self-government.

The Transkei constitution, which the South African Parliament approved in 1963, vests limited legislative power in a Legislative Assembly composed of sixty-four chiefs serving as *ex-officio* members and forty-five elected members. The Assembly may propose bills, which become law when signed by the state president of the Republic, on matters concerning the Transkei's finance, education, agriculture, local roads and public works, and justice—save for items falling within the jurisdiction of the South African police. In addition, the constitution lodges executive functions in a Cabinet composed of a chief minister and five ministers. The chief minister may allocate portfolios among his colleagues at his discretion, but all Cabinet members must be elected by the Legislative Assembly.

The election for the forty-five members of the first Assembly was held on November 20, 1963. It was expected that the Assembly, once it met, would choose between two contenders for the post of chief minister, both of them *ex-officio* members—Matanzima and Paramount Chief Poto. Each of the two, therefore, campaigned strenuously before the November election on behalf of candidates expected to support him. Poto's speeches during the campaign showed him leaning heavily

14. Transkei Territorial Authority, *Proceedings and Reports of Select Committees at the Session of 1961*, p. 49.

toward multiracialism; he argued, for example, that the Transkei should welcome any "non-African" prepared to "serve" under its government. Matanzima, on the other hand, came out flatly in favor of separate development. In December the Assembly elected Matanzima chief minister by a vote of 54 to 49. An analysis of the vote showed that Matanzima owed his victory to the *ex-officio* members; of the Assembly's elected members only twelve had voted for him.

The defeat induced Poto to organize an opposition party. Named the Democratic party, it held its first meeting in February, 1964; one week later Matanzima launched his own political organization, the TNIP.[15] One of TNIP's first acts was to endorse a Programme of Principles, which in substance expressed the same separatist sentiments Matanzima had aired in a manifesto issued during the campaign for election to the Assembly. Since then the two parties have been vying for the electorate's favor in several by-elections, with the results showing a small gain for the Democratic party. Some of Matanzima's supporters in the Assembly have defected to the opposition;[16] but there has also been a movement, slightly larger in number, in the opposite direction.[17] So far, therefore, Matanzima's power has not been seriously threatened.

What, one may ask, is Matanzima's separatist ideology? Nowhere is a precise and coherent formulation of it to be found. All that can be done is to trace the broad lines of Matanzima's reasoning as revealed by the TNIP's Programme of Principles and by various public statements he has made since he became chief minister.

Theoretically, Matanzima sees only two ways of ending white domination, which, as an African, he naturally resents. One is by establishing a multiracial society. He is convinced, however, that most South African whites do not wish to live together with Africans on the basis of individual equality; and since the whites have the power to enforce continued discrimination against Africans, an intermingling of the two races could not produce a different result. The alternative is separation of the races.

Central to Matanzima's espousal of separatism is the notion of a

15. *The Star,* 8 February 1964; *The Daily Dispatch,* 15 February 1964.
16. *The Daily Dispatch,* 15 February 1964.
17. One member, Shadrack Sinaba, was appointed TNIP chief whip after defecting from the opposition. He later resigned to form his own party, the Transkei People's Freedom party. He advocates independence for the Transkei at the earliest possible date and has accused Matanzima of temporizing on this issue.

Xhosa national culture with hereditary chieftainship as its most distinctive institution. If the Xhosa are not to lose their national identity, so the argument goes, it is imperative that the authority of their traditional chiefs be preserved. And the chiefs, being the "natural" political leaders of their people, must see it as their duty to work for the annexation of all the ancient Xhosa lands not yet under the authority of the Transkeian government—for the Xhosa homeland stretches from the Fish River to the Natal border, according to Matanzima, and includes, therefore, territories beyond the Transkei Reserve's present boundaries —the ouster of all whites (about 13,000 of whom now reside in the Transkei), and the widening of the Transkeian government's powers until full sovereignty is achieved.

The goals that Matanzima and TNIP thus emphasize—retention of chiefly authority, territorial expansion, Africanization, and sovereignty—are all clearly political. Little attention is paid in their statements to the problem posed by the Transkei's poverty and economic dependence on the South African Republic—a problem that so deeply preoccupied SABRA—probably because Matanzima and his supporters realize that the Transkeian government by itself could do little, if anything, to solve it.

The obvious elements of African nationalism in his political program suggest that under different circumstances Matanzima might have tried to widen his role by posing as the champion of all Africans who feel the oppression of white supremacy in South Africa. As it is, he has made no move in that direction. His brand of separatism, if we are to believe his pronouncements, remains firmly wedded to Xhosa (or Transkeian) tribal particularism. This suits the aims of the South African governments so remarkably well that Pretoria could do no less than give Matanzima its official backing, for which he professes to be grateful.[18] How deep his commitment to Xhosa traditionalism actually runs is, however, a topic for speculation. It is noteworthy, for example, that in its first year the Matanzima government made a dramatic gesture of joining with the opposition Democratic party in rejecting a proposal to use the vernacular instead of English or Afrikaans as the language of instruction in Transkeian schools.[19] There is room, then, for the suspicion that Matanzima's devotion to Xhosa

18. See, for example, Transkei Legislative Assembly, *Proceedings at the Meeting of Members of the Transkei Legislative Assembly, Held on 6th, 9th and 11th December, 1963, for the Purpose of Electing Office Bearers, Etc.,* p. 15.
19. *Transkei Legislative Assembly Debates,* 10 June 1964, p. 218.

particularism owes less to ideological fervor than to a calculated appraisal of the opportunities open to Africans for political expression and action in contemporary South Africa. There is no reason to doubt, on the other hand, that he truly favors the preservation of chiefly authority; but this is just as easily explained by self-interest as it is by ideology. In any event, the Transkei has made no visible progress toward fulfillment of TNIP's separatist program. It is of course true that Matanzima has been in power for only a few years, during which most of his energies have been absorbed, perhaps unavoidably, by administrative tasks and partisan politics.

Evaluation of the Separatist Challenge

It is worth emphasizing once more the central point made at the beginning of this essay: no political organization can be expected to challenge white domination in South Africa effectively if it depends in any way upon the support of the South African government, because a challenge to white domination in that country implies a threat to interests that government is bound to protect.

SABRA today is certainly not an independent organization. In 1961 it forfeited whatever opportunity it once had to function as a self-directed agent, though one may wonder whether it did not intend all along, despite all appearances to the contrary, to serve as a mere spokesman for and rationalizer of decisions taken elsewhere. It would be idle, however, to speculate on this question.

Nor can TNIP, for obvious reasons, be considered an independent organization. Matanzima's motives are not entirely clear. Some political observers of events in the Transkei are inclined to dismiss him as a mere henchman of Pretoria, but the majority of those who have had a chance to study him at close range have come away with a different impression. Opportunism, in all probability, is what chiefly motivates him to collaborate with Pretoria. The plain fact is that the Transkei's economic conditions give Matanzima—or any other political leader that might replace him—little bargaining power. For the Transkei has nowhere else to look but to South Africa for badly-needed budgetary support, development capital, and above all a market for its huge labor surplus. So long as such conditions obtain, the Transkei has no practical alternative but to stay, however reluctantly, within the political orbit of white-dominated South Africa.

The South African government is of course committed to bring about what it calls separate development, but the key to its true intention lies in the measures used, or assented to, to meet that commitment. It is not impossible that the Transkeian government will someday be allowed to expel white residents from its territory. It is even likely that the Transkei will be granted, at some distant date, legal sovereignty; according to the Ministry of Bantu Administration and Development, the South African government has already accepted the idea in principle.[20] The Tswana of western Transvaal, according to present thinking in official South African circles, are soon to be endowed with the political institutions the Transkei now has; if the same pattern is followed, a sovereign Tswanaland will eventually be allowed to emerge. In time, other reserved areas—such as the Ciskei and Zululand—may also be gradually advanced to sovereign status. Such a "creeping partition" would benefit Africans to some extent, since it would give those living in the reserves some scope for political and administrative advance. Yet it would not automatically result in a substantial disentanglement of the races. To achieve this, it would be necessary to repatriate the 50,000 or so whites now living in African areas to "white" South Africa—a task that could be accomplished without undue difficulties; it would also be necessary to improve material conditions in the African areas sufficiently to enable a sizable number of Africans to leave the truncated republic—of which there is little prospect, given the South African government's reluctance to step up expenditures for the economic development of those areas.

The Tomlinson Commission recommended in 1955 that 50,000 new jobs be created in the African areas each year for twenty-five years. This, in its opinion, would have permitted the reserves to accommodate about 60 percent of the projected total African population.[21] So far, the number of new jobs created there since 1955 is well below that recommended by the commission; in 1965 it probably did not exceed 10,000. Meanwhile, the demand for African labor in the republic shows no sign of slackening and in the future is expected to rise to even higher levels. The partitioning of South Africa into white-controlled and black-controlled states would thus leave most Africans seeking a livelihood in the republic's urban areas, where a regime of white supremacy would most certainly be maintained.

20. Communication to the author.
21. Union of South Africa, *Summary of the Report of the Commission for the Socio-Economic Development of the Bantu Areas within the Union of South Africa* (U.S. 61/1955), p. 184.

The government's *apartheid* policy has, until now at least, imposed no appreciable hardship on the white community in South Africa. At most it has resulted in a few minor annoyances, such as, for example, the need to comply with a regulation limiting the number of African servants who may "live in" with white families. The main thrust of this policy has been directed at matters lying at the periphery of white interests, such as the political and administrative structures of the Transkei and other reserved areas. It is a policy which, while it pays lip service to the idea of racial separation, carefully refrains from impinging upon the basic privileges secured by whites through domination over other races and which the government can therefore successfully defend, as indeed it has, before the white electorate.

It would seem, then, that there is little hope of ever seeing what SABRA called the separatist ideal come even close to being fulfilled. Yet this need not be the case. For some years now the South African system of white domination has been under attack from various quarters at home and abroad that cannot be as easily contained or controlled as were SABRA and TNIP. Their aim is to transform South Africa into a multiracial, non-racial, or African-controlled polity. There is every reason to believe that, as time goes on, the pressures they are exerting will grow stronger. If the past is any guide, however, the South African government can be expected to react by moving more closely toward, not away from, racial separation. There is little doubt, for instance, that external "non-separatist" pressures were much more influential than the arguments of Professor Olivier and Chief Matanzima in bringing about Pretoria's decision to grant "self-government" to the Transkei. It would be premature, therefore, to rule out the separatist solution to the South African problem. The irony of it is that, if realized, it will owe more to the efforts of those who advocate a united and democratic South Africa than to the separatist challenges of such organizations as SABRA and TNIP.

Government Policy toward
African Cult Movements:
The Case of Katanga

by Edouard Bustin

The political connotations of cult movements in a colonial context have been pointed out so often that they hardly need to be reemphasized here. Lanternari, for example, has described at length the characteristic features of religious and other associational movements in a society whose culture is pitted against another one in an unequal relationship.[1] In that respect a colonial situation is nothing more than a particularly acute form of cultural conflict where an institutional superstructure freezes the sociocultural stratification into what is from the viewpoint of the colonized a permanently unfavorable pattern. It

1. Vittorio Lanternari, *The Religions of the Oppressed* (New York: Knopf, 1963); Sylvia L. Thrupp, ed., *Millenial Dreams in Action* (The Hague: Mouton, 1962); Anthony F.-C. Wallace, ed., *The Ghost Dance and the Sioux Outbreak of 1890* (Chicago: University of Chicago Press, 1964); A.-J. F. Köbben, "Prophetic Movements as an Expression of Social Protest," *International Archives of Ethnography* 49 (1960): 117–64.

has been observed, however, that religious and other group phenomena
can also reflect the internal tensions of a society. Class distinctions
and class antagonisms, as well as frustrations and anxieties associated
with rapid social change, can, and frequently do, generate within a
politically independent society religious movements comparable to
those observed among subjugated people.[2] There is, therefore, no
reason to believe that cult movements, which were originally reactions
against colonial rule, automatically cease to exist once formal political
independence is achieved. But though they continue to function, different movements adjust differently to post-independence conditions.
The key problem for them is not unlike that which manifests itself
in the temptation of "permanent revolution" for secular movements:
having secured the right or at least the possibility to operate more or
less openly, will they find for themselves a place within the existing
social order, or will they continue to offer an outlet for the discontented at the risk of generating suspicion and antagonism on the part
of the new national establishment?

No religious movement, to be sure, views the problem in these terms.
Most of them, to the extent that they are truly nonsecular movements,
simply want to pursue their manifest aims free from governmental
interference. They expect greater tolerance from an African government
than from a colonial regime, but whether they receive it or not depends in a significant way on the extent to which they are willing to
"render their due unto Caesar" as well as on their ability to control the
faithful. Some movements, such as, for example, the Kimbangist movement (now called Eglise de Jésus Christ sur la Terre par Simon Kimbangu, or EJCSK), found no difficulty in fitting into a post-independence
situation. After nearly forty years of official hostility, Kimbangism was
authorized by Belgian colonial authorities shortly before independence,
presumably as a political concession in a region where passive resistance had reached alarming proportions. It was then elevated to the
rank of an officially recognized religion on the same footing as other
Christian faiths by President Kasa-Vubu, who, though not himself
a Kimbangist, was in a good position as the major political leader of
the BaKongo to appreciate the role played by the movement in the
awakening of Kongo national consciousness.[3] Kimbangist schools are

2. See L. Pope, *Millhands and Preachers* (New Haven: Yale University Press,
1942); E. J. Hobsbawn, "Methodism and the Threat of Revolution in Britain,"
History Today 7, no. 2 (1957): 115–24.
3. See René Lemarchand, "The Bases of Nationalism Among the BaKongo,"
Africa 31 (1961): 344–54; Laurent Monnier, "Notes sur l'ABAKO et le nationalisme
Kongo," *Genève-Afrique* 5 (1966): 51–61.

now subsidized by the state in the same manner as their Catholic and Protestant counterparts.

Without ever becoming quite as "established," the Lumpa movement in Zambia, which had been tolerated by the British, felt no particular compulsion to align itself with the Zambian nationalist movement and remained essentially nonpolitical. Ironically, it was the Lumpas' very "quietism" that precipitated a clash between them and the new African authorities of Zambia in 1965.[4]

On the other hand, the Kitawala, the Congolese offshoot of the Watch Tower movement, maintained an ambiguous attitude toward the new Congolese political elite. The Watch Tower doctrine, as interpreted by its Congolese followers, not only lent itself readily to the expression of anti-colonial sentiments but could also be brandished against any form of "evil" government—and the years following independence showed no lack of corrupt, tyrannical, and ineffective authority.

The frequency of religious undertones in the various Congolese uprisings since 1960 has been repeatedly recognized,[5] and no thorough analysis of Congolese religious movements after independence will be attempted here. The limited aim of this essay is to scrutinize the attitude of Congolese authorities in Katanga toward some of the best-known cult movements and to show the ambivalent feelings of the new African rulers toward a phenomenon which had long vexed their colonial predecessors.

Unlike the densely populated areas of the Congo's southern savanna —Lower-Congo, Kwilu, Kasai—Katanga had never been notable for the proliferation of home-grown cult movements. The most important foci of social change, the urban industrial centers of the Katanga copper belt, were relatively isolated from the major centers of traditional culture, and industrial manpower had to be drawn from neighboring British territories and from relatively distant regions of the Congo. It took time for industrial development and locally based salaried employment to penetrate the more densely populated areas of North Katanga. Not surprisingly, therefore, we find that up to the 1950's cult movements penetrated Katanga from or through neighbor-

4. James Fernandez, "The Lumpa Uprising: Why?" *Africa Report* 9, no. 10: 30–32.

5. R. C. Fox and W. DeCraemer, "The Second Independence: A Case Study of the Kwilu Rebellion in the Congo," *Comparative Studies in Society and History* 8 (1965): 78–109; B. Verhaegen, *Rébellions au Congo*, 2 vols. (Brussels: C.R.I.S.P., 1966 and 1969); Etat du Katanga, *La Rébellion dite Balubakat dans l'Etat du Katanga* (Elisabethville, 1961.)

ing Rhodesia. Examples are the Watch Tower movement, which later spread through the eastern half of the Congo under the name of Kitawala; the various offshoots of the Apostolic Faith Church, whose followers are known to non-members as Bapostolo; and the Watchman Healing Mission. It was not until after World War II that Kimbangism, having filtered from the Lower Congo through Kwango and Kwilu into Kasai, was imported into Katanga (without any spectacular success) by some migrants from Kasai and in forms somewhat different from the original creed. A number of non-Christian movements originated in the Congo but few of them in Katanga itself.

Non-Christian Movements under Colonial Rule

Excluding those associated with beliefs in sporadically recurrent rumors such as the alleged kidnapping of Africans by Europeans (Mitumbula), non-Christian movements suppressed by colonial authorities in Katanga can be divided into four major types.

The first type centers on belief in the resurrection of dead ancestors. A fairly common belief in all parts of the world, it usually associates the return of departed ancestors with a complete subversion of the relationship between the conqueror and the conquered. Elaborate ceremonies known as *Zemba* among the Lunda and *Mungonge* among the Tshokwe helped to diffuse the belief in Katanga and other parts of the Congo on two chronologically distinct but otherwise quite similar occasions.

In 1931–32 rumors heralding the imminent return of dead ancestors circulated among the Tshokwe of the Congo-Angola border. The return of the ancestors, it was claimed, would be accompanied by the demise of the colonial order; Europeans and Africans would exchange their respective social positions, and a golden age would begin. Villagers were urged to slaughter all black domestic animals and in certain cases to remove from their villages the chief objects of the *akishi* (spirits of the dead) cult, such as the *muyombo* (tree) and *mahamba* (life-size clay effigies of spirit incarnations). The movement died out rapidly, as such adventist beliefs often do, but two important chiefs —one a Tshokwe, the other a Lunda—were deposed by Belgian authorities for their parts in spreading the rumors, while a third chief fled to Angola.[6]

6. See the report by the Assistant District Commissioner of the Lulua District to the Governor of Katanga (29 February 1932) and attached correspondence between

An almost identical wave of rumors, followed by the same reactions, developed in 1950 in the Angolan border area of Texeira de Souza. To the slaughtering of black animals was added, in this case, the injunction that white clothes should be worn on the day of resurrection. Apart from unusually large sales of white cotton cloth in local stores, however, there were no further repercussions.[7]

The second type of non-Christian movement is distinguished by its use of vitalizing and immunizing objects. Belgian authorities could not and did not systematically suppress such movements, but they were more hostile than other colonial powers. Apart from missionary influence, the Belgian administration in the Congo was disturbed by the fact that people holding a certain amulet (*bwanga* or *dawa*) often believed that they were immune from the action of magistrates, tax collectors, and other representatives of colonial authority.

The best-known amulets in Katanga were Ukanga, Farmaçon, Tambwe, and Tshimani. Ukanga took many forms. The two most common were a brightly colored bottle capped with red feathers and a lancet containing various ingredients steeped in water from the first rainfalls of the season and a magical powder in the horn of a *kashia* antelope. The amulet, which appears to have originated among the BaTetela-BaKusu of the middle Lomami valley, became widely known in various parts of Katanga around 1930.

The use of Ukanga declined in the 1940's when Farmaçon became more popular. The name Farmaçon was apparently derived from the French "formation" (training), which referred in this case to "medical training." Farmaçon consisted of the injection of some kind of liquid with a hypodermic needle, or in some cases of the insertion of just the needle or some other sharp metal point, under the patient's skin. The popularity of Farmaçon reached its peak in the late 1940's in the Sandoa-Dilolo region[8] and even stimulated some enterprising people of neighboring Kapanga territory into launching their own version of it under the name of Konfirmash (or *Confirmation*).[9]

---

the District Commissioner and local administrators. On related movements outside Katanga, see Edouard De Jonghe, "Formation récente de sociétés secrètes au Congo Belge," *Africa* 60 (1936): 56–63.

7. Reports by the Territorial Administrator of Dilolo, 18 November 1950, and 5 February 1951; Report by the Territorial Administrator of Sandoa, 17 December 1950.

8. Territoire de Sandoa, *Rapport Affaires Indigènes et Main d'Oeuvre* (*AIMO*) 1948, p. 39.

9. *Rapport Sûreté,* Kapanga, Third Quarter, 1950. There was apparently some semantic confusion between *formation* (training) and *confirmation* (the Catholic sacrament).

Tambwe, like Ukanga, spread through Katanga in the 1930's. It too came in two versions. One, meant for adepts, consisted of a bracelet made of iron and antelope horn containing several magical substances (*Bizimba*). The other, for non-adepts, was a sausage-shaped roll containing an assortment of *Bizimba*—such as dirt from gravesites, crushed human bones, hawk feathers, and hairs and fragments from the heart of a lion or leopard—mixed with palm oil. In this second and presumably more powerful form the amulet was "fed" palm oil through a small aperture and kept in a box or washbasin along with coins and bills. Like other amulets, Tambwe was supposed to protect its possessor against various dangers, especially against disease, evil spirits, and prosecution for wrongdoing. In 1947 the price of the amulet was said to have ranged from 200 to 1,500 francs—a considerable sum for most Congolese. The popularity of Tambwe declined steadily after World War II, although it retained its appeal among certain groups, such as the BaSongye residents of Kongolo territory.

The use of Tshimani, a mixture of peanut oil and tree bark, spread from Kasai into the southeast in the 1930's and was replaced after the war by more "modern" practices, like Farmaçon. It supposedly gave immunity against snakebite, disease, and prosecution by the authorities; its adherents wore a bangle made of beads with two small wooden amulets around the arm or ankle.[10]

The third type of non-Christian movement focuses on witchcraft detection. Here, again, Belgian colonial authorities tried to intervene only when they suspected a possible violation of law and order. They forbade, for example, subjecting an accused sorcerer to various types of ordeals, especially ordeals by poison and by torture. Divination, which was generally tolerated by the administration, gradually replaced ordeals as a prelude to exorcism.

Witchcraft detection normally went along with the use of amulets in much the same way as a medical diagnosis is followed by a prescription. Diviners dispensed charms that were supposed to protect their bearers against spells. But the detection of witchcraft, as well as the preparation of charms against its effects, was considered most effective when practiced collectively, and diviners and those desiring protection against witchcraft often formed a single society. It is impossible, therefore, to draw sharp dividing lines among believers in the power of a certain *bwanga,* anti-witchcraft societies, initiation fraternities, and

10. Jean Vanden Bossche, *Sectes et Associations Indigènes au Congo Belge* (Léopoldville: AIMO, 1954), pp. 42–43.

organizations exercising some form of sociopolitical control. Nevertheless, witchcraft detection must be regarded as an important factor. The rapid spread and early success of the Watch Tower movement in Northern Rhodesia and the Congo was, according to most sources, linked to its emphasis on the elimination of witchcraft. And the same, to a certain extent, appears to be true of the propagation of other Christian faiths.

Finally, there are movements that try to establish "parallel hierarchies." Even the organization of independent African churches reflects, at least in part, the desire to create a purely African ecclesiastical hierarchy parallel to that of European churches. Some associations attempted to duplicate certain features of the colonial system in order to achieve what they viewed as a more satisfactory performance of functions normally discharged by the state apparatus. There was the *Pauni* movement, for example, which operated in Kivu and northern Katanga in the 1930's, whose dignitaries assumed the titles of judges, administrators, and *procureurs* in dispensing justice to the members.[11] Similar practices were also found in a movement called Les Belges. A movement known as Tutshikele emerged in the mid-1940's in the Dilolo area, from which point it spread to neighboring Sandoa. Its members claimed to be possessed by spirits of deceased Europeans and behaved accordingly, dressing and eating like whites and even claiming to speak a number of European languages.[12] The colonial administration took no measures against this movement. Perhaps it was flattered by what it viewed as an implicit acknowledgement of European superiority.

Christian Movements during the Colonial Period

The adaptation of the Christian creed to African needs followed various paths. So long as European and American missionaries insisted upon retaining both the organizational and the doctrinal control of Christian churches, the only alternative open to dissatisfied African converts was open dissidence. Schismatic or fissiparous movements have been a permanent feature of the history of Christianity in Africa. In Katanga, as mentioned earlier, the Watch Tower movement was

11. Ibid., p. 81.
12. *Rapport AIMO,* Territory of Sandoa, 1948: pp. 37–38; Vanden Bossche, *Sectes,* p. 66.

the first major manifestation of African aspirations toward religious independence.

The Watch Tower movement had expanded northward from Cape Town in the years preceding World War I and had found a particularly fertile soil in Nyasaland. After the war it appeared in Northern Rhodesia and spread among the Bemba of the Northern Province, where it has remained firmly entrenched ever since. Converts, led by Hanoc Shindano, built a community which they called Jerusalem near a river they renamed Jordan.[13] In 1925 a native of Nyasaland residing in Northern Rhodesia, Tomo Nyarenda "Mwana Lesa," introduced Watch Tower doctrines into the Congo, but after he practiced baptism by immersion so thoroughly that several of his converts drowned, he was arrested by the colonial authorities, escaped to Northern Rhodesia, and was finally hanged by the British in 1927.

The first of many Belgian bans on Kitawala was decreed in 1926. A second wave followed in 1930–31, prompting Protestant missionaries in Elisabethville to issue a vigorous condemnation of the movement. By that time, however, the movement had made many new converts, including some traditional chiefs, in the areas of Northern Rhodesia immediately adjacent to the Congo, and their infiltration into the Belgian colony became virtually impossible to stop, given the constant traffic across an artificial border and the presence of thousands of Rhodesian laborers in the mines of Katanga. By the mid-1930's the movement had spread in the direction of Dilolo and had made converts among the *évolués* in the urban centers of southern Katanga. The real breakthrough, however, came in the north. During 1937–38, Kitawala spread like a brush fire throughout this region. Sometimes hundreds of persons were baptized in a few days, and the movement made deep inroads into rural areas despite, or perhaps because, of its opposition to traditional chiefs. Kitawala continued to spread during World War II, especially in the North Katanga mining center of Manono and the Mwanza and Kongolo areas. Its success among salaried workers goes a long way to explain the widely held belief among European employers and officials that Kitawala was at the root of the 1945–46 wave of labor unrest in North Katanga. After 1947 the pressure of Belgian repressive policy in Katanga became so intense that members were forced to convene in small groups and constantly change the location of their meetings to escape detection. Rhodesian

13. Ian Cunnison, "A Watch Tower Assembly in Central Africa," *International Review of Missions* 40 (1951): 456–68.

influences continued to be felt, as the Watch Tower movement held frequent rallies just across the border. Periodic visits by traveling propagandists kept the faith burning. The movement even gained new ground in the mid-1950's, and during the last years of colonial rule it made a new thrust in North Katanga under the name—borrowed from Revelations, the movement's favorite part of the Scriptures—of "[Church of] Philadelphia."

The appeal of Kitawala to the Congolese is not easily explained. Different people were probably attracted by different aspects of the movement. The millenarian character of Watch Tower doctrines expressed itself in the Congo through adventist beliefs centering on the departure of all Europeans or on the reversal of the stratified order of colonial society. Teachings that concerned the evil roots of worldly hierarchies were interpreted, depending upon circumstances, against Belgian authorities, against traditional chiefs, or against both, and in recent years, sometimes even against African governments. Finally, as mentioned earlier, the movement's strong stand against witchcraft and its insistence that villagers rid themselves of all charms were more than a marginal factor in ensuring its success in communities where the web of spells and counterspells had become unbearable. More generally, Kitawala, like other independent churches, reflected the disappointment of many Africans at the bitter contrast between the professed ideals and the actual behavior of white Christians.[14]

The reaction to Kitawala in Katanga was such that for years any new cult movement, even if non-Christian, was automatically viewed as a disguised form of the Watch Tower movement. This was the case of the Watchman Healing Mission, for example, whose founder had indeed been exposed to Watch Tower doctrines before World War I, as well as of the Apostolic Faith Church—two movements that appeared in Katanga between 1953 and 1956.

According to its leaders in Katanga, the Watchman Healing Mission (WHM), also known as Mulenda Mission, was launched in 1909 by Eliotti Acirwa Kamwanya, a native of Nyasaland who had been trained by an American minister of the Watch Tower Society. Upon his return to Nyasaland from South Africa, Eliotti was deported by the British in 1916, but his work was continued by one of his disciples, Chilele. Eliotti was released in 1938 and allowed to return to Nyasaland, where he continued to evangelize until his death in 1955. He was

14. See Jacques E. Gérard, *Les fondements syncrétiques du Kitawala* (Brussels: C.R.I.S.P., 1969).

succeeded by Chilele, assisted by a new deputy, Andiford Kaliati.[15]

The teachings of WHM, which emphasized the curative virtues of prayer and forbade the use of medicaments, were introduced in the copper-belt area of Northern Rhodesia in 1946. Pita Kauto, a Congolese native who had resided in Northern Rhodesia, brought the WHM to Jadotville, Dilolo, Kolwezi, and Sandoa in 1953. The movement was outlawed by the Belgian authorities in 1954 and many of its members were arrested,[16] but official repression did not prevent the spread of the movement, especially in Dilolo territory.[17] The agitation reached a feverish pitch when a high WHM official from Northern Rhodesia toured Dilolo in 1958. Kauto was arrested, along with several other members of the sect, and sentenced to sixty days in jail. Upon his release he was placed under house arrest, but he somehow managed to reach Nyasaland in 1959. Appointed bishop by Chilele, Kauto returned to Dilolo in 1960 "to cause the banner of the Lord to be raised in the eyes of all the peoples of the Congo."[18]

The growth of the Bapostolo movement in Katanga is more difficult to trace. The parent movement, the Apostolic Faith Church, was founded by W. O. Hutchinson in Bournemouth, England, in 1908 and transplanted by him to South Africa in 1911. One of Hutchinson's aims was to "instruct and train Africans to communicate the word of God to their own people," and under European supervision "Bantu superintendents" were put in charge of the African clergy in each territory. But the church suffered from some serious rifts, and the name Apostolic Church has apparently been used by a number of dissident or even unrelated groups.

One such dissident was the prophet Marange (or Malangu), who founded a church at Umtali in 1924. Between 1953 and 1956 followers of Marange's African Apostolic Church introduced his teachings into Katanga. Petro Nawezi, a Lunda and a former Methodist catechist, was converted at Lusaka in 1953 following the miraculous healing of his wife and he, in turn, according to his own claims, baptized seven Congolese, five from Elisabethville and two from Dilolo.[19]

Within less than three years the movement had acquired enough of

15. "L'histoire et la signification de la WHM," memorandum to South Katanga provincial authorities, 17 October 1966.

16. *Rapport AIMO*, Territory of Dilolo, 1957, p. 40.

17. Idem, 1958.

18. "L'histoire et la signification de la WHM."

19. Letter by the representative of the "Eglise Apostolique Africaine Church" (*sic.*) to the Minister of Justice of South Katanga, 15 December 1966.

a following to stimulate competition and attract official attention. The Belgian administration outlawed all Apostolo movements in 1956, and four leaders of the movement, including Nawezi, were arrested. In 1957, eighty-two Bapostolo were indicted in Elisabethville and fifty-four were arrested in Dilolo territory. After his arrest, Nawezi decided to abandon some of the most conspicuous rites of the sect. He authorized his followers to shave off their beards (the wearing of a full beard had been the most distinctive mark of the Bapostolo), invited members to pray at home instead of gathering in the open air as they had done previously, and administered baptism with water carried in a cup, instead of by immersion.

These compromises caused his leadership to be challenged by one Pierre Musumbu. Two senior church officials from Northern Rhodesia effected a reconciliation at Lusaka in 1957, and Musumbu was appointed Nawezi's second-in-command. Though Musumbu left Katanga in 1958 to spread the faith in his home province of Kasai, the breach in the movement, far from the healing, was further widened by the factor of ethnicity that had come to dominate the Katanga political scene. While Nawezi was a Lunda, Musumbu and most of the followers of the movement were immigrants from Kasai. Soon the split in the ranks of the Bapostolo came to reflect the pervasive cleavage between so-called authentic Katangese and outsiders. Meanwhile, the colonial authorities had gradually relaxed their undiscriminating hostility toward African churches, and by early 1960, despite a continuing official ban on their activities, the bearded Bapostolo, wearing robes and carrying staffs, could be seen meeting in vacant lots in Elisabethville.[20]

The Apostolo were not the only churches to be affected by the problem of ethnicity. The Kimbangist movement, which had spread to non-BaKongo areas during the years it had been banned, was officially authorized in Léopoldville province in 1960. One of Kimbangu's sons, Joseph Diangenda, acting as the legal representative of the "official" Kimbangist church, went to Elisabethville to have his father's body exhumed. Kimbangu's remains were reinterred at Nkamba, the village that had been the center of Kimbangu's prophetic career and which his followers called Jerusalem. On the occasion of

20. An ordinance issued by the governor general on 8 May 1959 left the provincial governors free to decide which sects should be outlawed in their respective provinces. In Katanga a provincial arrêté outlawed the Apostolic Church, as well as a number of other sects and movements, on 25 August 1959.

this ceremony the church held an organizational conference, but non-BaKongo participants were disappointed by what they viewed as the ethnic imbalance in the apportionment of posts in the church's central administration. Of the twenty senior members on the board, eighteen were BaKongo. This was the source of a misunderstanding which eventually led a number of Kimbangists from Kasai and Katanga to form a dissident movement called Eglise Unie du Saint Esprit.[21]

Independent Religious Movements during the Katanga Secession

The end of Belgian rule was followed in Katanga by the almost immediate declaration of that province's secession from the rest of the Congo. From the outset, however, the "independent" state of Katanga had to face the determined opposition of a substantial portion of its population and the threat of military intervention by the central government. By September 1960 the latter threat receded into the background, following Lumumba's dismissal from the prime ministership, and the Katanga regime was able to concentrate on the suppression of domestic insurgency. In these circumstances the attitude of the Katanga authorities toward African cult movements was bound to be extremely cautious.

An ordinance was issued in October outlawing the activities of all associations of a political nature. Although a broad interpretation of this ordinance could have covered almost any nonconformist movement, Minister of Interior Munongo issued a decree the following month banning the activities of the Watch Tower association "under any appellation." This decision came as an unwelcome surprise to the officials of the Watch Tower Society in Belgium, where the movement had always been legal. Having been previously penalized for the faults of an unauthorized offshoot of their movement in the Congo, they had naturally hoped that Congolese independence would at last enable them to reintroduce some degree of orthodoxy in the propagation of their doctrines. In December the administrative secretary of the Watch Tower Society for Belgium sent a personal appeal to Moïse Tshombe (himself a Methodist) pointing out that Kitawala had never been

---

21. Pierre Konji, "Memorandum de séparation de l'Eglise du Christ sur la Terre par le Prophète Simon Kimbangu et la naissance de l'Eglise Unie du Saint Esprit," mimeographed (Lubumbashi, 2 August 1966).

acknowledged or recognized by his denomination. As he passed on the request to Munongo, Tshombe reminded his associate that the policies of the Katanga government "had been viewed rather critically, notably among African circles in the Federation of Rhodesia and Nyasaland, notably because of certain prohibitions," and suggested that the November decree might be aimed more precisely at Kitawala in order "to avoid offending, to some extent, African opinion in neighboring territories to the South."[22]

Munongo at first deferred to Tshombe's wishes and drafted a new decree in which the words "Watch Tower" were replaced by "Watch Tower-Kitawala," but because of the combined opposition of security agents and of certain Belgian advisers to any mitigation of colonial policy toward the movement, he subsequently decided not to issue the new decree. He told Tshombe in a letter that, much as he was attached to religious freedom, he though it best to maintain the earlier decree and suggested writing to the Belgian secretary of the Watch Tower Society that the authorization of their movement should be solicited again "in a good ten years" after any similarity between their church and Kitawala had become thoroughly obscured.[23] As a matter of fact, Munongo dispatched the proposed reply the very same day and sent a copy of it to Tshombe—although the copy, owing to a "clerical error," reached the president only three weeks later.

Despite suggestions by security agents that the Watch Tower movement could be utilized against the government by leaders of the Balubakat opposition in northern Katanga, the attitude of the Katanga authorities was probably not overly influenced by them, as the following passage found in a study of the North Katanga rebellion prepared by the secessionist regime around mid-1961 indicates:

It is well known that Kitawala, even in versions close to the Watch Tower, is hostile to any authority. It also opposes belonging to any movement whatsoever. Kitawala refused to join the BBK [i.e., Balubakat], and its members did not accept the BBK initiation. But while the BBK showed some understanding toward the Protestants, who also refused the *dawa*, it was intractable with the Kitawala. Unlike the Protestants, the latter refused to man roadblocks. . . . It seems that Kitawala might have been willing to enter into some sort of an alliance with the BBK, if only out of spite toward those who had harassed them. Their attempts were

22. Letter of 11 January 1961.
23. Munongo to Tshombe, 1 July 1961.

repelled. A case of this sort was the arrest of Chief Benze by members of Kitawala. The BBK showed no gratitude for this.[24]

The main spiritual support of rebel morale in North Katanga was not Kitawala but the more traditional *bwanga*. It apparently played a major role in galvanizing rural insurgents not only in North Katanga but in other rebel areas as well.[25] Meanwhile, despite the official ban on them, Watch Tower doctrines continued to circulate in the State of Katanga much in the same way as they had done under Belgian rule— along the rail line from Northern Rhodesia or simply through the mails.

The attitude of the Katanga authorities toward the Apostolo, Mulenda Mission, and other independent churches, though generally less repressive, was nevertheless characterized by overriding distrust. In 1961 Minister of Interior Munongo informed his subordinates that the Apostolic Church did not seem to present a threat to the security of the state (although the actions of individual members might be in violation of law and order and should in that case be punished), but that if they could prove that the Apostolic Church served as a facade for the Watch Tower movement, they should prosecute it accordingly. He concluded by stressing that the movement's activities should be watched closely.[26]

In September 1962 the Apostolo movement was banned in Dilolo. In November the district commissioner of Lualaba, the territorial administrator of Kolwezi, and a third official allegedly assaulted members of the Apostolic Church at Kolwezi.[27] In a subsequent letter justifying his actions to President Tshombe, the territorial administrator of Kolwezi claimed that "the association as a whole had become uncontrolled and uncontrollable," that many adepts, "in conformity with Kitawala practices," refused to carry any identification, and that they refused all medical care and spread "racial, anti-medical and anti-missionary propaganda."[28] On the same day that these incidents were taking place at Kolwezi, the mayor of Kikula township at Jadotville personally arrested fifty members of the Apostolo movement, all of them but

24. Etat du Katanga, *La Rébellion*, p. 26. Similar problems later emerged in the relationship between the Kitawala and the "Simba" rebels of Maniema. See Verhaegen, *Rébellions*, vol. 2, p. 21.

25. Verhaegen, *Rébellions*; Fox and De Craemer, "Second Independence."

26. Circular no. 3021/0529/404, 8 March 1961.

27. Letter by two members of the Apostolic Church to the Speaker of the Katanga National Assembly, 7 November 1962.

28. Memo. no. J.5/0830, 19 December 1962.

one being North Katanga BaLuba.[29] Four days later the Bena
Apostolo movement was outlawed throughout Katanga on the alleged
grounds that it had "definitely established links with the forbidden
association of the Watch Tower."[30]

Local Kimbangists did not fare much better. In several letters
addressed to the authorities in the fall of 1962, they requested permission to open churches in Elisabethville and Kolwezi.[31] Their request was turned down in December, but a few days later the Katanga
secession came to an end.

Government Policies after the Secession

The restoration of the central government's control over Katanga
led to a confused period in the relations between secular authorities
and independent churches. On the one hand, the Léopoldville government's general policy line toward such movements was one of greater
tolerance but, on the other, the administrative personnel of the former
Katanga "state" remained by and large in place and maintained, at
least for a while, its previous attitudes. Furthermore, as the Adoula
government leaned farther and farther away from its Lumumbist elements and faced the first outbursts of the so-called Mulelist rebellion,
its policy toward such movements as the Watch Tower became increasingly hostile. Tshombe's accession to the premiership in 1964
only accentuated this trend.

The vacillation of official policy in the months that followed the
end of the secession is illustrated by the Kimbangist church's complaints in the spring of 1963 that the provincial authorities in
Elisabethville appeared to remain unaware of the fact that their organization had been officially recognized by President Kasa-Vubu more
than two years earlier. The assistant public prosecutor, to whom this
complaint was presented, felt compelled to remind the provincial
Department of the Interior that "under the present circumstances,
the authorization of the church by a presidential ordinance should be
considered as implying the removal of any prohibition against it."[32]

29. Letter by the Mayor of Kikula "Commune" to the Director of Security Services
in Jadotville, 5 November 1962.

30. Arrêté Ministériel, no. 30/290, 7 November 1962.

31. Letters to Tshombe (30 October 1962), to Munongo (27 November 1962),
and to the District Commissioner of Lualaba (27 November 1962).

32. Letter by the Assistant Public Prosecutor to the Director of the Territorial
Service, 4 May 1963.

Watch Tower members also tried to take advantage of the change of regime. Less than one month after the end of the secession, three Rhodesian members sought permission to settle in a village near Sakania on the ground that they had relatives there. They soon ran afoul of the local authorities. One propagandist was arrested at the Sakania railroad station on 13 March, and a few days later the whole congregation was rounded up and sentenced to jail by Chief Serenge, the highest-ranking traditional chief of the area.[33]

The provincial administration at Elisabethville was divided over this incident. On the one hand, as one official in the Department of the Interior observed, the legal penalties against the Watch Tower movement were still technically in force and it might be preferable to uphold the traditional chiefs "who might not understand our new position" and whose cooperation was, in any case, "more useful than that of the few incarcerated members of a forbidden sect."[34] On the other hand, as the new provincial minister of interior, Alexis Kishiba, well knew, the central government's policy was "currently to tolerate the activities of this sect, pending new regulations concerning religious associations."[35] In this situation, the district commissioner of North Katanga instructed his subordinates that only those individuals who disturbed public order and tranquillity should be prosecuted.[36] Meanwhile, the Léopoldville government was reshuffled and revised its attitude toward the Watch Tower movement. In an emphatically worded circular, the new minister of the interior of the central government, Joseph Maboti, reminded all provincial presidents that his predecessor's tolerance had been unfounded and in support of his views he revived all the arguments once used by the Belgian authorities.[37]

Kishiba asked Léopoldville to clarify whether or not any distinction should be made between the Watch Tower Bible and Tract Society (Jehovah's Witnesses) and the Kitawala-Watch Tower.[38] Before he

33. Undated report of the Territorial Administrator of Sakania (*circa* late July, 1963).

34. Memo. by the head of the First Bureau of the *Direction du Service Territorial,* 2 September 1963.

35. Minister of Interior to the District Commissioner of North Katanga, 25 September 1963.

36. District Commissioner of North Katanga to Territorial Administrators in his district, circular no. 0310/i, 9 December 1963.

37. Minister of the Interior to Provincial Presidents, circular no. 2531/5674, 5 November 1963.

38. Letter of 16 March 1964.

could receive a reply, however, the Adoula government resigned and was replaced by a new cabinet headed by Tshombe. The reply that Kishiba eventually received from the ministry of the interior in Léopoldville, now placed under Munongo's direction, passed over the question of Jehovah's Witnesses and emphasized that pre-1960 ordinances against Kitawala and the Watch Tower were still in force.[39]

The provincial minister's caution was understandable, considering that a group officially called Jehovah's Witnesses had been lawfully organized in Léopoldville and was represented in Elisabethville by Shindano, speaker of the East Katanga legislature. Shindano took it upon himself to "authorize" the proselytizing activities of one Aron Kimba on behalf of Jehovah's Witnesses by a safe-conduct written under his official letterhead and addressed to Mufunga, the Lomotwa chief of Sampwe.[40] This may explain why shortly thereafter the assistant district commissioner of North Katanga informed the territorial administrator of Sakania that, pending an explicit prohibition directed against Jehovah's Witnesses, the latter group's existence should be tolerated, except in cases where "public order and tranquillity" were being directly threatened.[41]

The line drawn by the Elisabethville authorities between Kitawala or Watch Tower on the one hand and Jehovah's Witnesses on the other was too fine for local administrators to perceive. They understood that any movement to which the "Watch Tower" label could be affixed was still prohibited, and they reacted accordingly. They also knew of the Tshombe government's distrust of all unorthodox movements, particularly at a time when the spread of the so-called Mulelist rebellion into North Katanga seemed to coincide with the extension of the former Balubakat opposition to the Katanga secession. Indeed, the provincial government of East Katanga had just decided to outlaw the Apostolic Faith Church,[42] and it seemed likely that other cult movements would suffer the same fate. The provincial authorities therefore attempted to maintain a delicate balance between tolerance and repression. Local administrators kept reporting the existence of

39. Secretary General of the Ministry of the Interior to the Provincial Minister of the Interior of East Katanga, 16 July 1964.

40. Territorial Administrator of Mitwaba to the Director of the Territorial Service, 23 November 1964; *Chef de Poste* of Sampwe to the District Commissioner of North Katanga, 9 December 1964.

41. Assistant District Commissioner of North Katanga to the Territorial Administrator of Sakania, 18 August 1964.

42. *Arrêté Ministériel,* no. 201/106, 31 August 1964.

Watch Tower cells and expressing the view that from a practical stand-point any distinction between the Watch Tower movement and the Jehovah's Witnesses was impossible to draw.[43] The bafflement of local officials was probably shared by official representatives of the Jehovah's Witnesses in Léopoldville and in the United States. In rebel-held areas printed membership cards bearing side by side the designations "Kitawalisme, Religion Congolaise," "Watch Tower Bible and Tract Society," and "International Bible Students Association" (the latter two being used by the orthodox movement)[44] were being circulated without any sort of authorization.

Another source of friction had to do with the preparations for the 1965 general election. Tshombe and his associates were hoping that the election could be turned through careful manipulations into some sort of a plebiscite that would bolster the incumbent premier's legiti-macy and stature both on the domestic and on the international scene. In view of the administration's efforts to produce a massive turnout, the distinct lag in voter registration in areas where the Kitawala, the Watch Tower, and the Jehovah's Witnesses had been active was par-ticularly frustrating. Whether or not this attitude was common to all three denominations is impossible to detect from the record, but in any case local administrators were not inclined to quibble over this matter. "I reiterate my request," one of them wrote, "for measures to be taken in order to end the propaganda by [Jehovah's Witnesses] especially during this time when we are doing everything we can to ensure the success of the forthcoming electoral campaign."[45]

In exasperation, the director of the territorial service wrote to the governor of East Katanga on 1 February asking him to find out from the central government exactly what attitude to adopt toward Je-hovah's Witnesses.[46] Interior Minister Munongo, who had always been anxious to maintain a personal influence in his home area (he eventu-ally gave up his cabinet post and was elected governor of East Katanga in June 1965), saw no need to antagonize the speaker of the provincial

43. Territorial Administrator of Katanga to the District Commissioner of North Katanga, 16 December 1964.
44. The name "Watch Tower Bible and Tract Society" has been used by the "orthodox" movements in Zambia, Malawi, and Rhodesia, while the name "Inter-national Bible Students Association" has been used in Kenya.
45. Territorial Administrator of Mitwaba to the Director of the Territorial Ser-vice, 7 December 1964.
46. Director of the Territorial Service to the Governor of East Katanga, 1 February 1965.

legislature, who not only acted as the official representative of the Jehovah's Witnesses but was also believed to favor Munongo's local rival, Jean-Baptiste Kibwe. Possibly with the hope of securing at least the movement's benevolent neutrality, Munongo granted it a provisional authorization on 16 February. At the same time, however, he reserved for himself the option of a subsequent policy reversal by requesting the opinions of local officials on the advisability of allowing the movement to operate lawfully. Predictably enough, the response of local administrators was largely unfavorable.[47]

Meanwhile, individual cases involving Jehovah's Witnesses continued to be governed by the principle that only those specific activities that were in violation of law and order would be prosecuted. This "neither war nor peace" policy was also applied to other sects, such as, for example, the Apostolo. It is nearly impossible to determine with any degree of certainty to what extent this policy was part of a nationwide strategy by Tshombist forces or a tactical response to the volatile political situation in Katanga. In any event, the policy was apparently continued for a while by Governor Munongo after Tshombe's fall from office and the establishment of the Mobutu regime.

The Jehovah's Witnesses themselves pursued their activity with a clear conscience, as suggested by Shindano's secretary in a note: "To be sure, the current regime forbids any activity by political parties. Religious associations, however, may continue to pray. For this reason, I invite you to pray and to praise the Lord."[48] Whether or not this interpretation of General Mobutu's intentions was actually warranted, the provincial government's disposition toward nonconformists was far from benevolent. The provincial department of the interior had just completed a fairly exhaustive survey of a number of associations, both secular and religious, such as the Watch Tower, the Apostolo, and a few others, and the conclusions released in 1966 were undiscriminatingly hostile to all sects.[49]

The wheels of government were meanwhile grinding in a different direction in the capital city of Kinshasa. The result was the almost simultaneous passage of two contradictory measures: a presidential

47. Territorial Administrator of Lubudi to the Director of the Territorial Service, 18 October 1965; Territorial Administrator of Kasenga to the Director of the Territorial Service, 13 September 1965; chief of General Administration to the Director of the Territorial Service, 13 September 1965.

48. Letter to Provincial Minister Kibwe, 21 February 1966.

49. Memo. from the Provincial Minister of the Interior to the Governor of East Katanga, 15 March 1966.

ordinance permitting the incorporation of the Jehovah's Witnesses as a nonprofit organization,[50] and a decree by the governor of South Katanga banning all offshoots of the Apostolic Church family, the Jehovah's Witnesses, and the Mulenda Mission.[51]

The outbreak of the first Kisangani mutiny diverted much official attention from the problem of religious freedom, but local officials in Katanga were still confused about what attitude to adopt toward the various movements listed in Governor Munongo's decree. A number of Jehovah's Witnesses who had been arrested in Baudouinville before the passage of President Mobutu's ordinance were apparently kept in jail for several months, while some of the Apostolo who had been arrested immediately after issuance of Governor Munongo's ban were released. The Apostolo and the Mulenda Mission, realizing that despite their being lumped together with the Jehovah's Witnesses in Munongo's ban President Mobutu's recognition of the latter movement did not actually extend to them, submitted petitions for separate authorizations in the fall of 1966.

Curiously, while independent African churches were meeting throughout this period with the growing displeasure of the provincial authorities, one group, the Lumpa, escaped official hostility. The reasons for this difference of treatment are not entirely clear, but one may assume that two factors played a part. First, although ethnically related to populations living in the Congo-Zambia border area, the Lumpa were clearly a refugee group seeking shelter and not propagandizing for their faith. Second, the circumstances under which the Lumpa sought refuge in the Congo undoubtedly worked in their favor, at least initially. The first refugees reached the border post of Mokambo, where they eventually settled in a village of their own, in February 1965—when relations between the Tshombe government and its African neighbors, especially Zambia, were acutely strained. The refugees, who were disenchanted with the Kaunda government, indicated upon arrival that they considered themselves Tshombe's subjects and not Kaunda's. It is not inconceivable that the Tshombe government's welcoming of the Lumpa refugees was in part motivated by the consideration that their presence on the border would provide some leverage on the Zambian government. There were rumors that the Lumpa might reenter Zambia with weapons supplied to them by

50. Ordinance no. 66/353, 9 June 1966. Two other ordinances extended the same recognition to the Eglise Unie du Saint Esprit, a non-BaKongo splinter group of the Kimbangist church.
51. *Arrêté* no. 30/37, 11 June 1966.

Tshombe.[52] The Zambians dispatched several envoys to Mokambo to appraise the Lumpa's intentions and to persuade them to return to Zambia. But the number of Lumpa refugees streaming into the Congo continued to grow throughout 1965.

Tshombe's fall from power resulted in improved Congo-Zambia relations and in joint efforts by the two governments to repatriate Lumpa refugees. Both countries preferred to use persuasion rather than force. When this failed, the Lumpa were permitted to remain in the Congo, though at some distance from the border.[53]

After an initial display of tolerance, the Mobutu regime stiffened its attitude toward all religious associations, including independent churches. During its much-publicized conflict with the Roman Catholic Church (1972–73), the government not only asserted the unqualified primacy of state over church but also made it clear that it would not tolerate any sort of mobilizational activities by religious groups that might infringe upon the single party's monopoly of social organization. Protestant denominations were persuaded by a skillful blend of threats and incentives to coalesce into a single confederation known as Eglise du Christ au Zaïre (ECZ)—a move that made it possible for the government to deal with them collectively, while at the same time quietly stifling nonconformist sects. A 1972 act made it unlawful for churches and sects to engage in any form of proselytism unless they could meet a certain number of prerequisites and obtain official recognition as religious nonprofit organizations. All churches were given three months to file for legal recognition with the department of justice, though the Catholic Church, EJCSK, and the newly created ECZ were exempted from the need to resubmit applications, a privilege subsequently extended to the Greek Orthodox, Jewish, and Islamic faiths.

Faced with the alternative of a costly and cumbersome procedure, established Protestant groups more or less grudgingly accepted membership in the ECZ. For the independent churches, on the other hand, the options were far less attractive. They could seek affiliation with the ECZ, but they knew that their applications stood little chance of being favorably reviewed by the established Protestant denominations;[54] or

52. Report by the Assistant Territorial Administrator of Mokambo, 29 June 1965.
53. Territorial Administrator of Sakania to the District Commissioner of North Katanga, 19 February 1966.
54. By spring 1972, 45 independent churches, including 24 from Shaba (Katanga), had applied for affiliation with the ECZ. No such application was filed by the Watch Tower movement or by Jehovah's Witnesses, nor was any anticipated, according to the Secretary General of the ECZ. Communication to the author, April 1972.

they could seek legal recognition in their own right but would then have to face the government's stringent criteria. These included a deposit of $200,000 in a local bank, evidence that the founding officer held a graduate degree in theology, and convincing proof that he was not a dissident from another church—a set of conditions that no independent African church could reasonably be expected to meet. It seemed most unlikely, therefore, that any independent group other than, of course, the EJCSK, could hope to retain any sort of legal existence.

Conclusion

The developments in Katanga reviewed here show that feelings of annoyance and frustration play a considerable part in determining the attitude of secular authorities toward unorthodox religious movements. In the case of colonial authorities, these feelings are intensified by the awareness that colonized peoples do not really accept imperial rule and by the inclination to view all spontaneous "native" organizations, whether religious or secular, with suspicion. But even governments of newly-independent countries must face up to the basic problem that nonconformist movements pose. For while these movements do not create alienation, they appeal to the alienated. Not only are all governments interested in the preservation of law and order; they are also interested in seeing to it that public authority is not ignored. On this last point, officials of newly-independent countries are, understandably, particularly sensitive.

"If the Belgians outlawed the Watch Tower," said one Congolese official privately, "it is probably because they resisted imperialism. Should we hold this against them?" To which another immediately replied: "If so, why do these people refuse to vote, to be innoculated or to send their children to school now that we are independent?" This exchange accurately sums up the ambivalence of official feelings toward nonconformist sects in many an African country. It is possible, indeed probable, that the attitude of public authorities toward such movements is influenced to some extent by the different administrative traditions of different colonial powers, but even where such traditions had established a pattern of greater tolerance, occasional clashes have occurred. Although it had not been outlawed by the British, the Watch Tower movement and its offshoots, for example, have been banned or restricted in Malawi, Zambia, and Kenya.[55] Fundamentally, relations between secular authorities and religious nonconformists are characterized not so much by mutual suspicion as by lack of a common base of reference. This hampers the process of communication, and so long as it does, a certain amount of misunderstanding is bound to continue in the dialogue between church and state.

55. In 1967 a serious incident occurred in the Kabompo district of Zambia's Northwestern Province. Zambian officials had previously denounced the sect because of its members' refusal to send their children to school (*The Times*, 22 June 1967). Jehovah's Witnesses were banned in Malawi by an Executive Order of 20 October 1967 (*Sunday Mail*, Salisbury, 19 November 1967). Kenya banned the Watch Tower and all related organizations in 1973 (*Daily News*, Nairobi, 27 April 1973).

The Infrastructure of
Technical Assistance:
American Aid Experience
in Africa

by John D. Montgomery

Few would now deny the difficulty of transferring technology from a developed society to an underdeveloped one, even when the knowledge required already exists in usable form and the social institutions involved are receptive to change. American experience in providing technical assistance to African countries illuminates the range of problems encountered when neither of those conditions prevails. Many of the bromides offered about American foreign aid in the 1950's, drawing on events in other parts of the world, were tested in Africa in the 1960's and found wanting. By 1970 foreign aid analysts were much less sure than they had been about the importance to be attached to the personality traits of the "overseas man," for example, or the desirability of using assumed cultural similarities as a basis for introducing innovations in an underdeveloped society.[1] Though advanced with the laudable intention of countering naïve views about the universality of technology and the ease of its transfer, these turned out to have been hastily conceived and largely impractical notions. They were bound to be discarded eventually, but the extraordinary difficulties encountered in Africa speeded up the process.

It is to be regretted that the experience gained in Africa should have had so little influence on American aid policy. Most of the changes made in the American aid program in the 1960's—the increased emphasis given to loans rather than grants, the sharp limitations put on the magnitudes of financial commitments in Africa, the preference shown for using the services of private contractors instead of promoting governmental careers in technical assistance, and the plan to substitute international agencies for American initiatives—came about mainly in response to domestic political pressures. For a decade, foreign aid, like most other manifestations of foreign policy, did not undergo any comprehensive examination of its own experience. But its costs were too great and its constituency too remote to permit aid to survive on the basis of faith alone. Each successive review was a greater challenge to its original assumptions.

Early in the 1960's the Kennedy administration had opted for a new approach to foreign aid based on the liberal economic growth model, using ever more sophisticated and comprehensive forms of country programming, and treating aid as a series of instruments that could be orchestrated in accordance with regional needs. The Kennedy approach called for more careful attention to the social dimensions of development than had prevailed in the 1950's, when programs had been designed primarily according to technical criteria in order to reproduce Western systems of education, health, and agriculture in the underdeveloped world. The Kennedy country approach demanded more area expertise than had been needed before, especially in dealing with the newly emerging and little known countries of Africa. Moreover, since the African continent was scheduled to receive only small amounts of capital assistance, it now became necessary to examine closely the processes by which technical assistance could be rendered

1. Harlan Cleveland, Gerard J. Mongone, and John Clarke Adams, *The Overseas Americans* (New York: McGraw-Hill, 1960); Jahangir Amuzegar, *Technical Assistance in Theory and Practice: The Case of Iran* (New York: Praeger, 1966).

most effectively in that region. Accordingly, in 1961 the aid agency contracted with Boston University's African Studies Program to conduct research on developmental processes and to train aid technicians in the arts of rendering assistance in Africa.

There is reason to believe that this perspective on technical assistance is even more relevant to the needs of American aid in the 1970's than to the decade for which it was prepared. For as the Nixon administration proceeds with its reorganization of foreign aid, separating capital and military aid from technical assistance and transferring much of the dollar volume to international agencies, it is likely that the American contribution to Third World development will be increasingly associated with technical assistance. Such a specialization of functions, leaving capital aid and the more conventional forms of cultural and technical interchange to international agencies, would exploit an American comparative advantage in applied technology. It would also take advantage of a widespread popular concern in this country with finding ways to improve the quality of life. In the underdeveloped countries this would mean concentrating our aid activities on raising popular standards of health, education, and nutrition, as well as addressing the more abstract economic goals proposed in national development plans. And finally, it would contribute substantially to developing technical skills in the countries where they are scarcest. These objectives seem especially relevant to the opportunities ahead in Africa, where already the largest portion of American aid— about half—is in the form of technical assistance.

If technology is to be increasingly recognized as the favored instrument of American development assistance in the seventies, it is all the more important to find ways of accumulating knowledge and experience in the art of rendering technical assistance.

A Typology of Technical Assistance Projects

Induced technological transfer involves three major elements, which, though interdependent in practice, can be examined separately: (1) the environmental conditions in the donor country, which shape a technology to fit local resources and needs; (2) the transmission process involved in the communication of skills and knowledge; and (3) the conditions affecting receptivity to the innovation, as measured by the infrastructural capabilities an aid-receiving society develops for adapting and supporting the new technology.[2] The first and third of these elements are least understood, the second having engaged the attention of a few social psychologists and anthropologists interested in the broad processes of induced cultural change. Many Westerners have gradually become conscious of the problems involved in transferring Western skills and knowledge to others.[3] But they continue to ignore the infrastructural prerequisites of technology, not so much because they deem them unimportant as because they take them for granted.

Foreign aid is frequently offered as a package of administrative units called projects. Apart from the commodity and "commercial" import programs used in emergencies to close a country's foreign exchange gap,[4] most aid involving technology consists of small-scale efforts to change traditional ways of producing goods or rendering services. Project aid may be defined as the extension of technical assistance, with or without a capital component, to sectoral activities affecting a large number of people and offered either to improve the economic conditions of a given clientele or to increase the technical capabilities of a specific professional or subprofessional group. The United States, in contrast to the United Nations, normally offers technical assistance as a component of a funded development project. This approach has two major advantages: first, it gives individual technicians access to American funds and the opportunity to influence the host government's cooperative ventures; and second, it assigns them specific targets by which to measure their performance. But it also involves the risk that the technician may end up concentrating his energies on the easily solvable and often relatively unimportant problems that were identified when the aid was first planned. Aid projects, like other bureaucratic entities, have a way of perpetuating themselves independently of their continued social utility. Only by carefully selecting and so designing a project as to permit great flexibility in its operation and

2. John D. Montgomery, "The Challenge of Change," *International Development Review* 9 (1967): 2–8.

3. Everett M. Rogers, *Diffusion of Innovations* (New York: Free Press of Glencoe, 1962); W. F. Lionberger, *Adoption of New Ideas and Practices* (Ames: Iowa State University Press, 1960).

4. See John D. Montgomery, *The Politics of Foreign Aid* (New York: Praeger, 1962), pp. 85–93, 185–86; Joan M. Nelson, *Aid, Influence and Foreign Policy* (New York: Macmillan Co., 1968), pp. 49–50; Jacob J. Kaplan, *The Challenge of Foreign Aid* (New York: Praeger, 1967), pp. 291–93.

even, where necessary, experimentation can this danger be averted.[5]

Technical assistance projects are sharply focused according to function, location, time, personnel, and costs. In some cases they are expected to influence fundamental economic and social characteristics of the host country. Though they differ widely in their approaches to this long-range objective, they can be grouped into three basic types of activity: the pilot, the demonstration, and the diffusion project.

Pilot Projects. A pilot project may either seek to determine the prospects of applying well-known Western techniques in a new situation or explore alternative ways of meeting a technical objective. In either case it may also be used to test cultural responses and make it possible to predict the probable effects of social change once small-scale experiments are replaced by large-scale operations.

The Gbedin Swamp Rice project in Liberia provides an illuminating case study of the advantages and limitations of pilot projects. An official report issued in 1955 publicly labeled it a success because it proved that a new crop could be cultivated in Liberia's bush lands;[6] but four years later the United States government officially abandoned the project and Liberia's President Tubman called it a failure because it did not displace traditional preferences. Paradoxically, both opinions appear to have been justified. It was a successful pilot project, but because its lessons were ignored it led to a costly failure as a demonstration project.

As originally conceived, the project was to be a modest test of the hypothesis that Liberia could grow swamp rice cheaply enough to augment the limited supply of red-skinned rice grown along uplands that were being cleared by the traditional slash-and-burn method. Neither American nor Liberian technicians were aware of tribal scorn for swamp rice as "hunger" food, to be eaten only in time of famine. Nor did the Gbedin planners know that by tradition volunteer women were the sole cultivators of swamp rice crops until they requested that each clan supply labor according to a quota and it was discovered that the best workmen were unavailable. Unenthusiastic and undisciplined small boys were provided in their place—an expensive substitute, as it developed. Encouraged by the precedent, still smaller boys began to demand pay for the chore of bird watching (or, more accurately, "bird

5. Arthur T. Mosher, "Administrative Experimentation as a 'Way of Life' for Development Projects," *International Development Review* 9 (1967): 38–41.

6. U.S., Foreign Operations Administration, *Liberian Swamp Rice Production: A Success* (Washington, D.C., 1955).

scaring") in the swamp rice fields instead of working voluntarily as they had in the traditional planting. The scale of the enterprise called for the clearing of new swamplands, construction of water-control systems and, in some cases, mechanical drilling for seed planting—all involving the use of heavy equipment that would not be available to individual farmers. The expansion of the Gbedin project thus showed that new techniques would imply far-reaching changes in the rural way of life.

Other problems of a technical order also appeared. Some of the dams and dikes built to control the flow of water broke down, and the dikes had to be bulldozed over. The first efforts to grow swamp rice took place on fifty-odd small, scattered plots belonging to various clans and chieftaincies. In half the cases the seed was furnished by the government; in the others, to test the economic feasibility of the project the seed was sold. But in both situations work stopped on many of the sites soon after the chief American technician went home on leave, largely because of local taste preferences for red-skinned rice and a widespread reluctance to work in swampy areas. Soon after the American returned, however, the aid mission initiated a larger swamp rice demonstration project at Gbedin, without examining the reasons for the slowdown. Under government financing and with the support of a new extension service, training programs, and a free seed distribution program, Gbedin was to become a showplace of American technology. Heavy mechanical equipment was introduced to supplement the system of clan-supplied labor, but it soon became apparent that the demonstration was taking on life of its own. As its scale and costs rose, it became increasingly difficult for either government to disengage; as its technology became more advanced, it became increasingly difficult for the local economy to absorb.

Early evidence that swamp rice could be grown in Liberia was not sufficient basis for moving toward new large-scale techniques or to introduce on a large scale hitherto unacceptable foods. Government support was not a sufficient reason for converting successful small-scale individual operations into a large demonstration project when neither the techniques nor the product were locally desired.

The Gbedin scheme illustrates the consequences of moving too fast in applying technical knowledge to solve problems that were not defined in terms of economic, cultural, and social needs. It also demonstrates the difficulty of using small-scale success as the basis for large-scale operations.

Demonstration Projects. The purpose of a demonstration project is to dramatize an innovation whose technical merits are already known to experts. In foreign aid, of course, there can never be absolute certainty of technical success; but a demonstration project is not normally undertaken until serious technical doubts have been laid to rest.

The Gondar Public Health College and Training Center in Ethiopia, which combined a medical school, a provincial hospital, and a preventive medicine program into one spectacular project, relied on techniques that were well established in the medical profession. The project ran into serious difficulties not because of doubts among the members of the medical team about the value of the techniques used —there were few differences of opinion among them, and such as were expressed had to do with minor matters of curriculum and management—but because of cultural resistance and weak administrative support.

To the villagers in the Gondar region the measures envisaged by the demonstration project meant something more than just better medical treatment. They implied drastic changes in community living patterns. The project technicians realized from the very beginning that the local population would not acquiesce in such changes on the mere advice of outsiders. For in an Ethiopian village, as in many other small and relatively isolated communities throughout the world, the stranger is a natural object of suspicion. Almost as soon as work began on the project, local medicine men, despite deep divisions among themselves and bitter competition for patients, quickly united to oppose the Western technicians who came to their villages. Careful preliminary work had to be done before rural health centers could be set up in the Gondar region. It was learned that by first inviting village leaders to meet with them formally, health officials could usually make their presence more or less acceptable in the villages, though often at the cost of having to work through local *debtera* (spiritual healers), *woggesha* (herbalists), or *zar* ("specialists" in psychosomatic practice). In some villages, however, health officials were unable to win the support of local leaders; and though health centers were nevertheless established there, they were shunned by all patients except those who had absolutely no hope of treatment by traditional methods.

The project's administrative difficulties centered on two problems: inducing Ethiopian officials to make timely decisions, and establishing and maintaining proper channels of communication between them. The source of these difficulties lay in the nature of the Ethiopian

regime, a tradition-laden bureaucracy dominated by the strong personality of the emperor. Retention of many decisions of state in the
emperor's hands led to hesitancy and encouraged delay on the part of
ministers and subordinate officials, many of whom were never sure of
the limits of their responsibility and authority. Even when power was
delegated, tradition-minded officials tended to postpone decisions as
long as possible to reduce the risk of failure or reproach. Documents
were often conveniently misplaced or lost, especially if they required
an action deemed distasteful. "Something that must be performed in a
month's time, else dire disaster will befall, will eventually be completed in a year," an Ethiopian staff member of the Gondar project
once remarked philosophically, "and with relatively minor repercussions." Only a crisis, real or imagined, could change this attitude.
"Use of long-range planning, or, indeed, planning of any type, and
anticipation of problems," a foreign observer pointed out, "is still
virtually unknown to government officials. However, in the face of
crises which could easily have been foreseen and aborted, the official
machinery moves rapidly and effectively. A sense of when and how to
accept a crisis situation may help to accomplish the almost impossible."

The creation of a technical advisory committee in 1954 helped to
overcome some administrative difficulties. The committee was composed of three members, representing, respectively, the Imperial Ethiopian government, the World Health Organization, and the American
aid mission in Ethiopia. It administered a joint fund in its own right
made up of Ethiopian and American deposits. It had direct access to
the Minister of Health, and if necessary it could approach the
Emperor himself. It was also empowered to implement specific measures directly through United States and World Health Organization
channels. The mere knowledge that the committee possessed these
capabilities usually persuaded Ethiopian officials to treat its requests
seriously and process them through ordinary administrative channels.

Despite the ingenuity shown in the design of these institutional
arrangements, the Gondar project fell short of expectations. In 1959,
after five years of operation and an American aid expenditure of
$418,000, difficulties were still being experienced in assuring timely
budgetary action, following correct purchasing procedures, and developing a reasonable phasing-out plan. Still, the project could not
be described as a wasted effort. A considerable number of Ethiopian
medical technicians were trained, and the usefulness of preventive
medicine at local levels was effectively demonstrated. Of greater

relevance here are the object lessons that the project provided: that one could, at least in some instances, take advantage of certain indigenous cultural traits and administrative processes to ensure the survival of newly established institutions once Western technicians were withdrawn; that it might be advisable at times to experiment with existing practices in order to find cooperative solutions to problems of social change; and that caution should be exercised in anticipating public acceptance of Western techniques in less-developed countries.

Even when a demonstration project is publicly accepted, it may sometimes fail to achieve its purpose. Modern equipment and new construction may be welcomed while their purposes and intended uses are not. Just as many foreign-aid technicians have reported that other governments appear at times to welcome American dollars and material but reject American advice, so aid administrators have encountered cases where the appurtenances of a demonstration have won out over its substance.

A range management project in Somalia illustrates the feelings of qualified success a technician experiences when he sees his demonstration equipment serve a useful, but unintended, public purpose. To reduce overgrazing caused by nomads moving with their herds from one water hole to another, a group of American technicians proposed to install a series of carefully spaced permanent stock ponds near Afmadu, in southern Somalia. They planned to use these ponds to demonstrate the economic advantages of keeping small, select herds in a limited area where the animals could have plenty of water and adequate grazing within short distances. The installation of new watering facilities visibly pleased the local population; more than that, it attracted nomadic tribes from distant areas, so that grazing in the Afmadu region became once again inadequate. When the technicians tried to convince the local notables of the wisdom of either restricting grazing rights in the area or of instituting compulsory destocking, they met with a firm refusal. To fence off land and thus deny its use to others would have meant violating a time-honored Somali custom: Somali herders could not be persuaded to give up the known benefits of a nomadic existence for the sake of speculative advantages described by outsiders. An opinion poll taken shortly thereafter in the region showed that most of the inhabitants welcomed the installation of the ponds as a useful government contribution to public well-being, although a few thought that the ponds were too close together to serve the needs of nomads. None viewed the undertaking as a range management project. In the end, the project managers agreed to allow the stock ponds to be used as water holes, to build new ones in dry areas, to encourage stock raising by private entrepreneurs, and to organize long-term range management training programs.[7]

A demonstration project may also suffer from an "excess of success." The experience of a South African community development project, Entokozweni (Place of Happiness), illustrates this phenomenon so vividly that it seems appropriate to cite it here, even though it was not an American aid project.[8]

Entokozweni was a family welfare center that catered to the needs of about 130 African families living in a Johannesburg suburb of more than 60,000 people. It was financed by both public and private sources. Its activities included a day nursery, a children's club, a women's club, a school, a social welfare center, and a public health program. It had a racially integrated staff. There was little harmony between the white and black members of staff, but this did not prevent the welfare center from becoming immensely popular with the families it served. Indeed, the demands for its services soon began to overtax the center's physical facilities. New nursery school enrollment, for example, had to be stopped after only one year of operation because of lack of space. The center had clearly been designed for far fewer people than those who needed and sought its services.

Because the South African government refused to provide the necessary funds, the center was unable to expand its facilities. With the limited means at its disposal, it did what it could to accommodate as many people as possible; by attenuating the family basis of its operations it was eventually able to serve about 2,000 persons. After about twelve years of activity, it was nevertheless forced by the government to close its doors. With the hardening of its *apartheid* policy, the South African government found it increasingly more difficult to continue to provide financial support, however meager, for a welfare project that did not fit in with that policy, and it is probable that the popularity Entokozweni enjoyed and the expectations it generated weighed heavily in the government's decision to terminate the project.

It is possible, then, for a demonstration project to succeed too well.

7. Arthur H. Niehoff, ed., *A Casebook of Social Change* (Chicago: Aldine Publishing Co., 1966), chap. 11.
8. Violaine Junod, "Entokozweni: Managing a Community Service in an Urban African Area," *Human Organization* 23 (1964), reprinted in Niehoff, *Casebook of Social Change*, chap. 10.

If it creates the desired contrast with traditional ways and its services are accepted, it may succeed in stimulating new wants the government is unwilling to satisfy.

Diffusion Projects. Diffusion projects are concerned with the direct spread of knowledge, assuming both its soundness (perhaps as a result of a pilot project) and its acceptability (presumably because of success in a demonstration project). The target groups may vary in size and nature from a small number of specialists to a broad, perhaps even an illiterate, mass. Many, perhaps most, technical assistance projects are of the diffusion type.

Universities have played a substantial role in American diffusion projects. In 1967, forty-eight American university teams were operating in Africa under contracts with the Agency for International Development.[9] Though on balance the universities' involvement in diffusion projects has probably resulted in positive contributions to technical assistance, it has caused considerable dissatisfaction. Critics have charged that universities do not provide adequate logistical support for project teams, that the members of these teams are often less well trained for overseas service than government technicians, and that academics tend to be too preoccupied with their personal status and prestige to exhibit the flexibility of conduct required in an aid project.[10] For their part, university spokesmen have pointed to the rigidity of contractual arrangements and the detailed agency control over the activities of university teams as the principal obstacles to a more effective performance.[11]

Whatever the merits of these complaints, the fact remains that a university is not well equipped to cope with the delays and uncertainties inherent in aid project management. For financial and other reasons it can rarely afford to keep personnel and plans in abeyance during the long periods needed by government agencies to complete numerous formalities. The experience of Ohio State University, which agreed to assist in establishing a vocational-technical training program

9. U.S., Agency for International Development, *Operations Report: Data as of June 30, 1967* (Washington, D.C., 1967); idem, *AID-Financed University Contracts as of December 31, 1967* (Washington, D.C., 1967).

10. Walter Adams and John A. Garraty, *Is the World Our Campus?* (East Lansing: Michigan State University Press, 1959).

11. John W. Gardner, *AID and the Universities: A Report to the Administrator of the Agency for International Development* (New York: Education and World Affairs, 1964).

in Sierra Leone under a government contract, provides a typical case.[12] The initial plan called for a two-year project beginning in December 1955, but the signing of the contract, because of United States government procedural requirements, had to wait until February 1957, and approval for sending university personnel and equipment to Sierra Leone was not obtained until February 1958. Thus the project got underway more than a year after it was supposed to have been completed. The delay forced Ohio State University to change the composition of the project team. And by the time the team arrived in Sierra Leone, the curriculum under which the project was to be conducted had been substantially revised by the country's educational authorities. There no longer was any real need for curriculum advisers, and the shortage of teachers—one of the basic reasons for undertaking the project—had eased markedly.

Diffusion projects require a high degree of mutuality between donor government experts—who may act as advisors, teachers, or extention workers—and host government personnel. To carry out pilot and demonstration projects little is actually required of the host government, apart from its consent, and it is not uncommon for such projects to be staffed almost entirely by foreign technicians. Whereas in diffusion projects, at least those financed by the United States government, foreign experts are usually outnumbered, and always outranked, by host country nationals. Diffusion projects therefore court certain failure if a high degree of cooperation and mutual understanding between the two groups cannot somehow be assured.

Ohio State University found in Sierra Leone, for example, that even though the project seemed doomed, it was not easy to abandon it. The prospect of terminating it appealed neither to the Americans involved, who feared that they would thus lose "face," nor to the authorities of Sierra Leone, still a British dependency then. The reasons were, as one British official put it, that they feared that they would "lose the immediate aid including equipment grants; secondly, [that they would] find it very much harder to get U.S. technical aid on other projects possibly of greater importance to [them], and thirdly, [that] it would no doubt be turned against [them] locally." Nevertheless, differences in their educational philosophies proved too great to permit any meaningful cooperation between the Americans and the British in Sierra Leone. While the Americans argued that the London City and Guild Examination did not suit the needs of Africans, the

12. Gardner, *AID and the Universities.*

British insisted on maintaining it as a qualifying requirement for Sierra Leone graduates enrolled in the vocational training program. Although the Ohio State University contract called for the training of technical teachers, the British authorities believed that such training was no longer required. Whereas the Americans thought that they were to serve as consultants, the British wanted them as instructors. Though the contract required the Ohio State team to set up an electrical workshop, the British authorities could not be persuaded to supply the necessary power because they did not consider the workshop necessary. In a last-ditch attempt to provide some of the teacher training for which they had been recruited, two members of the Ohio State team offered Saturday morning demonstration classes to the entire staff of the vocational school, only to encounter resentment because of the implied suggestion that American instructional methods were superior to British ones. After eighteen fruitless months the project was, with great reluctance, terminated.

Not all diffusion projects operate within the framework of formal training institutions. Some of them, for example, make use of community development, public health, or agricultural extension programs to change citizen behavior directly. The participation of foreign technicians in such roles is especially sensitive.

Most technicians realize that at some time their advice is going to have to be accepted, modified, or rejected. Their greatest disappointments have usually accompanied the most ambitious projects, especially those of the "diffusion" category where large-scale social change was desired. Yet it is precisely in the field of mass change that the greatest hope lies for significant improvement in African ways of life. It is therefore important to test the feasibility of proposed widespread changes through the judicious use of pilot projects and then to investigate their acceptability and administrative feasibility by suitable demonstration projects. While the ultimate responsibility for mass changes in citizen behavior rests with the leadership of the host country, external advisors accept joint responsibility when their aid contributes to errors of judgment that could have been avoided by better project design and sequence.

The Problem of Evaluation

Bilateral aid projects are more difficult to evaluate than any other form of government operation, involving as they do two governments, a mixture of political and economic purposes, and uncertain techniques, as well as all the other difficulties of assessing public activities. Aid operations are vulnerable to political attack in each country. The best defense is the greatest precision in identifying the impact of development operations, leaving their evaluation as a separate task to be carried out independently. The most obvious sources of information are the technicians involved, but their opinions are often self-serving and in any case have limited value because of their usual ignorance of the long-term consequences of their work.

Individual Technicians' Views. In assessing their own difficulties and experiences in Africa, American technicians showed more concern with problems of policy and administration than with those involving Africans, or with the adequacy of Western technology, or even with the difficulties of technological transfer. In the period 1959–1961, a team of American aid technicians under the direction of John H. Ohly interviewed nearly 1,000 returnees from overseas assignments in an attempt to "capture and record" experiences that might contribute to a better understanding of technical assistance. Only 66 of the interviews (or "debriefings") involved technicians returning from Africa, since American aid activities on that continent were then only beginning to get underway. But a content analysis of these interviews conducted at Boston University developed information not otherwise available to administrators of United States aid in Africa.

The first correlation of responses showed some connection between mission organization and communications system and the technicians' view of mission success. The highest correlations were between reports of relative failure[13] and culture conflict (.9) and between the sense of failure and the technician's low opinion of his superior officer (.9). High correlations also occurred between perceived failure and reported indifference to Americans on the part of host government personnel (.7).

Mission "rigidity," or inability to respond to changing needs, as judged by the respondents, correlated highly with low morale (.9) and a low degree of mission autonomy (.9). There were also correlations between rigidity and the degree of cultural difference (.9),[14] lack of

13. "Failure" is defined in this study as a low evaluation of the success of a mission.

14. Culture conflict was also associated with "inadequate communication with the host government" (.8) and the belief that many of the host personnel were incompetent (.8).

host cooperation (.8), and frustration of the host government's needs (.8). Rigid missions were also viewed as those that considered their purposes or nature as "technical" (.7). An administrative lesson can also be drawn from the strong correlation between a high evaluation of a superior and frequent communication with him (.9).

Political, economic, and institutional difficulties probably combine to make Africa the most complex setting for foreign aid. Yet it was not the African setting but American policies and operations that provided American aid technicians with their greatest problems. Evidence of the need for reorganizing the aid agency was nowhere more urgent than in the field missions that were just beginning to function but were carrying into Africa the bureaucratic baggage that had been accumulated on other continents.

Critical-Incidents Study. In 1961 Paul A. Schwartz of the American Institutes for Research joined with the author in examining the experiences of veteran technical assistants who were then in training for an African assignment. The expectation was that their experiences in other parts of the world would suggest means of analyzing technical assistance operations—a pilot project for American foreign aid that would be useful in selecting and training personnel and in organizing their activities more effectively.

The critical-incident technique was first used during World War II to gather quantifiable data regarding organized human experience. The method has been successfully applied to analyzing the work experience of a variety of occupations, from airline pilot to clergyman. The method requires the respondents to report specific occurrences (not impressions or attitudes) that they personally observed and that they judged to be favorable or unfavorable in connection with an aspect of their work (their own effectiveness, for example). When enough of these incidents are collected, the job itself can be defined operationally in terms of the specific factors that are "critical" determinants of the outcomes achieved. Between 3,000 and 15,000 separate events may have to be collected to get a complete catalogue of the significant factors of a given occupation.

The technical assistant's role is more complicated than that of most of the other occupations that have been so studied, since it is not only ill defined in its objectives but also cross-cultural in setting and multidimensional in terms of technical skills required. For these reasons it is possible that an even larger number of incidents might be necessary to bracket this occupation. Only about 500 incidents could be gathered from the trainees available in the year's time at Boston University, and they covered experiences in many different parts of the world from 1956 to 1961. Obviously the task was only begun, but it was carried far enough to demonstrate the feasibility of pursuing this approach further.

The findings will not be reported here, since the data are so few. But the incidents collected strongly suggest what technical assistants who have had overseas experience consider to be the central factors in effective performance. Incidents suggesting a limited number of specific factors were cited repeatedly as either disturbing or as contributing to "success" as perceived by the technicians themselves. Significantly, the incidents revealed that many of the most important perceived difficulties are problems that lie outside the control of the technicians or their supervisors. There is also a sizable number of self-generated problems brought about by fixed attitudes or other basic personal characteristics of the technicians themselves. These are appropriate matters for training or, even more importantly, for selection. But it is significant that the possibility that general cultural factors or professional deficiencies may be responsible for want of success does not appear to be strong in the minds of the technicians themselves.

Impact Evaluation. One of the primary difficulties in evaluation procedures, regardless of the skills and sensitivities of the evaluators, is the tendency to consider only the question of whether the project accomplished its intended goals or not and the cost of doing so. The difficulty with such an approach is that it ignores the unplanned and unexpected consequences of a foreign aid project that may be more important than the original mission itself.[15] It is important, therefore, to assess both the planned and the unplanned impact of project activity.

The immediate consequences of an induced innovation may be misleading if judged only in terms of its technical feasibility. A thoroughgoing evaluation of a project's impact will include the changes it promotes among individuals, institutions, and society at large observed in accordance with the different rates at which these changes occur. While individuals in an aid-receiving country who are directly

15. John D. Montgomery, *Foreign Aid in International Politics* (Englewood Cliffs, N.J.: Prentice-Hall, 1967), chap. 4; Albert O. Hirschman, *Development Projects Observed* (Washington, D.C.: Brookings Institution, 1967), pp. 9–34.

exposed to a technological innovation are likely to respond to it fairly rapidly, institutions change so slowly that the impact of an innovation on them may not be felt for some time. And members of the society at large, changes in whose behavior is the ultimate purpose of technological innovation, may take even longer to react. Indeed, one should also consider various infrastructural changes in the host society.[16] For if a technological innovation is to take root, its introduction must be followed by the formation of new technical and entrepreneurial classes, the emergence of new values and priorities, and the development of new economic interests and political action groups. Such changes, even though they may take a long time to come about, are of vastly greater importance than the purely technical ones that may be immediately observed in the target groups of foreign aid operations.

The problem of evaluating foreign aid projects is thus exceedingly complex. Only through an immense research effort by social scientists in and out of universities can there be any genuine hope of solving it. Among other things, more needs to be known about the varying elements of receptivity to social change in aid-receiving cultures. This at least is what the experience gained from America's involvement in aid to Africa during the past two decades suggests.

16. Samuel P. Hayes, Jr., *Evaluating Development Projects*, UNESCO Series: Technology and Society (Paris, 1966).

Manpower Requirements and Allocation of Educational Resources in Underdeveloped Countries

by Idrian N. Resnick

Cost-benefit analysis, the cultural approach, and the manpower requirements technique are the major tools for planning the allocation of educational resources in underdeveloped countries. While cost-benefit analysis has been used operationally in Argentina and applied in individual studies of various countries,[1] it has certain drawbacks—for example, the impossibility of measuring the widespread indirect benefits and costs associated with education—that make its application

1. See, for example, Samuel Bowles, "The Efficient Allocation of Resources in Education: A Planning Model with Applications to Northern Nigeria" (Ph.D. diss., Harvard University, 1965); C.R.S. Dougherty, "A Cost-Benefit Analysis of the Colombian Educational System" (Paper delivered at the Development Advisory Service Conference, Sorrento, Italy, September 5–12, 1968).

to educational planning difficult and of somewhat dubious value for most underdeveloped countries. The cultural approach, the specification of the objective function simply in terms of the proportions of the population that should receive various levels of education, is used in francophone Africa. Most underdeveloped countries, however, tend to view educational expenditures largely in economic terms; they prefer the manpower requirements technique, which treats education as a source of high- and middle-level manpower and which has the great advantage of employing rather simple methods for calculating the skilled labor "required" to achieve specific development goals.

In planning manpower requirements, use is sometimes made of the "Tinbergen model." Though there are several forms of it,[2] the model basically involves a linear regression relating enrollments and outputs at each educational level to aggregate production. This nets the amount of various types of educated manpower required by the economy to grow at a particular rate.

More frequently, however, use is made of the so-called Mediterranean approach.[3] A manpower survey is made to determine the stock of skilled labor in each of the occupations listed in the International Labor Organization's International Standard Classification of Occupations (ISCO). To this is added the flow of the educational system, broken down by type of output (lawyers, doctors, economists, agricultural technicians, etc.). An estimate is then made, covering the period of the development plan, of the demand for various types of skilled manpower, as defined by ISCO. Vacancies are added to this demand estimate, and mortality, retirement, and emigration are subtracted from the stock and flow figures. Finally, the supply and the demand are compared on an occupation-by-occupation basis to determine the excess or deficiency. The education plan thus becomes a program to channel students into instructional pipelines in numbers approximating manpower requirements as closely as resources permit. The short-run goal is to minimize the supply-demand gap; the long-run goal is to eliminate it altogether.

While much can be said in favor of the manpower requirements

2. See Jan Tinbergen and H. Correa, "Quantitative Adaptation of Education to Accelerated Growth," *Kyklos* 40 (1962): 776–86; Jan Tinbergen *et al., Planning Models of Educational Requirements for Economic Development* (Paris: OECD, 1964); Jan Tinbergen and H. C. Bos, *Econometric Models of Education* (Paris: OECD, 1965).

3. See Herbert S. Parnes, *Forecasting Educational Needs for Economic and Social Development* (Paris: OECD, 1962); idem, ed., *Planning Education for Economic and Social Development* (Paris: OECD, 1963).

technique, its various shortcomings are also worth noting. To begin with, what should be understood by "high-level manpower" is not entirely clear. Harbison defines high-level manpower as people with "two years of post-school certificate work or its equivalent." His definition includes all "administrators, executives and managers of sizeable establishments in government, commerce, industry, education, etc.; professional personnel; technical, sub-professional and supervisory personnel . . . teachers . . . army and navy officers and police officers . . . judges, members of parliament, government ministers, local government councillors and senior staff."[4] Parnes and Thomas define high-level manpower in terms of specific occupational classifications and educational requirements normally associated with those occupations.[5] Zack also uses an occupational definition, but his definition covers only those occupations that "should be filled by individuals with university training, or university coupled with experience."[6] There is, then, little agreement as to the precise meaning of high-level manpower.

More important, however, are certain substantive problems. The manpower-requirements technique assumes that technical coefficients are fixed (zero elasticity of factor substitution) and that increases in the supply of manpower will either fail to bring about changes in its relative price or meet with a completely unresponsive demand.[7] There are also problems on the supply side. Several economists have questioned the somewhat rigid links that the manpower-requirements technique assumes to exist between specific occupations and educational attainments. The level of education of job holders in various high-level occupations, they have pointed out, varies widely from country to country.[8] Most categories in the occupational classification

4. Frederick H. Harbison, "High-Level Manpower for Nigeria's Future," in *Investment in Education,* Report of the Commission on Post-School Certificate and Higher Education in Nigeria (Lagos: Federal Ministry of Education, 1960), pp. 51–52.

5. Parnes, *Forecasting Educational Needs,* App. B; Robert L. Thomas, *Survey of the High-Level Manpower Requirements and Resources for the Five-Year Development Plan, 1964–65 to 1968–69* (Dar es Salaam: Government Printer, 1965), p. 2.

6. Arnold M. Zack, "Ethiopia's High-Level Manpower—Analysis and Projections," mimeographed (Addis Ababa, 1964), p. 4.

7. Bowles, "Efficient Allocation," p. 4.

8. See Frederick H. Harbison and Charles A. Myers, *Education, Manpower and Economic Growth* (New York: McGraw Hill, 1964), pp. 186, 191–2, and 198; Bowles, "Efficient Allocation," pp. 7–9; James Blum, "Educational Attainment of Occupational Categories of Workers in Selected Countries," in *Planning Education,* ed. Parnes, App. D.

system are therefore likely to be associated "with a *range* of educational preparations rather than a single educational background."[9]

Going further, there are two major defects that so far have received relatively little attention. One is that the manpower-requirements technique underestimates additions to the stock of high-level manpower. The other is that the use of international standardized job classifications induces planners to express demand for manpower in terms of occupations rather than skills.

Underestimation of Skilled Manpower

As already noted, the first step in the Mediterranean approach to educational planning is to undertake a manpower survey of the country's skilled manpower resources. Calculated additions to the surveyed stock, once demand estimates are made, include only the outputs of formal educational institutions (secondary and above), formal training facilities in private industry, and immigration. No attempt is made to determine whether or not changes in the stock of high-level labor have been greater than these calculated outputs. Some manpower analysts admit that certain jobs, particularly those requiring skilled craftsmen, may be filled by people with less than secondary education when secondary school graduates are not available in sufficient numbers. Others believe that employment and education should not be too closely linked. But no suggestion has been made that the flow of "uneducated" high-level manpower should be estimated, despite the probability that this type of manpower is available in significant quantities in many underdeveloped countries.

The process of change creates certain forms of knowledge and skill that are required for, and further stimulate, development. They are acquired, in part, as the result of job experience, training programs, imitation, and instruction received from parents and other members of the individual's community. Experiences of this kind coupled with other modern phenomena, such as mass communication in various forms, add to the stock of human capital as the economy progresses.

The hypothesis that human capital is endogenous to development falls within the theory of the aggregate production function. The argument that human capital contributes to output differently than labor

9. Parnes, *Forecasting Educational Needs,* p. 41.

(in the traditional sense of the term) suggests that the aggregate production function includes at least two types of labor: skilled and unskilled. If no further distinctions were made, the only problem would be to estimate the parameters of the system in order to determine the relative importance of human capital in changing output. The hypothesis presented here, however, postulates that the skilled labor, human capital, is given by the sum of the outputs of the educational system and increases of uneducated skilled labor.[10] The supply of skilled labor in the present formulation thus becomes a function of aggregate output and of an institutional parameter for the educational system. The former relationship is the important feature of the hypothesis, in that growth in aggregate production brings about the creation of supplies of skilled labor outside the educational system. The problem of estimation then becomes one of discovering the parameters of all the independent variables in the production function and of finding the coefficient that describes the relationship between changes in aggregate output and changes in the supply of uneducated skilled labor.

As long as secondary education is not compulsory, a certain proportion of the total labor force will be uneducated. Most workers in this category will enter employment in unskilled jobs. Assuming no institutional or other kinds of barriers to learning skills on the job, some uneducated workers will acquire skills and techniques through their participation in the production process. To what extent this will occur will depend upon the personal capabilities and ambitions of individual workers. As pointed out earlier, skills may also be learned outside actual job situations, from technical literature and from persons who previously acquired them. As aggregate output increases, therefore, the stock of uneducated skilled labor may be expected to increase as well.[11] Uneducated workers will also acquire skills when drawn into skilled positions and trained on the job in a situation of excess demand for skilled labor over and above that met by the supplies from the educational system. When the demand is fully met by the supplies of educated labor, uneducated workers will no longer be taken on and those who have been employed previously will be replaced by educated workers if the returns from such replacements are

---

10. The term refers to labor with less than a secondary education.

11. There are circumstances under which the stock of uneducated skilled labor might decrease as aggregate output increases: if a larger proportion of the labor force completes a secondary education, even though not required to do so; if productive processes become more capital-intensive; or if population declines.

greater than the costs. Where preference is shown for educated over uneducated skilled labor despite equal productivities, a noneconomic variable would have to be introduced in the production function to explain this preference. In an excess demand situation of this kind, changes in the stock of uneducated skilled labor depend on (1) changes in output, (2) changes in supply of educated skilled labor, (3) the gap between the demand for and the supply of skilled labor, and (4) the relative marginal productivities/costs of educated and uneducated labor.

In those countries that have little uneducated high-level manpower flowing into the labor market, filling high-level requirements from the educational system or by importing foreign manpower are of course the only options open to the manpower planner. But in other countries his choices are wider, and before reaching a decision he should: (1) compare the productivities of the two types of skilled labor; (2) compare the costs of training uneducated labor with the costs of educating labor; (3) relate differences in market prices, if any, to differences in productivity, if any, between uneducated and educated manpower; (4) estimate opportunity costs involved in supplying skilled manpower with and without various educational inputs; (5) examine curricula in the educational system at all levels in order to determine which is best suited for learning various jobs, and (6) evaluate the manpower plan in light of the possibility and desirability of concentrating educational resources in those areas where manpower is not supplied without education and allowing other high-level requirements to be filled with uneducated labor.

The hypothesis presented here thus suggests that in many underdeveloped countries the elasticity of substitution between educated and uneducated skilled workers is likely to be positive. By discarding the false assumption that certain types of high-level manpower can only be provided by the educational system, many development projects could be undertaken sooner than has been thought possible thus far, and with less waste of scarce human resources.

Inappropriate Measurement

The other major weakness of the manpower-requirements technique which has not received as much attention as it deserves is that it measures supply and demand in terms of occupations rather than skills. This stems from its application, rigidly at times, of the ILO's International Standard Classification of Occupations (ISCO):

> The occupations identified and coded in the international standard classification are defined in terms of the work customarily performed in most countries by the workers concerned; the definitions provide descriptions of their functions, duties and tasks, and occupations or workers performing similar types of work are brought together in larger groups.[12]

Occupational definitions were first developed in the 1930's by the United States Bureau of the Census. With the establishment of the ILO, they were applied to Western European economies—a justifiable procedure, in view of the many similarities to be found in the occupational duties of industrial workers in Western Europe and in North America. Not only was the state of technological knowledge comparable within competing industries, but a whole range of factors led to the absence of wide divergences in labor productivity.[13] Trade unions, apprenticeship schemes, the level and type of education, the standards of living, and the industrial composition of the labor force were all similar enough in these countries to make occupational classifications useful measures of comparison.

Such similarities are not to be found, however, in any comparison involving developed and underdeveloped countries. The productivity of unskilled labor is considerably lower in underdeveloped countries, owing to extreme differences in health, climate, the relation of the worker to his task and product, and the nature and relative value of payoffs for effort. Disparities in skilled-labor productivity arise for the same reasons, as well as because of the absence of certain skills in the worker in the underdeveloped country that are usually commanded by his counterparts in developed economies. Diversity in training, exposure to different capital, and non-uniform possession of complementary skills such as literacy give rise to international variations in the productivity of skilled workers in the same occupations. Dissimilar productivity and techniques of production lead to the evolution of different occupational tasks. Moreover, owing to differences in the relative supply of various skills, tasks that by ISCO definitions are associated with one occupation are often performed by people in other occupations. ISCO definitions tend to compartmentalize functions:

12. ILO, *International Standard Classification of Occupations* (Geneva: ILO, 1958), p. 2.
13. The reference here is to output per man-hour when labor is applied to nearly identical plants and equipment.

their application to underdeveloped countries causes high-level manpower to be viewed as having little cross-occupational substitutability,
while in practice functions are likely to be variable and many types
of manpower highly substitutable.

The application of ISCO definitions to underdeveloped countries
comes from various sources: the education and training of nationals
in foreign countries, union acceptance of occupational classifications
as a means of obtaining higher wages, the presence or dominance of
foreign firms in the industrial sector, technical assistance, an often
blind belief by government officials in the superiority of foreign
techniques, and a general tendency to explain the failure of workers
to meet "standards" by the lower formal educational achievements of
high-level manpower.

The consequences of this application of international occupational
definitions and standards are far-reaching. Since wages are usually paid
on the basis of occupations, nationals in underdeveloped countries
receive higher wages than are justified by their productivity. Labor
unions fight for the designation of workers with international occupational titles, even though the workers do not possess the skills associated with those titles in developed economies. Where "equal pay for
equal work" between nationals and foreigners is a government policy,
equality is generally determined by title. Since occupational entrance is
often determined by some educational prerequisite both in the public
and in the private sector, artificial barriers to the localization of high-
level jobs are more than likely to emerge. And where these qualifications are rigid and unjustifiable from an economic point of view,
resources are either wasted on securing a higher-cost (educated) worker
than is necessary or factors go unemployed while they wait for complementary (unnecessary) educated manpower to be produced to put
them to work. This, in turn, leads to an excess supply and/or mis-
allocation of educational resources: either too much is spent on education in general, if the pure manpower approach guides these
expenditures, or the wrong kinds of manpower are produced.

The application of imported standards leads to capital intensity,
where labor is the relatively abundant factor. Because of its low-skill
concentration and the lack of complementary labor and capital, this
labor tends to be economically inefficient. The nurse, for example, is
trained to perform a range of duties including many tasks that could
be carried out efficiently by aides but which are occupationally reserved for her. At the same time, there are many skills that she could

have been taught during her training period but are reserved for the physician. In practice, the nurse carries out functions far below her skill level and training because of a lack of lower-skilled operators within whose duties these jobs would ordinarily fall. Given the excess demand, particularly in the medical market, and the attempts to meet it, choices have to be made. Current occupational task definitions tend to make these choices uneconomic and, in some cases, socially undesirable. The decision most frequently made is to reduce the service or quality of output for all product recipients. Better results could be achieved if the reduction in quality were pushed to the lowest skill level rather than spread across the occupations. Physicians should devote full time to those duties that can be performed only by people with their training and knowledge; clerical work, sutures, dressings, injections, minor examinations, etc., should be assigned to lower-skilled operators. If the same process were undertaken at each skill level, inefficiencies would be substantially reduced. At the same time, the reallocation of functions would provide a clearer picture of the actual stock of skills as a basis for calculating real shortages.

Planning would become easier in some respects and more difficult in others. Instead of calculating the manpower required on an occupational basis, estimates would be made in terms of skill requirements. A knowledge of different skill packages (production functions) and the relative costs of obtaining labor with these skills would provide the basis for rather simple calculations; the production of manpower would change over time as relative prices altered. Of course, the educational facilities for producing labor with the kinds of skill concentrations suggested do not exist at present. But this difficulty, though real, is not insurmountable in the underdeveloped country itself; and as for students who would be sent abroad, it is possible to think of them taking courses providing specific skill training rather than the current degree packages which lead to knowledge consistent with present occupational definitions. In addition, it would be necessary to persuade governments and employers to rearrange their productive processes along the lines suggested—admittedly a most difficult task.

Not only is there evidence that high-level occupations can be filled by people with less formal education than is generally required,[14]

14. See statistics on India in Blum, *Educational Attainment*, App. B; and Republic of Zambia, *Manpower Report* (Lusaka: Government Printer, 1966), App. C, especially Table C16.

there are also some theoretical grounds for doubting the links between occupational designations and their functions. The theory of the production function in its simplest form treats labor as a homogeneous factor. It does so in order to draw attention to the fact that the critical division of effort is between land, capital, and labor. It thus emphasizes the different nature of these three factors. Land tends to be fixed in supply, does not lend itself to accumulation, and makes its contribution to production through its natural powers; capital can be accumulated, can replace itself, is capable of having large amounts of energy concentrated in it, and depreciates with use; labor cannot be accumulated in its unskilled form, is dexterous, and has rejuvenative productive power—it tires the longer you use it, but recoups with rest. The distinctions, of course, are oversimplified: the very heart of human capital theory is that labor has enough of the properties of capital to be fruitfully analyzed in the same theoretical framework. However, simple production function theory facilitates the understanding of the concept of substitution.

When labor is no longer regarded as being homogeneous, it becomes necessary to reexamine the concept of substitutability. The more precisely labor is defined in terms of skills, the less substitutability there will be among units of labor. Typically, occupations rather than tasks and skills are discussed when labor is differentiated. Workers in different occupations are often interchangeable because there is always an unskilled element in their duties and many of the skills and tasks in the productive process looked at as a whole are performed by labor in various occupations.

But the skill mix within occupations is institutionally, rather than technologically or economically, determined. It evolves over time and is explained by the habits, prejudices, and distribution of power of labor, management, government, and professional groups. Few would contend that the result has been sorted out by the market and, however arrived at, has yielded an efficient division of tasks; if anything, the reverse is now being argued.[15]

Conceptually, it should be possible to analyze the functions of different labor units in a production process and arrange tasks in a technically and economically efficient manner. The range of labor tasks, given the technological constraints of land and capital, could be

---

15. See Ralph E. Berry, Jr., "Competition and Efficiency in the Market for American Hospital Services" (Ph.D. diss., Harvard University, 1965).

ranked by degrees of difficulty and length of time it takes to acquire a skill. If we obtained a perfect classification in which there were no inseparable connection between skills of one level and those of another,[16] we would be able to construct a labor-production expression with each skill denoted separately. Given the technology of capital and land, if each of these skills were regarded as factors, the elasticity of substitution among them would be zero. If it were not possible to fully separate skills along these lines, there would be some overlapping of the rankings, but the junctions would be technical and not institutional as they are now. In terms of optimal technical efficiency, it might be desirable to combine various skill mixes in particular workers. With these modifications we would obtain a new production-labor expression and the elasticity of substitution between labor units might be, though not necessarily, greater than zero.

This entire process would result in a new set of isoquants showing the combinations of unskilled and skilled labor possible to obtain various levels of output. It would be different from the present occupational set, since it would involve a different skill mix for labor. Providing the new arrangement resulted in a reduction of costs for various output levels, it would be superior to the skill mixes in use at present. Defining the labor side of the production function along skill lines would also tend to make functions similar internationally. It would eliminate the hidden factors that once exposed currently lead us to the view that functions are not similar.

The practical implications of this approach to manpower planning lie on the production side of labor skills. It has already been noted how current skill mixes find their way from developed to underdeveloped countries. An efficient combination of skill mixes in the former does not imply that technical and economic efficiency will coincide in the latter. But knowledge of technical optimality and some idea of the range of possible skill combinations will provide a basis for two kinds of decisions: (1) the optimum labor combination, given present relative prices for different types of labor, and (2) the best future combination, given the relative costs of producing different labor skills. This, in turn, will provide a guide for manpower production in general and educational planning in particular.

---

16. This is conceivable but not practically possible. It takes no skill to hold a piece of raw material being fed into a precision machine but a high degree of skill to feed it in correctly.

Modifications for Educational Planning

The foregoing arguments showed the need for introducing quantitative changes in the manpower-requirements technique. The two shortcomings discussed can be overcome by modifying the analytical techniques of manpower planning. The supply hypothesis—that human capital is created by the development process, as well as by the educational system—is pertinent to all countries in the long run and to many countries also in the short run.

But the hypothesis can also be used to improve manpower estimates on the demand side. One of the chief criticisms in the literature on manpower planning is that the manpower requirements technique assumes fixed technical coefficients of production. The hypothesis implies that coefficients are variable. Accepting this implication would lead the analyst to estimate the elasticity of substitution among factors. The elasticities of substitution between capital and high-level manpower would be of particular interest; but so also would be those between uneducated and educated high-level manpower.

The presence of a stock of uneducated high-level manpower in a country suggests that the elasticity of substitution between uneducated and educated labor may be substantially above zero in some high-level occupations. To the extent that there are variable factor proportions in the production processes of a particular country, producers may choose among various combinations of factor inputs for each level of output, including alternative combinations of uneducated and educated skilled labor. The demand for high-level manpower, particularly educated manpower, will thus depend partly upon the supply of uneducated skilled manpower. To put it another way, adequate analyses of demand depend upon proper supply estimates.

How the hypothesis can be quantified in a manner useful to manpower planners is a subject that requires further examination. One approach might be to find the relationship between aggregate output and the supply of "uneducated" (less than secondary) high-level manpower over the short-run planning period. The obvious shortcoming of this method is that one must have an adequate time series to estimate the parameter of the suggested relationship between output and the supply of manpower. Such series are generally not available in underdeveloped countries, and there are also no *a priori* grounds for choosing among the various possible forms that relationship might take. For example, projections of short-run trends would give planners entirely different estimates if they assumed linear, rather than non-linear, or lagged, rather than leading, functions. Furthermore, it is not simple to project the output itself.

Where manpower data are limited, another approach may be used. In order to measure the magnitude of the stock of uneducated high-level manpower and the rate at which that stock has increased in recent years, the manpower analyst may introduce a series of questions into his manpower survey designed to discover: (1) the educational attainment of workers currently employed in high-level jobs; (2) the date at which workers entered their current jobs; (3) the rate at which new high-level jobs have been added to the total; and (4) the rate of turnover in high-level occupations. This information will give the planner a rough estimate of the annual rate of entry of uneducated workers into high-level positions. This rate may then be projected for the short-run planning period. The planner may next group high-level occupations according to the range of educational attainment of workers in the jobs. This would give an indication of those occupations that are not filled by uneducated manpower and, therefore, must, *ceteris paribus,* be filled from the educational system or through imports.

It must be reemphasized that this is a method of introducing the manpower supply hypothesis into manpower planning where data do not permit a more sophisticated approach. Productivity data are not provided by this method, nor are the various elasticities of substitution. Prices are neglected entirely. The chief advantages of this method are that it is simple and does not require limiting assumptions, that it lends itself to short-run analysis and may be easily incorporated in other manpower supply-and-demand analyses, and that it relies upon data that are available in underdeveloped countries and easily collected.

The incorrect classification of occupational functions arising out of the use of ISCO can be remedied, but the means required involve practical difficulties unlikely to be met in correcting the underestimation of supply. The ultimate aim is to be able to distinguish the skill component of productive processes in the entire economy. But the distinction would have no impact if the implications were not translated into changes in the duties of labor working in specific industries. For if it is possible to group skill requirements in a productive process according to their level of difficulty, it follows that functions should be reallocated in the private as well as in the public sector, so that each worker performs as much of his work as possible within his skill range.

A reallocation of functions along these lines will require, in the first instance, a microanalysis of the entire labor contribution to the productive process so as to divide it into technologically inseparable segments. For in every establishment there will be some operations which cannot be separated regardless of whether or not they contain skilled and/or unskilled aspects. Technological "packages" will have to be examined in detail so as to specify their part in production in terms of their skill contribution. In turn, the "skill contribution" will have to be determined with respect to prerequisites and the training time necessary to acquire it.[17] Prerequisites will include such things as literacy, the ability to read blueprints, knowledge of various levels of mathematics, and technological knowledge of a certain field (mechanical engineering, etc.).

Within a hospital, for example, certain functions are inseparable, such as filling syringes and giving injections, although the first may be considered an unskilled and the second a skilled operation. Making beds, turning patients, and carrying trays are unskilled functions; answering patient calls, aiding semi-ambulatory patients, and administering pills and liquid medications are low-skilled functions; changing bandages, giving injections, administering to minor emergency ailments, and even sewing certain kinds of wounds are skilled functions; and operating, diagnosing, prescribing, and counseling are high-skilled functions.

Reasoning along these lines, one could group labor tasks into four general categories: (a) those requiring no prerequisites or training time; (b) those requiring prerequisites but no specific training or breaking-in time; (c) those requiring training but no prerequisites; and (d) those requiring both prerequisites and on-the-job training. Within each of these one might arrange tasks, as far as possible, according to the time required to acquire the necessary skills. What would emerge would be essentially an input-output table of labor in the productive process.

These groups and their subdivisions could then be ranked according to the input time required for each skill. Finally, the tasks could be grouped into occupational packages, satisfying two constraints: that

17. Prerequisites might prove difficult to assess along these lines. While it may be known how long it takes to acquire a medical degree, it might be difficult to define the time it takes to become literate.

workers be fully employed[18] and that all required tasks be performed.

While this analysis may appear at first glance to be time-consuming and difficult, it need not become too complicated. Basically, what is needed is a knowledge of which tasks can be shifted away from higher to lower skilled labor and which skills can be shifted upward from primarily unskilled occupations to skilled jobs. Looked at in this way, it should be possible to carry out a relatively simple analysis using current occupational divisions to determine which operations could be rearranged on a task-by-task basis.

The result would be that skilled operators would be freed to undertake more of those tasks for which they are peculiarly equipped and that other workers would contribute more to production with the lower skills that are often associated with their present occupations. To the extent that there are no serious technological constraints to prevent such rearrangements, manpower constraints in any establishment would be reduced, for with a general downward shifting of tasks, relative demand will move toward the less-skilled occupations for which prerequisites and training-time inputs are smaller.

In summary, the manpower-requirements technique used in many African and other underdeveloped countries can be significantly improved with the introduction of a few simple changes that would provide better estimates of supply and refine analysis of demand. These changes call for an economic rather than an institutional classification of tasks. Their chief advantage is easy application in underdeveloped countries. Formal education and training is not the only source of skilled manpower, and the current assumption that it is results in considerable underutilization of scarce human resources. This underutilization can be substantially reduced, if not eliminated, by including the skilled labor supplied by sources other than the educational system in manpower estimates.

18. It is possible to think of some part-time employment within this constraint.

A Comparative Analysis of
Industrial Relations Systems
in French West Africa
and the Gold Coast

by Elliot J. Berg

There has been considerable writing in recent years about African labor, the bulk of it focused on trade unionism and, in particular, the political aspects of trade unions. Few studies have appeared, however, that are concerned with the broader industrial relations environment within which African trade unions have operated, and comparative analyses of African systems of industrial relations are rare.[1]

1. The International Labor Organization study, *African Labor Survey* (Geneva, 1958), provides much useful background, but as is usually the case with surveys of this sort, it is very general in scope and legalistic in tone. A recent book by B. C. Roberts and L. Grefié de Bellecombe, *Collective Bargaining in African Countries* (London: Macmillan, 1967), is explicitly comparative in intent and does contain observations and information of a comparative kind. While it is a noteworthy first step toward comparative analysis in this area, it too is quite general, largely descriptive, and based heavily on documents available in Geneva.

The lack of comparative studies is surprising as well as unfortunate, since one of Africa's continuing sources of interest for social scientists is precisely its potential for study of the process of institutional transfer and social change on a comparative basis. Into African areas with similar cultural, social, and economic systems were injected a variety of new institutions, including industrial relations institutions. The study of how these institutions were adapted to the new environment can tell a great deal about the process of social change, as well as about the nature of the colonial relationship. The evaluation of industrial relations institutions is of particular interest to students of comparative industrial relations, especially since studies of non-Western systems of industrial relations are still very few.

A description and comparison of some of the main aspects of industrial relations in British and French colonial territories in West Africa, using French West Africa and the Gold Coast (now Ghana) as units of comparison, is presented in this study. The focus is on the period before independence, roughly the years between World War II and the late 1950's. Much of what is covered is meant to be explanatory and tentative, since so much about the two areas in the colonial period remains obscure. A comparison of French West Africa and the Gold Coast is not, of course, the same as a comparison of French and British African colonies in general. Nonetheless, the analysis here should shed some light on the general character of industrial relations in British and French colonial Africa.

The Characteristics of the Two Industrial Relations Systems

The major differences between the French West African and Gold Coast industrial relations systems can be summarized by considering in turn the trade union movements, the organization of employers, the role of government, the structure of collective bargaining, and dispute patterns.

Trade Union Organization. The major differences in trade union organization between the two areas were: (1) a greater degree of political involvement and ideological concern in French West Africa; (2) less attention in French West Africa to the development of trade union institutions in the sense of organizational machinery and procedures, and less activity at the shop level; (3) a smaller degree of dif-

ferentiation in French African trade union structure along economic
or occupational lines, and a greater degree of centralization of authority at the territorial level.

It is not easy to define and measure the "politicalness" or degree of
ideological commitment of a labor movement, and it is even harder to
compare these qualities.[2] All labor organizations have interest in
issues beyond those of bread and butter, and all mix some politics
with some job-oriented and institutional (union-building) activity.
The relative importance of the two components of union activity
varies among countries and over time within countries. It is nonetheless fairly clear that the mix of activities contained relatively more
politics and ideology in French West Africa than in the Gold Coast; in
the allocation of trade union energy, time, and money, the French
African unions gave relatively more attention to political issues than
did the Gold Coast unions and relatively less to job-oriented or union-
oriented activities.

One indication, rather intangible, is to be found in the marked
differences in the language of trade unionism and trade unionists
in the two areas. Marxist thinking of one shade or another permeated
the writing and speech of French African unionists. In the Gold
Coast labor movement the mainstream of thinking and writing contained much less in the way of political or social philosophy or concern and very little of a traditional Marxist flavor in particular.

A firmer clue is the fact that the divisions within the labor movement in French West Africa were apparently due almost exclusively
to political factors arising either from local political circumstances or
from the rival union situation inherited from France, itself largely
ideological in nature.[3] In the Gold Coast, political disagreements
played a much less important role; only for a brief period in the early
1950's and again in the year before independence were they at all
significant. Even then the ideological content was slight, and in any
event the conflict existed almost entirely at the Trade Union Congress

2. For a discussion of some of the semantic and conceptual problems see E. Berg
and J. Butler, "Trade Unions," J. S. Coleman and C. Rosberg, eds., *Political Parties
and National Integration in Tropical Africa* (Los Angeles and Berkeley: University
of California Press, 1964).

3. Throughout the colonial period the unions in French Africa were grouped into
rival centrals attached to the three main French union centrals, the Confédération
Générale du Travail (CGT) (communist); the Confédération Générale du Travail—
Force Ouvrière (FO); (socialist); the Confédération Française des Travailleurs Chré-
tiens (CFTC) (Christian socialist).

level. Trade union splits in the Gold Coast had their origins for the most part in job-oriented conflicts. In the 1950's, for example, first railway engineers and then maritime workers seceded from the railway union because they felt the railway clerks were running the union and that their particular interests were not being taken into account. There were also some breakaways that reflected ethnic particularism or regional conflicts.

In the evolution of every trade union movement two related sets of structural questions arise. The first involves the form of organization to be adopted; the second relates to the distribution of functions and power among the various layers of union structure.

Between French West Africa and the Gold Coast some fundamental differences arose in these structural matters. According to the theoretical blueprint of union structure in the French-speaking areas, workers were organized in *syndicats professionels,* occupational unions most often industrial in scope. Electricians in XYZ Company in Dakar would be organized with all other XYZ workers in an XYZ Company Section Syndicale, a local unit of the Construction Workers' Union of Dakar. The structure then rose horizontally (geographically), as well as vertically (occupationally). The Construction Workers' Union of Dakar joined with all other Dakar unions in a kind of city central or district council—a *union locale* or *régionale,* which was grouped with other *unions locales* on the national level into a territorial federation—a *union territoriale* (after independence *union nationale*). The Construction Workers' Union of Dakar would also be grouped with construction workers in other parts of Senegal in a Construction Workers' Union of Senegal.

The key organizational unit, where true authority in the labor movement resided, was the geographical federation, the *union territoriale.* The "house" (or enterprise-level) unions never had much vitality. An all-French West Africa-wide organization came into being after 1951 but was mainly a coordinating body with little authority. Industrial unions, except among teachers and railwaymen, existed more on paper than in reality, though after 1956 they assumed a somewhat more important role in negotiations. Throughout most of the history of the labor movement in French-speaking Africa, the territorial (national) federations handled grievances for all workers, bargained on most important questions, and decided the major strikes as well as leading them.

In the Gold Coast a different structure emerged. The basic unit became the "house" or company-wide union. Industrial unions developed in mines and railways and in a few other sectors, as in French West Africa. But most unions were limited in scope to a single company. The Trades Union Congress, which existed at the top before independence, was a relatively powerless body, with little money, few full-time staff workers, and limited control over the constituent unions. Authority in the labor movement of the Gold Coast thus tended to be more decentralized than in French-speaking Africa, and the geographical bodies so important in the French West African union structure had no counterpart there.

The French West African unions were less concerned than Gold Coast unions with organizational matters, with improving the union's institutional position, and with procedures and administrative machinery. They had less presence at the shop or office level, though in neither area did the labor organizations have much of a hold among the rank and file. There are a number of indicators of these differences.

1. In French West African trade union affairs of the period there seems to have been very little preoccupation with matters relating to internal union machinery; neither trade union administration nor structural problems were much discussed at conventions, except occasionally and when they bore on broader political issues.[4] Among unions of comparable strength in the two areas, the internal administrative machinery was more developed in the Gold Coast—committee structure and branch organizations were more articulated, for example, in the Gold Coast Mineworkers' Union or railwaymen's organizations, than in the mining or railway unions in French West Africa.

2. The most direct impact of unions on workers is normally in the area of grievance handling. The French African unions played a significantly smaller role with respect to grievances than did the Gold Coast unions. There was very little formal grievance machinery in either place, but consultation and negotiation machinery at the shop or office level was more frequent in the Gold Coast. In the bigger private firms and government departments there was a fairly well-

4. At the UGTAN (General Union of African Workers) convention in Conakry in January 1959, for example, there was considerable discussion of "corporatism"— that is, tendencies toward job-oriented union positions as opposed to "revolutionary" unionism. But this apparent discussion over union structure was simply the overt manifestation of basic political differences that could not prudently be discussed openly.

developed system of joint consultations. In 1953–54, for example, some 47 such committees were functioning in private enterprises and 125 in public services.[5] Individual grievances in French Africa, on the other hand, were almost invariably handled by the representatives of the trade union central, not the local representative. At the local level, the labor law provided (as in France) for the election of workers' delegates (*délégués de personnel*), who were to act as spokesmen on grievances. Although the unions usually put forward slates at these elections, and so were represented in this sense at the local level, there was an ambiguity in the relationship between workers' delegates and trade unions that did not exist in the Gold Coast. It is not clear, in any event, that the worker delegate system functioned satisfactorily, though very little is known about how it worked in practice.

Equally little is known about the actual functioning during these years of one other shop-level institution: the joint classification committees, provision for which was included in collective agreements. These committees, composed of worker and employer representatives, were intended to resolve grievances related to job gradings.

The presence of labor courts, and the absence of comparable institutions in the Gold Coast, further contributed to the dilution of a trade union presence at the shop level in French Africa. Not only was there in the French West African system less face-to-face discussion between unions and employers about local issues and grievances, but these issues were less frequently settled directly by the parties. Mediation and conciliation by labor officers were general in both systems, however.

3. Accounting and financial problems absorbed far less leadership energy in French West Africa than in the Gold Coast. The Gold Coast unions operated on locally-raised dues revenues to a greater extent and were much more concerned with financial reporting, both within the labor movement and between the unions and the government. The French West African unions could exist without much dues income, thanks to provision by municipalities of office space in a *Bourse du Travail* and the French administration's practice of allowing civil servants to be "detached" with pay for union duties.

4. Broader efforts at rank and file education were made in the Gold Coast. Soon after the formation of the first university in the late 1940's, an Extra-Mural Department was set up, which sent out trade

5. Gold Coast, *Annual Report of the Labor Department, 1953–4.*

union tutors throughout the 1950's and held frequent in-service training courses for trade unionists. In 1953, the Trades Union Congress, with the help of the British TUC and the International Confederation of Free Trade Unions, set up a Workers' Education Association, which was supposed to concern itself with rank-and-file education, though what it actually did is obscure. In French Africa the only union education efforts were those that took union leaders abroad, though the Christian unions in Senegal did set up some courses in the late 1950's. This seems to have been the only effort of its kind in all of French West Africa before independence.

The Organization of Employers. Differences in trade union organization were matched by differences in employer organization in the two areas. In French Africa almost all employers were members of an industry-based trade association; there were over 120 such associations in French West Africa in the early 1950's. Through their trade association most employers belonged to one of the two major groups that did most bargaining for employers: an organization of employers in manufacturing and construction (Union Syndical des Industriels, UNI-SYNDI), and an organization of employers in trade, commerce and service (Syndicat des Commercants Importateurs et Exportateurs, SCIMPEX). (Where there were expatriate planters, as in Guinea and the Ivory Coast, they had their own organizations.) Each of the two major employer associations maintained an office with paid staff in each of the territories, in Dakar, and in Paris. Finally, overseas employers formed a special section in the French Employers Association (Comité National de Patronat Français, CNPF).

In Ghana employer organization was much sketchier. The big mining companies, with one major exception, were members of the Chamber of Mines, which bargained for its members over wages and had a joint policy on conditions of service. There was a variety of trade associations and numerous chambers of commerce, but there was no joint bargaining other than in the mining industry. The Ghana Employers' Association, composed of most of the important British enterprises, was a poorly financed, loosely organized group, which played no significant role in collective bargaining. Some employers in commercial enterprises attempted late in the colonial period to organize along racial lines: the Indian Merchants Association, the Syrian Merchants Association, etc. But when in 1958 these associations were urged to bargain collectively with a newly formed Union of Distributive

Retail and Allied Workers, they were unable to do so effectively. British-based firms had relations with the British Overseas Employers' Federation, but the links were less formal and less continuous than were those that tied the French overseas employers to the French Employers' Association.

The Role of Government. In both areas government wage decisions were the major determinants of the general level of wages and the wage structure. In the Gold Coast the government influenced general movements in wages through its position as employer of over half the nonagricultural labor force. Private-sector wage changes tended to follow those of government, but there were substantial variations between firms and industries, and the whole process of private sector wage determination was decentralized. There was, for example, no statutory minimum wage until after independence. Decisions about non-wage conditions of employment were also decentralized and varied fairly widely from firm to firm.[6] The scope for determination of these conditions by the parties was relatively large, since the law was not extensive on these matters.

In French Africa it was otherwise. There was first of all a statutory minimum wage (*salaire minimum interprofessionelle garanti*, SMIG), which affected privately as well as publicly employed workers and which became the effective rate for unskilled labor throughout the territory. Furthermore, the change in the SMIG was the basis of discussion for changes in the wages of skilled workers. And finally, the scope of bargaining was highly restricted: all the basic conditions of employment were set down by law—overtime rates, vacations, etc. The law also prescribed the form of collective contracts, including directives as to what had to be included in the agreement. The government role in the negotiation of collective agreements was more direct than in the Gold Coast, since agreements were negotiated in the presence of government officials and could be "extended" to cover entire industries, thereby acquiring the force of law.

With respect to wages, bargaining procedures were more or less the same in all the territories of French West Africa. There existed in each territory a tripartite (government, employers, union) Labor Advisory Committee (Commission Consultative du Travail), whose

6. Cf., *Report of the Ghana Employers' Association of Terms and Conditions of Service, 1957.* See also Roberts and Grefié de Bellecombe, *Collective Bargaining,* chap. 5.

main, almost exclusive, function was to discuss changes in the SMIG. The "bargaining" procedure consisted of the two parties presenting the government representative with conflicting claims as to how much the cost of living had gone up since the last SMIG revision.[7] In states other than Senegal demands also focused on closing the gap between the SMIG in Senegal and other states. More meaningful wage bargaining took place when the time came to discuss the wages of graded workers—that is, those in skill categories above that of unskilled laborers. These discussions took place in tripartite territorial joint councils (*commissions mixtes*), also under the chairmanship of a government official. In these councils collective agreements were worked out. In the French areas, therefore, the procedures of wage determination and collective bargaining in general were highly structured.

In the Gold Coast the instrument of wage changes in the public sector was the wage or salary commission, a body of experts, usually chaired by an expatriate called in from Britain. The major wage changes after World War II were based on the recommendations emanating from such commissions: the Harrigan Commission in 1946, Korsah in 1947, Lidbury and Gbedemah in 1951 and 1952, Waugh in 1957. Between commission reports, bargaining took place mainly with respect to cost-of-living adjustments; public sector unions demanded, and generally won, cost of living allowances. But what usually happened was that between commission reports, "anomalies" in the wage structure and dissatisfaction with cost-of-living allowances led to accumulation of grievances and consequent pressures that were temporarily dealt with by the succeeding salaries commission.

Bargaining over wages and conditions of employment in the private sector almost invariably involved demands by unions that employers meet government rates or conditions. Changes in the general level and structure of wages of privately employed workers did tend to follow government changes, though larger enterprises retained considerable flexibility. The important point is that the government's role in determining private-sector wages and conditions, either through direct wage regulation or by legislation, was far less significant than in French Africa.

Colonial administrations in French Africa were not uniformly more

---

7. In periods of price stability, as in the mid-fifties, bargaining revolved around arguments as to what was suitable to include in the minimum subsistence budget (*budget du minimum vital*), the composition and cost of which was the peg around which all discussions over wages took place.

"interventionist" in industrial relations matters than the British administration in the Gold Coast. In several respects the roles were reversed. Thus, in matters of political activity French administrations generally took a more permissive line toward the trade unions. In 1949–50, when there were a number of serious "incidents" in the Ivory Coast and Upper Volta, the authorities in those territories did move to suppress overtly political acts by the trade unions. But the normal response of the colonial administrators was to play the political game themselves, manipulating where they could trade unions as they tried to manipulate political parties and other groups.

Related to this was the policy regarding the scope of activity allowed to civil servant organizations. In the Gold Coast, as throughout British Africa, civil servants had particular restrictions put on them, especially insofar as their activities touched political nerves. In French West Africa this was decidedly less of a concern, and trade union activities among civil servants were subject to fewer constraints.

Finally, the British were a good deal tougher about accounting practices than were the French. In the Gold Coast trade unions were required by law to register with the Registrar of Trade Unions and to submit annual reports on membership and finances. Proper reporting and accounting were taken seriously by the Registrar of Trade Unions, who subjected the unions to a continuous flow of nagging letters and complaints about inadequate financial accounting.

The French West African unions were not exposed to the same controls. It is true that in the beginning years formal regulation by law was more extensive than in the Gold Coast. In the latter country, for example, the Trade Union Ordinance that appeared just before World War II required registration and financial accounting as a precondition for union recognition. In French Africa the 1937 legislation authorizing unions had accounting regulations, educational qualifications for membership and leadership, and prohibition of political discussion by some of the new associations of wage earners. In 1944 most of these restrictions were swept away. Between 1944 and 1952 there existed a peculiar legal situation in labor matters: it was not clear which laws applied to Africa and which did not. African trade unionists claimed that the French Constitution was applicable in certain matters of African labor law. They therefore refused to comply with unfavorable legal provisions supposedly in force in French West Africa. Thus, the registration and accounting provisions of the 1937 law on trade unions were ignored after 1944, and the unions sent in no reports. In the Labor Code of 1952, the omnibus labor law governing industrial relations until independence, no provision was made for registration and regulation of financial practices.

The Nature and Structure of Collective Bargaining. The structure of bargaining—like the union and employer organizations themselves—was more centralized in French West Africa than in the Gold Coast. In the Gold Coast typical negotiations took place between the management of a given plant or company and the employees of that company. In some of the bigger firms bargaining was on an establishment rather than an enterprise-wide basis; the United Africa Company Employees' Union, for example, did not negotiate for all the employees of the UAC in the Gold Coast, since important subsidiary companies had their own unions. In a few cases, bargaining took place along craft lines, though this was rare; the main example was in the railways, where the skilled locomotive engineers had their own union and negotiated separately. In some cases, too, there were approaches to industry-wide bargaining. The most important example was in the mining industry, where the Mines Employees' Union and the Chamber of Mines bargained for most mines and companies. The African Manganese Company, however, which employed approximately 20 percent of the mineworkers in the country, was not a member of the Chamber of Mines and bargained directly with the union.

In French West Africa matters were more complicated. In each of the territories union and management representatives selected by the government met with government representatives in the territorial joint councils (*commissions mixtes*), where they worked out long collective agreements covering large blocks of workers. In some territories, as in Senegal and Dahomey, there was one basic agreement covering all African workers; in other territories there were two agreements for African workers—one for all manual workers, the other covering all office workers. Expatriate European workers were covered by separate agreements.

That these arrangements involved more centralized decision-making in the French African areas is clear. Wage decisions made in any of the territories (the Ivory Coast, for example), were influenced by employer and government representatives in Dakar (where the government of the Federation of French West Africa was located) and in Paris. Employer policies on wages and other labor matters were often set on a broader basis than the territory, because of a concern with territorial "whipsawing," whereby an increase granted on the territorial level could become the target wage of unions in other territories;

employer organizations in each territory often had to clear with Paris before making final offers in wage discussions in the Labor Advisory Commission or the joint councils. With respect to conditions of employment, Paris played an even more decisive role; for it was in Paris that the big legislative decisions were made, such as in the substantive provisions of the Labor Code of 1952, which applied to all the overseas territories of France.

All of this suggests a second major difference in the nature of the industrial relations systems in the two areas, as evidenced in the collective-bargaining process: the Gold Coast system was much more "indigenous," or "inward-looking," involving essentially domestic considerations, while the French West Africa arrangements were outward-oriented, embedded in the colonial relationship.

In French West Africa one general issue dominated collective bargaining: equality of treatment of wage earners, and in particular equal pay for equal work. Trade union demands were invariably focused on the existence of "unjustified" wage differentials between African and French civil servants working in the African administrations, between workers in private industry and workers in the public sector, and between workers in one territory and workers in others within the Federation of French West Africa. The essence of trade union strategy was a kind of generalized "whipsawing," frequently using expatriate conditions as the lever or target.

The process is illustrated most dramatically in the civil service. An adjustment of civil servant salaries in France was normally followed by a comparable adjustment of the salaries of Frenchmen at work in the colonial territories in West Africa. But these adjustments in Africa led to a widening of differentials between Frenchmen and African civil servants doing comparable jobs, a situation that generated insistent demands by African unions for equalizing increases. Up to 1957, near the end of the colonial period, this procedure dominated discussions of civil servant salary policies and invariably led to increases in African civil salaries.

Private-sector employees had two comparison groups: African civil servants, who enjoyed better conditions, and European (French) workers in private employment. Not only were demands for private-sector wage increases generated by increases granted in the public sector, but equally favorable fringe benefits were sought and frequently won.

In discussions over statutory minima a similar kind of whipsawing occurred. Here the target was the narrowing of what can be called "the Dakar differential." The SMIG in Senegal was always the highest in the federation, and in territories other than Senegal it served as the reference point in bargaining over minimum wages.

Thus the issues and strategies of collective bargaining in French colonial Africa depended to a unique extent on the special conditions of French colonial rule. The main grievances sprang from the connection with France and the presence of French administrators and wage earners in Africa. This was far less so in the Gold Coast or in British colonies generally. The issue of overseas allowances for expatriates in the civil service did exist in the Gold Coast and was a source of grievance, as were differences in leave provisions and other fringes. But the issue was faced squarely in the early 1950's insofar as the public sector was concerned, and it did not arise again as a major source of organized protest in the public sector, nor was it an overwhelming issue in the private sector. Into the public-sector salary structure there was put an inducement in the form of an overseas allowance, which was recognized to be necessary to recruit expatriate civil servants and hence was limited to expatriates.

Strike Patterns. In certain basic respects work stoppages in both the French areas and the Gold Coast displayed common characteristics. First of all, most work stoppages in both areas were short demonstrations, lasting one day or less; many of these were spontaneous in character—that it, not organized by local union leaders. In both areas, too, most stoppages were limited to the workers of one enterprise and were, insofar as one can tell from the strike descriptions contained in official reports, essentially "defensive" in nature; they were the result of some action by management felt by the workers concerned to be unnecessary or unjustified. These stoppages were really a method of airing a grievance, or of initiating bargaining.[8]

Where differences in strike patterns appear most clearly is in the character of big strikes. In the Gold Coast before 1958 there were three large-scale strike movements. Two of them, in 1947 and in 1955–56, were long strikes in the mining industry; the third was the semigeneral political strike of 1950. In French West Africa the major strikes were sometimes on an industry basis, such as the railway strike of 1947–48, which lasted five months in some areas, but they generally tended to involve larger blocks of workers, such as all government

8. Analysis of strike histories given in Labor Department reports in the Gold Coast between 1947 and 1959 indicates that some 300 out of a total of almost 500 work stoppages during these years were "defensive" in this sense.

workers (Senegal and the Ivory Coast in 1959) or all workers in the private sector (Senegal, 1957), and frequently engaged the African wage-earning community in general protest demonstrations (1952 and 1953 stoppages throughout French West Africa). Major French West African union efforts were thus not only broader in coverage than those in the Gold Coast but were strikes against the government itself. A typical union effort was a one- or two-day protest demonstration by most workers in a territory against a government wage decision. The substantive issue in many of the general or semi-general strike movements was often equality of treatment; this was true for the railroad strike in 1947 and the private-sector strike in Senegal in 1957. There also occurred in French West Africa a kind of stoppage without counterpart in the Gold Coast: stoppages aimed at influencing labor lawmakers and those who applied the law at the local level. This type of stoppage was common from 1952 to 1954, when the new Labor Code for the Overseas Territories was being debated in France, and when it was later applied in Africa.

Explanatory Factors

We have thus far described certain key characteristics of the industrial relations systems of French West Africa and the Gold Coast, pointing out similarities and especially differences in the two systems. Any attempt to explain these differences is complicated by the fact that in colonial situations whole institutional systems, in industrial relations as in other spheres, were introduced as part of colonial rule. It is possible in these circumstances to regard colonial industrial relations systems as simply little mirror images of metropolitan systems, distorted here and there perhaps but still essentially French or British.

Now it is obvious that the colonial inheritance goes a long way in explaining why the industrial relations of French West Africa and the Gold Coast developed as they did up to independence and why they evolved differently in the two areas. This is especially so in the French areas, where the relevant institutions were more directly imported and in greater detail. In British Africa the principle of "voluntarism" in collective bargaining was reflected in labor law and in a greater diversity in such matters as wage determination; there was therefore greater scope for indigenous adaptation.

But neither the French system nor the British system was absorbed wholesale. A process of selection and adaptation took place, and African conditions and needs determined which parts of the colonizers' industrial relations' institutions would be rejected or modified. Moreover, even to the extent that most of the differences in patterns can be explained by reference to the different colonial inheritances, it is still important to spell out the process involved; certain elements of the transferred institutions were especially critical in shaping the evolution of the system as a whole, and these should be identified.

That there were local options, so to speak, is illustrated by certain aspects of trade union development. With respect to French Africa, there was much in the local trade union situation that was familiar from French trade unionism: the ideological and political bent, the shaky presence of the unions at the shop level, the general indifference to financial matters, and the casualness of administrative structure. It could have been otherwise in French Africa, however. The CFTC and FO centrals, for example, did tend to give higher priority to job-oriented issues and spoke the language of "non-politicalness"; they offered significantly different orientations than the CGT unions and their offshoots. Their audience, however, was always limited; CGT unions, and unionists in the CGT tradition, remained dominant throughout the colonial period.

In the Gold Coast, similarly, it is hardly an inherent characteristic of the British system that the labor movement is non-political; yet in the Gold Coast, relative non-politicalness was a fact for most of the unions throughout most of the colonial period.

The evolution of trade union structure suggests even more clearly the existence of options and the fact that adaptations were made. The Gold Coast's unions developed as small autonomous company unions, and where there was more than one firm in an industry no centralized industrial union developed, except in mining. But it cannot be said that this occurred because unions in Britain are this way. Recent British trade union history has seen the sharp reduction of numbers of unions and continual amalgamation into bigger units. The Gold Coast unions might just as easily have developed along general union lines and still have remained within the British tradition. Elsewhere in the British Empire, in fact, national unions were the dominant form, as in Sierra Leone and East Africa, for example.

It is the same with union structure in French West Africa. In France the national confederations are the center of power. In French West Africa the West African-level organizations were always weak;

real power was in the hands of the geographical federations in each territory. Local unions and industrial federations were, for the most part, paper organizations, sacrificed to the territorial federation. In building this kind of union structure, African unionists in French West Africa often ignored legal requirements as to trade union organization. For in French Africa, as in France, the labor law said that only people who worked on the same or related crafts or industries could join together in unions. But the African trade union leadership generally disregarded this part of the law. Often they enrolled members directly into the ranks of the geographical organization, the territorial federation, even if they belonged to no local union. This was for a long time the despair of French labor officers, but it was common practice.[9]

It is necessary, then, to search for local factors and forces that guided the process of institutional selection and adaptation and shaped the development of the local industrial relations systems. Three related aspects of trade union organization will be considered here: the nature and extent of the political commitment, trade union structure, and the intensity of institution-building or organization-oriented activities.

Trade Union Organization. In the Gold Coast a variety of factors "explain" the distinctive characteristics of the labor movement. An important element was the wage-setting mechanism, especially the fact that individual firms retained considerable autonomy in fixing their wages and terms of employment. This encouraged union concentration at the enterprise level and the emergence of a company-based or "house" union as the key organizational unit.

This tendency was reinforced by other aspects of the environment. In an export economy, where there is in effect no internal competitive product market, even in the nascent manufacturing sector, there are no significant product market pressures inducing large-scale organization either among unions or employers. Nor was there any ideological impetus or a general spirit of proselytizing which might have encouraged drives to organize the unorganized and thus stimulate units of organization wider than the firm. Though this was partly due to

9. In 1950 the labor inspector of Guinea reported that the CGT in Guinea consisted of a few regularly constituted unions plus a mass of individuals who were members only of the geographical federation. (Inspection Territoriale du Travail de la Guinée Française, *Rapport Annuel 1950*, p. 56.) The Inspector General of Labor in 1951 commented on the generality of this phenomenon and its undesirability. (Inspection Générale du Travail de l'A.O.F., *Rapport Annuel 1951*, p. 148.)

the scarcity of union leadership and funds, it is also evident that there was little sense of mission among most Gold Coast trade union leaders.

Administrative, organizational, and regional factors further increased the propensity to small-scale organizations on the trade union side. Where geographically scattered unions existed, central union headquarters were frequently incapable of servicing the minimum needs of component units.[10] Slipshod accounting and mishandling of union funds led local union organizations to hesitate in sending money to higher echelons for fear that it would be misspent or misappropriated. Fast and loose use of union funds was in fact a major plague.[11]

Administrative shortcomings and misuse of union funds aggravated centrifugal tendencies. They added to existing feelings of regional separateness or ethnic differences, thereby making amalgamation of unions harder and even stimulating the dissolution along regional lines of such interregional organizations as existed. The most troublesome region was Ashanti, where general sentiment for separatism was greatest. The Kumasi Branch of the Agricultural Department Workers' Union broke away from the national union in 1957, and the Ashanti Branch of the Cadbury and Fry Employees' Union stopped sending its dues to headquarters after 1954.

Finally, there appears to have grown up a considerable amount of loyalty to company or to craft. In the railway and harbor workers union, first railway enginemen, then maritime workers seceded because they felt the railway clerks were running the union and that their interests were not taken into account. Between clerical workers and manuals there were signs of distrust. Leaders of strong company unions argued that only workers in one company had the "sense of oneness" necessary to cement a union together; they cited the failure of the early (1947) Mercantile Workers' Union, which had quickly fallen apart.

10. In their 1956 report to the Registrar of Trade Unions, the Patterson Zachonis Employees Union, for example, noted that branches for some time refused to send dues to headquarters in Accra because: "We had no cooperation from Accra since the last Annual Conference held in Accra in 1953; matters referred to Accra had received no attention and our letters had not been replied to; the HQ is not functioning and its administration has deteriorated."

11. See, for example, "Joint Report of Inquiries into the Functions of the Trans-Volta Togoland Regional Union of Agricultural Department Workers Union, Appendix to Minutes of the 7th Annual Delegates Conference of the Agricultural Department Workers Union," mimeographed, 4–5 August 1956; "Report of Committee of Enquiry, the Obuasi Urban Council Employees Union," mimeographed, 1956?

Another set of explanatory facts is "political" in a broad sense, relating to the creed or ideology of the colonial administrators, the policies of the administration (which were partly the consequence of administrators' ideology) and political forces within the Gold Coast. The Gold Coast colonial administration, first of all, took a consistently hard line in support of "voluntarism," and this led to a legal framework that indirectly encouraged enterprise-wide unionism in a number of ways. Social legislation was relatively sketchy, restricted largely to protective laws, and such conditions of employment as were specified in the law were distinctly minimum (as against "effective") conditions. Collective bargaining, conciliation, and negotiation were strongly encouraged, and direct government intervention in determination of private sector wages and conditions was not common.

The law on trade unions probably encouraged the development of "house" unionism in one special way: it permitted groups of workers as small as five in number to form themselves into a trade union. This meant that employers could, if they wanted to, easily disturb or break a union giving them trouble by stimulating separatist groups to form their own union. Dissident groups within each union were also allowed to separate from the union whenever they suspected that their interests were not being advanced by the leadership of the union.

British administrators and labor officers took a purist position on the desirability of non-political trade unionism, which they combined with a devotion to "sound unionism"—i.e., well-organized, well-administered, self-supporting unions. It is easy to see why administrative officers should have taken this position; it was in accord with their general desire to avoid political disturbances along the carefully laid path they saw leading to full independence for the Gold Coast. But there is more to it than this; political expediency does not explain, for example, why representatives of the British labor movement who were serving as labor officers in the colonial government or as advisors to the African unions should have shared this dedication to non-political-ness and "sound" union development. One factor may have been their recognition that their role as technical-assistance people could only be effective to the extent that the Gold Coast unions were anxious to become "real" unions, not political agencies. It also seems probable that they had an understanding of the needs of basic institution-building, upon which their vision of "proper" trade union development rested.

In addition to these "positive" factors, there was an important negative one: that the British administration in the Gold Coast would not hesitate to crush any serious wandering from the non-political path. This was how they reacted to the one political adventure of Gold Coast unions, the general strike of 1950, and trade unionists knew they would react the same way if a similar situation arose.

African political dynamics were also important in shaping the Gold Coast system. The relationship between the Convention People's Party, which was the dominant nationalist party after 1949, and the trade unions was quite complicated.[12] Two aspects are relevant here: (1) the biggest and best-organized unions (UAC Workers Union, Public Works Department Union, Mines Employees Union, most of the railway unions) were not involved or interested in political affairs; (2) the CPP in the early 1950's tried to gain control of the unions and the labor movement as a whole by putting its people in control of the Trades Union Congress and shifting authority to the TUC. Throughout the 1950's, therefore, most important unions were unwilling to give greater power to the TUC, because to do so would involve control by the CPP. This was a major factor rendering the TUC impotent until the situation was changed by law after independence with the Industrial Relations Act of 1958. It also helps explain why union leaders so insistently argued that unions should be non-political, a view that was not only a matter of conviction but congenial to their self-interest as they saw it.

In explaining the distinctive feature of French West African trade union development, two factors are of major significance. The first is the peculiar political context: the colonial relationship was ill-defined, the French were morally and politically committed to an ideology of equal treatment for Africans and Frenchmen, and the metropolitan governments of the period were weak and unstable. The general implications of this situation will be considered below; with respect to trade union development, it encouraged such political propensities as existed in the unions, gave much potential political bargaining power to the unions, and made the equality issue an effective bargaining device. Free movement of people was one of the principles of the French Union, and many Frenchmen came to work in West Africa, including so-called *petits-blanes,* men of little skill or training who competed with Africans for jobs and provided grist for the equality issue.[13]

The second major factor was the method by which wages were determined. Geographical bargaining meant that geographically-based union organization was stimulated. That the basic unit of union

12. See Berg and Butler, "Trade Unions."
13. E. Berg, "The Economic Basis of Political Choice in French West Africa," *American Political Science Review* 54 (1960): 397–98.

sovereignty was the territorial rather than the West Africa-wide organization is explained partly by political factors—the territory rather than the French West African federation was the predominant political unit —and partly by the fact that wage determination was made on a territorial basis. Also, since government determined so much of the wage structure and conditions of employment, what was most useful was an agency capable of creating a political impression, one that could call all the workers out for one- or two-day demonstrations.

The territorially-based general-type unionism that developed in response to these conditions was not torn by the centrifugal forces so much in evidence in the Gold Coast's unionism. Although clerical-manual differences existed and were in some territories given official recognition in separate unions and collective agreements, they do not appear to have caused the same intraunion conflict; the non-manual leadership of the unions seems to have given rise to far fewer protests. Nor did administrative problems, misuse of funds, or regionalist and ethnic separatism cause comparable strains.

The reasons for this are not entirely clear. One probable factor was the different role of ideology in the two areas. As noted earlier, ideological elements were always more substantial in French West Africa's unionism than in the Gold Coast's. Preachment of the unity of the working class, especially in the colonial situation, may have served to dilute separatist sentiment among wage earners. Another factor was that union administration was not so absorbing an issue to French African unions as it was in the Gold Coast, and it was less likely therefore to give rise to internal controversy. Moreover, the greater role of government in wage determination and in fixing conditions of work and the greater centralization of bargaining gave less scope for division on the basis of local particularisms. Lastly, the equality issue, around which so much of the bargaining revolved, was undoubtedly a unifying force since it involved general grievances arising from the colonial situation.

Employer Organization. In the Gold Coast there was no stimulus to employers to bargain together, except in the mining industry. Private firms were relatively free to adjust their own wages and conditions of employment. As with the unions, there were few competitive pressures in product or factor markets to encourage wider organization of employers. The disparate size of firms was also a factor. Leading firms such as the United Africa Company felt it preferable to work out their own conditions on the grounds that they had little to gain from joining with other employers, while smaller employers feared domination by the UAC.

In addition there was a political factor. The main expatriate firms were reluctant to engage in joint action with each other and with other employers, partly because the history of such joint action was bitter to many Africans and evoked fears of imperialist conspiracy. The Association of West African Merchants, along with the import quota arrangement from which it benefited in the immediate postwar period, was one of the main elements in the Gold Coast disturbances of 1948. To avoid stirring old memories or new fears among Africans, many of whom tended to regard the expatriate firms as part of the colonial apparatus, the large employers—virtually all expatriates—shied away from employer organization.

In French West Africa employers organized more widely and more readily. French employers are more accustomed to joint negotiation than are British employers; there were fewer political overtones in their organizing than in the Gold Coast and, most important, the wage-setting mechanism in French West Africa was such as to encourage them to organize. When they were consulted on the minimum wage and when they negotiated the wage of skilled workers, all employers bargained together because all were directly affected by the outcome. There was also less reason for major firms to be reluctant to bargain in common, since they had less scope than did employers in the Gold Coast to determine their own conditions of employment.

The Bargaining Pattern and the Role of Government. The importation of the French custom of statutory minimum wage determination by region, with the statutory minimum being not only an effective rate actually paid to large numbers of workers but also the key rate in the wage structure, was especially important in shaping the French West African system of bargaining. It was the same with the highly articulated wage structure, which involved grouping all skilled workers into six or seven broad categories, all in practice linked to the SMIG. Other crucial elements, such as permissiveness toward civil servant participation in trade union affairs, also were in some measure projections of the French system.

In the Gold Coast there was less of this kind of direct influence, because the British system was much less structured and because no particular set of wage-determining institutions or approaches was "necessary" in the sense that the adoption of French wage-fixing institutions was necessary.

There were, nonetheless, alternatives in French West Africa. If, for example, wages had been determined on an all-French West Africa basis, instead of by territory, the structure of the labor movement and other major features of the industrial relations system might have been different; more authority would probably have gone to all French West Africa union bodies, for example, and also industrial unionism would have been stimulated. This was, in fact, beginning to happen after 1956, when industry-wide collective agreements were negotiated. Why did the structure of bargaining not take this form from the beginning?

The territory became and remained the major unit of wage determination because all parties concerned preferred it, and underlying this preference was the fact that the territories differed substantially in terms of income levels. Thus, for government a French West Africa-wide minimum wage would have been too rigid and would have risked forcing up wage levels in the very poor territories of the interior. Employers wanted territorial wage determination for the same reason and because they recognized that the risk of political concessions was greater the larger the scope of conflict. The unions in the richer territories were not keen on federation-wide bargaining because it would have restrained wages in their territories. There was also a political factor of some importance: the French confederations, to which the African unions were tied informally, favored territorially-based unionism and bargaining because they feared the separatist tendencies manifested from the early 1950's in all French West Africa-wide organizations.[14]

Differences in the political context, in the nature of the colonial situation in the two areas, are basic to understanding the variations in the two industrial relations systems. In the Gold Coast the nature and outcome of the colonial relationship was never in doubt, nor after 1950 was there much uncertainty even about timing. It was clear to all concerned that the Gold Coast would be independent, and soon; by 1951, the country already enjoyed a fairly large degree of self-government.

French Africa, in contrast, lived under greater uncertainty about the character of its relationship to the metropole, about the ultimate outcome of the relationship, and about the timing of change. The French African territories had some political autonomy after 1945. But they were not self-governing to any significant extent, and constitu-

14. *Bulletin de Liaison des Travailleurs des Pays Coloniaux*, no. 33 (Paris, 1953), pp. 4–5.

tionally they were part of an indissoluble French Union. They did not in principle have the right to independence. It was not until 1956 that the word "independence" even came out into the open in general political discussion.

These specific differences in the political environment are important in explaining the differences in the two industrial relations systems. In all their dealings with African subjects, British administrators in the Gold Coast could posture as high-minded trustees—holders of a disinterested stewardship. They could act with that ineffable self-confidence which was so striking a feature of the British colonial style. They could crush political strikes when they occurred. They could insist on developing "sound" unionism and properly functioning institutions, in industrial relations as in other areas. In confrontations with Africans over wage policy or other economic issues, they could righteously defend the long-term public interest and demand "responsible" behavior on the part of trade unionists or other Africans.

French colonial administrators in West Africa, on the other hand, could not make convincing appeals to economic responsibility. The uncertainties of the political connection that bound Africa to France and the need to avoid social disturbances that might raise questions about the nature of that connection forced them into a much more defensive position. Most important for them was the keeping of the peace, particularly after disturbances began to spread in North Africa in the early 1950's. The French administrators were caught in special contradictions created by the doctrine of equality between Frenchmen and Africans; on both moral and political grounds they were thus vulnerable to African trade union attack. Under these circumstances it was extremely difficult for French administrators to maintain a principled position and to avoid concessions, especially when any threats of social disturbance arose.

Conclusion: Environmental Change and Institutional Adaptation

In one sense, the industrial relations institutions that emerged in French Africa between World War II and the accession of French West Africa to independence around 1960 were especially "functional" or well suited to West African conditions. Trade union organizations and collective-bargaining relationships were in line with organizational needs and capacities on the one hand, and in harmony with the structure of decision-making power on the other. Few restrictions were put on civil servants or other public employees in their trade union activities. Legal requirements regarding registration and financial reporting were ignored before 1952 and absent from the law after 1952. The attitude of government and employers toward work stoppages was in general tolerant. The government largely relieved trade unions of financial worries by an arrangement allowing civil servants to collect their pay and serve as full-time union officials. There was relatively little insistence by government officials or employers on the virtues of union self-sufficiency and solid organization at the local level. All of this meant that the trade unions had their hands free, so to speak, for substantive issues.

Union structure was similarly "functional." The vaguely delineated organizational arrangements, with the emphasis on geographically-based organizations, was an efficient adaptation to French African realities. Given the centralization of decision-making on labor matters, the broad scope and coverage of legislation, the tendency for the SMIG to be the effective rate for unskilled workers and to determine rates of change of all wages, the existence of labor courts, a solicitous inspectorate of labor, and the *délégués* system, there seemed little to be done at the shop level and hence not much point in building shop-level institutions of any strength.

From the point of view of the immediate interests of African wage earners and even the African community as a whole, the system worked well. The trade unions in French West Africa enjoyed a position of prominence in political and economic affairs during these years. In some of the territories (Guinea and Niger, especially) they provided top political leadership. On the economic side, the trade unions and the peculiarities of the bargaining system led to a higher level of real wages, especially in the public sector and the poorer territories, than would otherwise have prevailed and to conditions of work and wages considerably better than those in neighboring countries.

In the Gold Coast the situation was different. In many respects the policies and institutions that evolved during the same period seemed out of joint, unsuited to local needs and possibilities. The unions never had more than a marginal impact in political or economic terms. They were for the most part half-formed institutions, weak, divided, small, poor, preoccupied with the forms of trade unionism rather than the substance, developing organizational machinery, laboring over account books, sitting in consultative and negotiating bodies that dealt only with minor issues of the workplace. They never came to grips with the fact that big advances might have been possible through legislative or administrative channels.

Judged only by their serviceability to African wage earners and their adaptation to local possibilities and local power structures, the industrial relations institutions of the Gold Coast were thus less functional or suitable than those in French West Africa. But when account is also taken of the adaptability of the two systems to conditions of independence, a different judgment is called for. For the French West African system could not survive in recognizable form once colonial rule ended. It was too specialized, too dependent on the peculiar features of the colonial environment at a particular phase of colonial rule. Independence removed almost entirely the political and moral force behind demands for equality of treatment between expatriates and locals, and it thus stripped from the unions their main weapon and removed from the bargaining system what had been its main concern. Independence also brought the new states face to face with budget effects of wages policy, which, combined with an awareness of their political fragility, led them to take a far less genial view of strikes than had the colonial administration—particularly strikes of civil servants and semi-general protest demonstrations of the kind common earlier. They did not hesitate, therefore, to forbid such strikes, requisition strikers when they occurred, and even fire strikers—an act almost without precedence in the earlier period. They could, and did, decapitate union leadership by changing the practice of civil servant detachment for union duty. And they did not hesitate to jail unionists, freeze wages, and severely control union activity. In most of French-speaking West Africa, independence thus brought into being state-dominated trade unions serving mainly ceremonial functions, and the withering of genuine bargaining.

The colonial system was disfunctional in another sense. It led to levels of wages and salaries which were too high in the sense that they severely constrained possibilities for local financing of public-sector development expenditures. One consequence of this was that the problems of independence were exacerbated by the need to deflate real wage levels in French Africa. This brutal confrontation with economic reality, which was postponed during the colonial period because the appeal by the French for "responsibility" was always strongly countered by the African appeal to "justice" and "equality," has been a basic source of political and social instability throughout the French-speaking areas, and particularly in the poorer territories of Dahomey and Upper Volta.

In Ghana, also, independence brought dramatic changes. Full government and party control over the unions was imposed by the Industrial Relations Act of 1958, and independent trade unions disappeared. Strikes and other union activities were closely regulated, and the unions were fully absorbed into the machinery of the governing party. In much of the public sector the negotiation and consultation machinery fell into disuse. But what is most striking is the extent to which the system developed under colonial rule persisted throughout the N'krumah regime and up to the present. Before the 1966 coup which ousted N'krumah, the trade unions continued to spend much of their energy on institution building, on perfecting their organizational machinery, and on job-oriented issues. In the private sector negotiations and discussions went on much as before. And despite the change at the top, with the newly dominant TUC playing a major role as the political and ideological agent of the party, most of the trade union officials at the lower levels continued to work at negotiations with employers, grievance handling, and similar matters. In part this was due to institutional inertia and to the fact that there was not much else that could be done. But it suggests that precisely because the Gold Coast system gave priority to local matters and because of the efforts to construct genuine trade union machinery and engage in genuine bargaining with employers, the inherited institutions were able to survive more recognizably. Unlike the French West African arrangements, the Gold Coast system did not depend on particular characteristics of the colonial regime, except in certain respects—the degree of autonomy, or independence from government. It was more general, based on more solidly universal and persistent problems arising out of the relationship between employers and the employed.

There is not much doubt, then, that the industrial relations institutions and policies of the Gold Coast involved more institutional development than did those of French West Africa. It involved relatively more people in dealing with problems of a more basic and enduring kind, and it taught them more about the complex task of administering organizations and resolving problems. It created an institutional base, a set of established procedures and habits of mind which, though it was neither large nor firmly rooted, could grow and develop. In this sense the colonial industrial relations experience had a broader modernizing impact in the Gold Coast than in French Africa, and this is probably the most important criterion of all in evaluating any set of institutions in modernizing countries.

The "Protestant Ethic" of
the Mourids of Senegal

by Mark Karp

It is no exaggeration to say that no Moslem brotherhood in Africa
has attracted as much attention as the Mourids of Senegal. Already
sizable, the literature on the history and life of the Mourids continues
to grow.[1] Some of it is sympathetic to the Mourids; some is not. Curiously, however, none of it contains more than oblique references to
the brotherhood's most distinguishing, and indeed quite extraordinary,
feature: its "Protestant ethic." Though Moslems, the Mourids exhibit
in all essential respects the same "ethic" that Max Weber ascribed to
the Calvinists and their Anglo-Saxon counterparts, the Puritans. To
act in accordance with Mourid principles means that disciples must
work diligently and leaders must save and invest as much as possible,
not in response to material incentives but for the sake of the world
beyond. It is in this respect that the Mourids stand out as a unique

1. The latest additions, in English, are Lucy C. Behrman, *Muslim Brotherhoods
and Politics in Senegal* (Cambridge, Massachusetts: Harvard University Press, 1970),
and Donal B. Cruise O'Brien, *The Mourides of Senegal* (Oxford: Clarendon, 1971).

phenomenon in the Moslem world as well as in the non-Islamic part of Africa.

The Mourid phenomenon is more than a *curiosum*. It deserves the attention of anyone with a broad interest in some of the questions that the current state of economic development theory poses. Weber's hypothesis—that a social ethic shaped by certain religious beliefs is the decisive factor in economic development—has never been effectively tested, despite the enormous growth of critical literature on the subject since the publication in 1905 of *The Protestant Ethic and the Spirit of Capitalism*. A major difficulty has been the impossibility of divorcing the influence of the ethical norms emphasized by Weber from that of other factors on the economic development of the Western world given the tacit assumption, shared by Weber's supporters and critics alike, that those norms were uniquely associated with the religious tenets of Protestant sects. With the emergence of Mouridism, that assumption can no longer be maintained. As will be shown, the religiously-motivated economic conduct of the Mourids fits Weber's hypothesis in all its essential elements so well as to provide, by observing the effects of that conduct in an historical context and environment vastly different from that of Western Europe and North America, a useful basis for judging the validity of the hypothesis.

Origin and Growth of the Brotherhood

The Mourid brotherhood was founded by Amadou Bamba in 1886. While not the first Moslem brotherhood in Senegal, it received unusual attention at the time because of the relatively large following which Bamba was able to attract almost immediately. Much of the explanation of Bamba's rapid gain in popularity is that he profited from the breakdown of the traditional political order and the social disorganization that occurred among the peoples of the area when the French tightened their grip over what was to become the colony of Senegal, now an independent republic.

The influence of the French in Senegal dates back to the seventeenth century, when they established a number of trading posts there; but only in the late nineteenth century did they gradually extend their full military and political control over the interior regions. In 1877 severe friction developed between the French and Lat Dyor, the thirtieth and last ruler (*damel*) of the Cayor. Roughly encompassing the territory between Saint Louis and Dakar—generally regarded as the heartland of the Wolof, the largest ethnic group in Senegal—the Cayor had been an independent kingdom since the sixteenth century. The French decision to build a railway between Saint Louis and Dakar brought vigorous protests from Lat Dyor, who saw the project as a threat to his state's independence. In 1882, after a futile exchange of correspondence with the French authorities, he took up arms against them. Four years later, at about the same time that Bamba launched his religious movement, Lat Dyor died in battle and the Cayor fell under French control.

In these circumstances, the initial French reaction to Bamba and his religious movement was one of extreme wariness. The French feared that Bamba would capitalize on his sudden popularity to start a new war against them. They became particularly suspicious when they found that several members of Lat Dyor's family, into which Bamba's father had married, and many of the *damel's* former supporters had rallied around him. They also learned that he kept in close touch with some individuals who had been forced to flee Senegal because of their anti-French activities.[2] On two occasions they banished him—the first time to Gabon and the second to Mauritania— for a total of twelve years. Thereafter the French attitude toward him gradually changed. After the end of World War I, they even bestowed certain honors upon him, partly in recognition of his assistance in recruiting Senegalese for the French army and partly, one may surmise, out of a sense of guilt for the mistreatment inflicted upon him earlier without any real evidence against him. Even so, the French authorities deemed it prudent to keep him under surveillance until his death in 1927.

The literature currently available on the rise of the Mourid movement is largely based on the account left to us by Paul Marty, a remarkable French administrator with a scholarly bent and a contemporary of Bamba. Marty was the first to recognize that the Mourids were more interested in economic than in political power.[3] He believed, however, that the Mourid movement depended on Bamba's personal leadership to such an extent that it would not survive his death.[4] In this regard he could not have been more mistaken.

In 1912, according to Marty, Bamba had less than 70,000 followers.[5]

2. Medoune Thiam, *Cheickh Ahmadou Bamba* (Conakry, 1964), p. 7.
3. Paul Marty, *Les Mourides d'Amadou Bamba* (Paris: Leroux, 1913), p. 112.
4. Paul Marty, *Etudes sur l'Islam au Sénégal*, 2 vols. (Paris: Leroux, 1917), 1: 287–88.
5. Marty, *Les Mourides*, p. 144.

In 1952 a French mission sent to investigate agricultural conditions in Senegal, the Portères mission, estimated that about 300,000 adult males belonged to the Mourid brotherhood. The mission cited no figures for total membership, but it thought it not unreasonable to suppose that at least one-third of the country's population might be Mourid.[6] In 1957 a French administrative estimate put the number of adult males belonging to the Mourid brotherhood at approximately 400,000, and there were some who, on the basis of this estimate, claimed a total membership of one million.[7] Whatever the true figure, there is no doubt that the brotherhood's numerical strength has increased substantially since Bamba's death.

Nor did the death of Bamba cause any serious problems of leadership, even though no man could be expected to command as much prestige within the brotherhood as did the founder. A few days after Bamba died, a family council met and chose Mamadou Mustapha Mbacké, his eldest son, to succeed him. When Mamadou Mustapha died in 1945, he was replaced by his brother Falilou Mbacké. The present head, or Khalifa-General, of the Mourids is Abdou Lahatte Mbacké, another son of Bamba, who was elected to the post by a family council after Falilou's death in 1968. So far, therefore, only Bamba's sons have been elevated to the Khalifate-General. The candidacies of both Mamadou Mustapha and Falilou were contested, the former's by two of Bamba's brothers and the latter's by Mamadou Mustapha's eldest son, Cheickh Mbacké. There was some tension as a result, but in both cases the Mourids' strong sense of discipline and solidarity prevented it from splitting the brotherhood into rival factions.

It was also after Bamba's death that the brotherhood's pyramidal structure of authority, for which the brotherhood is noted in Senegal, took on a clearly recognizable form. At the base lies the huge mass of disciples (*talibés*). Immediately above them are the sheiks, who are chosen by the disciples through a ritual act of submission—unlike the sheiks of other Moslem brotherhoods, who are appointed by higher authority. The act of submission, called *njebbel* in Wolof, is voluntary but total, since a disciple must unflinchingly obey his superior. It is not, however, irrevocable. Should a disciple become dissatisfied with his sheik, he might, as he sometimes does, leave him and submit to

6. Mission Roland Portères, *Amenagement de l'économie agricole et rurale au Sénégal*, 3 vols. (Dakar, 1952), 1: 102–4.
7. See Vincent Monteil, *L'Islam noir* (Paris: Seuil, 1964), pp. 127, 265, and 265n.

another.[8] Above the sheiks are the Khalifas, who in turn answer to the Khalifa-General. The chief source of their power and prestige is descent from some revered Mourid figure, such as a particularly illustrious relative or disciple of Bamba. Their authority is gradually being eroded, however, by an increasing tendency among the sheiks to pledge direct allegiance to the Khalifa-General, whose hand is thus further strengthened.[9]

His powers are already considerable. The Khalifa-General acts as spiritual leader of the brotherhood, as sole organ of the brotherhood's formal relations with the outside world, as sponsor of an annual pilgrimage (Magal) to the tomb of Bamba, and as custodian of the huge mosque that houses the founder's tomb at Touba.

What has particularly distinguished the brotherhood and contributed most to its growth, however, has been its economic performance. Throughout Senegal's recent history, the Mourids have been in the forefront of economic activity. Around 1912 they launched a colonization drive that brought many hitherto unused lands under peanut cultivation. Relying chiefly on the dara, a type of pioneer settlement in which able-bodied young men led by a sheik work the land collectively, the Mourids pushed aggressively ahead, overcoming many hazards. Except for a brief interruption engendered by Bamba's death, the drive continued unabated until 1945, when the government, alarmed by allegations—later disputed[10]—that Mourid cultivation practices threatened to exhaust the soil, took measures to restrain it. Agricultural expansion then gave way to urban migration. Many Mourid disciples can now be seen working as artisans and petty traders in cities, and their leaders are known to have made several investments there, mostly in real estate. Peanut cropping, however, continues to engage the energies of the majority of the brotherhood's members.

To appreciate the role of Mourid cultivators in the Senegalese economy, one must see it in the context of the country's resource availability. Senegal has few known economic resources, and of these only the peanut crop can yield a significant monetary income. Peanuts account for three-quarters of the country's exports and for nine-tenths of the government's fiscal revenue. How large the Mourid share in Senegalese peanut production is cannot be said for certain, since it

8. For details, see Cruise O'Brien, The Mourides, pp. 84–88, 101–9.
9. Ibid., p. 123.
10. CINAM et SERESA, "Rapport général sur les perspectives de développement du Sénégal: La région arachidiere" (Dakar, 1961), chap. 1.

has not been measured statistically. According to one observer, it is one-quarter;[11] according to others, and this is the more common estimate, it is one-half.[12] Moreover, it has to be remembered that it was the Mourids who in past years spearheaded the drive for peanut production. They set an example that induced many others to imitate them[13] and won them recognition as the most dynamic element in the country.

The Doctrine of the Two Ladders

In addition to the Mourids, there are two important Moslem brotherhoods in Senegal: the Khadiriya and the Tijaniya. Founded in Bagdad twelve centuries ago by Sidi Abdel Khader Jilani, the Khadiriya has a sizable following in many parts of the Moslem world, though its membership in Senegal, while not inconsiderable, is now smaller than that of the Tijaniya (which claims to have the largest) or of the Mouridiya. The Tijaniya takes its name from Ahmed el Tijani, who founded the brotherhood in Morocco near the end of the eighteenth century. It gained many adherents in various parts of North and West Africa, but its main center of activities remained in Morocco. Thus both the Khadiri and Tijani brotherhoods of Senegal, though they function autonomously, are actually branches of organizations that have their principal centers elsewhere. Both are imported movements that spread in Senegal as the result of Mauritanian proselytizing efforts during the nineteenth century.

By contrast, the Mouridiya originated among the Wolof, whose traditions probably helped to shape some of its most singular features. This is not to say that the Mouridiya is an ethnic sect. While Wolof still make up the majority, Serere, Diola, and Toucouleur are now also found among the brotherhood's members. Nor is it, strictly speaking, a purely Senegalese movement. Mourid communities have sprung up in Mauritania, Mali, Guinea, Ivory Coast, and even in Zaire, though they are too small to enable the brotherhood to exercise much influence in those countries.

---

11. Cruise O'Brien, *The Mourides*, pp. 214–15.

12. Monteil, *L'Islam*, p. 267.

13. Fernand Quesnot, "Influence du Mouridisme sur le Tidjanisme," in *Notes et études sur l'Islam en Afrique noire*, Centre de Hautes Etudes Administratives sur l'Afrique et l'Asie Modernes (Paris: Peyronnet, 1962), p. 122.

In many respects, the Mouridiya does not differ from the other Senegalese brotherhoods. They all belong to the mystical world of Sufi Islam. Sufism began in the Middle East during the ninth century, possibly earlier,[14] as an ascetic reaction to the increasing worldliness of established Moslem institutions. In the tenth century it went through a partial transformation. The belief that Sufi mystics were endowed with charisma (*baraka*) gained currency and eventually led to their veneration as saints. Despite strong objections by orthodox Moslem scholars, who pointed out that the notion of an intermediary between man and his Creator was contrary to the letter and the spirit of the Koran, the cult of saints continued to gain in popularity. Some Sufis organized their followers into brotherhoods. The movement spread to North Africa, where it has been particularly strongly entrenched ever since the fifteenth century. From there it penetrated the western part of the continent.

In French-speaking Africa Sufi mystics are popularly referred to as "marabouts." Some marabouts play leading roles in brotherhoods, in which case they usually carry the title of sheik. Those who do not often serve as religious teachers. In West Africa it was customary in the past for peasants to support these teachers by growing food for them on a special field, which became known as the Wednesday field, for Wednesday was the day the peasants usually reserved for its cultivation. Nowadays Wednesday fields are cultivated to provide gifts to sheiks. This is true of the Mourids, as well as of the Tijanis and the Khadiris. There are many practices and beliefs that the Mourids share with the other brotherhoods. The strict discipline observed among the Mourids, for example, though it has evoked much comment in and out of Senegal, is not a unique Mourid trait. The difference between the Mourids and the other brotherhoods is, in this respect, at best only one of degree. All of them preach that a disciple should obey his sheik.

Much as the Mourids have in common with other maraboutic groups, there is nevertheless, in addition to differences in origin and in internal organization which have already been noted, a profound difference in doctrinal orientation between them. Like all ascetics, the Mourids aim to achieve spiritual perfection by practicing self-denial, but they reject the general Sufi idea that the material world is a threat to spiritual development. Mourid doctrine, which consists of the interpretations the brotherhood's leadership places upon Bamba's views on

14. See Monteil, *L'Islam*, pp. 121–22.

Islam, holds that asceticism must be practiced not by renouncing the world but by living in it, by combining ceaseless activity with rigorous abstention from self-indulgence.

This is clearly shown in the Mourid attitude toward labor. The doctrinal justification for it is based on two statements attributed to Bamba: "To work is one of the duties of a slave of God" (in Wolof, *ligey si diamou yalla la bok*), and "work is part of the action of following God" (*ligey si top yalla la bok*). In the first statement, Bamba's followers are simply asked to recognize the fact that man must work in order to live. Man has no choice in this matter, if he wants to survive on this earth, as the reference to him as a slave emphasizes. The explanation offered for the necessity of work is, of course, in purely theological terms. God has willed that man should work. He is master of all creation and man is His slave. In the second statement, the notion of constraint is absent; there is no reference to man as a slave. Work is a worldly activity that the believer voluntarily undertakes to prove his faith.[15]

A distinction is thus made between the work a Mourid has to do to support himself and his family and the work he may additionally engage in to show his religious devotion. But he must not indulge himself by consuming the fruit of his extra effort. He must part with it. "He who works in his own interest," Bamba is reported to have said, "his toil shall be entirely wasted."[16] The extra labor can have spiritual value only if its fruit is donated to a superior in the brotherhood.

One branch of the brotherhood, the Bay Fall, believes that "only through work can one secure the blessing and the grace of God."[17] Its members do not observe any of the customary religious obligations of a Moslem, such as daily prayers or the Ramadan fast. In this they follow the late Ibra Fall, one of Bamba's most devoted disciples, who held that he had no need of rituals or prayers since he meant his whole life to be a service to God. The Bay Fall form a small group, however. Only about 500 families, according to Abdulaye Fall, their present Khalifa and a son of Ibra Fall, belong to it.[18]

For the majority of the Mourids work is not the only means by

15. For details, see Abdulaye Wade, "La doctrine économique du Mouridisme," mimeographed (Dakar, 1966), pp. 15–18.
16. Cruise O'Brien, *The Mourides,* p. 51.
17. Ibid., p. 150.
18. Interview with the author, 9 March 1965.

which a man can show his faith. He can also do it through prayer. Work and prayer, said Falilou Mbacké in 1965, are two ladders to Heaven; the Mourid, who aspires to enter Paradise, may use either ladder, or both, to climb to his goal.[19] The late Khalifa-General was thus echoing sentiments expressed earlier by the brotherhood's founder. In 1903, in an open letter to his followers, Bamba defined membership in the Mourid brotherhood as limited to those who were willing to work, to learn to pray, or to do both, and ordered the expulsion of all others.[20]

It is sometimes alleged that among Mourids only agricultural labor has religious value. It is difficult, however, to find a basis for this notion. Bamba's writings certainly do not provide it. Most Mourids, it is true, work on the land, but this is due to the lack of superior economic alternatives and not to a religiously-dictated preference. One of the brotherhood's leading personalities, Mamadou Mahmoun Mbacké, categorically rejected the claim that Mourid doctrine accords religious significance to agricultural labor. All remunerative work, he declared, is religious vocation.[21]

The doctrine of the two ladders has no precedent in Islamic tradition. Vincent Monteil has tried to show the contrary, but the most he could produce as evidence was a *hadith* (saying) in which the Prophet Mohammed indicated his approval of work to support one's family by rating it equal to prayer.[22] Clearly, this is not the Mourid view of the religious significance of work. It is the additional labor, the fruit of which must be donated to a sheik, and not the work done to support one's family that, according to Bamba's doctrine, has spiritual value.

Among Mourids no particular importance is attached to the form of a disciple's contribution to his superior. Contributions can be made in money, goods, or labor services. Most Mourids work as independent peasant producers who after the harvest contribute as much money to their sheik as they believe they can afford. Many of them also cultivate a Wednesday field for him. Others work on the sheik's land, or in *daras,* especially those who have no land of their own. Khalifas, as well as the Khalifa-General, also own lands that their personal followers cultivate. A part of the fees of Mourid urban associations, called

19. Interview with the author.
20. Thiam, *Bamba,* p. 12.
21. Interview with the author. See also Portères, *Amenagement de l'économie agricole,* p. 103.
22. Monteil, *L'Islam,* p. 263.

dairas, is regularly remitted to religious leaders. City residents also pay a special fee, the *allarba,* as a substitute for work on a Wednesday field. In addition to all these more-or-less regular payments, contributions are made on numerous special occasions, of which the annual *Magal* to Bamba's tomb is the most important. It is generally estimated that at least 200,000 Mourids gather at Touba during the annual event, leaving the equivalent of nearly one million dollars in the hands of the Khalifa-General.[23]

The Sin of Ostentation

So far it has not proved feasible to estimate, even broadly, the total amount that Mourid disciples contribute each year to their marabouts. Nobody doubts, however, that the steady flow of contributions has enabled a relatively small group of men to accumulate considerable wealth. Some Mourid marabouts are counted among the wealthiest people in Senegal. This concentration of economic resources, drawn from a mass of poor but indefatigable workers, into the hands of a religious elite has caused much speculation as to how these resources are ultimately utilized.

There are those who believe that personal consumption takes up nearly all of the leaders' resources. Others dismiss this notion, pointing out that had the leaders frittered away their resources on luxurious living they would not have been able to command the loyalty of their followers for as long as they have. They maintain that the Mourid community is a static system of collective security in which reserves are accumulated by the marabouts and redistributed within the community as the need for them arises. Finally, there is a group that argues, with greater reason, that investment absorbs most of the Mourid elite's resources.

Like those of other maraboutic groups, the disciples of the Mouridiya expect their leaders to live and conduct themselves in a manner that will reflect prestige upon the brotherhood. A Mourid marabout's expenditure on consumption is therefore higher than that of a *talibé,* though it is far from lavish—as anyone who has visited the Khalifa-General and other members of the Mourid elite can attest—and certainly much smaller than his means allow. His expenditures on charity

23. Ibid., p. 266.

are also modest. Though he enjoys a reputation for generosity, the Mourid marabout's charity is limited to helping those members of the brotherhood who, for one reason or another, cannot work and have no other means of support. It is investment that taxes his resources and energies most. Had it not been for his willingness to invest the large means put at his disposal, the brotherhood would not have been able to go through its remarkable economic evolution. It was his capital that financed the brotherhood's agricultural expansion between 1912 and 1945 by advancing subsistence means, seeds, animals, and tools to the cultivators; that, even after the government forbade the acquisition of new lands, enabled the cultivators to increase agricultural output through intensive methods of cultivation by purchasing modern mechanical equipment; and that is now financing the Mourid surge into the cities by advancing funds to disciples who want to start new businesses and by undertaking various direct investments.

A key question is whether there are any religious principles governing the economic behavior of the marabout. Curiously, one can find no mention of this point in the existing literature on the Mourids, which on the other hand devotes so much space, even if the views expressed in it are not always accurate, to the influence of religion on the behavior of the disciple. The resulting picture is that of a Moslem order strikingly lacking in doctrinal consistency: the sheiks are presumed to be free to engage in secular activities to satisfy their personal material ambitions, while the disciples must toil to fulfill a religious duty.

The truth is that the Mourid leadership feels no less bound by Bamba's teachings to practice asceticism in worldly activities than its disciplined followers.[24] A marabout is not expected to work, and the doctrine of the two ladders therefore does not apply to him, but he must not indulge himself by allowing his personal consumption to exceed the requirements of his position in the Mourid community. "Be like the small donkey that carries a load of millet on its back but does not eat it," said Bamba,[25] and the Mourid leadership has taken this statement to mean that a marabout should not consume more than

24. Unless otherwise indicated, the discussion of Mourid doctrine as it applies to the marabouts is based on research conducted in Senegal in the spring of 1965 at the invitation of the Faculty of Law and Economics of the University of Dakar and with the generous financial assistance of the Ford Foundation. The views presented are those that were expressed unanimously by the Khalifa-General and other leading figures of the Mourid movement in separate interviews carried out with the help of Abdulaye Wade of the University of Dakar.
25. Marty, Les Mourides, p. 52.

he has to. Were he to do so, he would be guilty of ostentatious conduct, which Bamba regarded as one of the worst offenses against God. He repeatedly admonished his followers to avoid it, in any form. "Do not wear fancy clothes," he wrote, and "do not pray for the sake of ostentation, but in order to please God."[26] Consumption in excess of one's needs is therefore condemned. It can serve no other purpose, as far as the Mourids can see, than to satisfy the urge to display one's wealth.

For the marabout, then, the question is what to do with excess resources. He cannot hoard them. Indeed, he has a positive horror of hoarding. It is known that Mourid Khalifas and sheiks, nearly all of whom live in the countryside, keep the large sums they collect from various sources in their home safes no longer than is absolutely necessary before forwarding them to a bank, where they will earn interest, or disposing of them in some other way. For the Mourids define hoarding as "contemplation of wealth," which is as reprehensible in their eyes, and for the same reason, as unnecessary consumption.

For Bamba, the justification for the marabout's accumulation of wealth was that it could be used to relieve the poverty of the Mourid community. If used for any other purpose, it could have no religious or moral value. "He who keeps all his possessions and does not give to the poor," he preached, "will be unhappy before he dies."[27] In taking this stand Bamba was simply reiterating a basic tenet of Islam—to give alms to the poor. But the Mourid elite could not take this injunction literally. Indiscriminate giving could not be reconciled with the doctrine of the two ladders, since it would encourage indolence among the *talibés*. Hence it was decided that charity should be extended only to those needy disciples who through no fault of their own could not temporarily secure employment and to those who because of age, illness, or some other misfortune were unable to work. The remainder of the marabouts' considerable resources was to be invested in such profitable activities as could be found.

Oddly enough, while the Mourids tend, in a sense, to confuse hoarding with consumption—or, if you will, with "unnecessary" consumption—they are quite clear on the difference between hoarding and saving. They understand that when an individual saves he parts with his income and provides resources to others; that saving, in other words, is a form of spending. They also understand that savings, if profitably invested, will raise social income. Savings and investment

26. Ibid., pp. 52, 262.
27. Ibid., p. 262.

are therefore seen as capable of fulfilling Bamba's expectation that accumulated wealth would be used to lift the Mourid community out of its poverty without impairing the doctrine of the two ladders. For the Mourids, therefore, the chief justification for saving and investing is religious. It is an activity that, in keeping with their ascetic principles, must be undertaken continuously, insofar as investment opportunities permit, without regard for the increased consumption possibilities it may offer to the investor in the future.

This economic philosophy, based on religion, determines Mourid attitudes toward many aspects of life. The Mourids are not attracted by political ideology; the need to protect economic interests is all that inspires their limited participation in political affairs. Though Mourid leaders have often been accused of opposing modern education for their followers, their attitude toward it actually depends on what is proposed to be taught. Apart from religious instruction, which they themselves provide, they oppose the teaching of subjects that have strictly cultural value and thus represent a form of consumption, while they not only endorse but actively encourage any kind of training likely to lead to increased efficiency of production. It was at their request, for example, that the French authorities established an agricultural school in 1932 at Diourbel.[28] They favor technological progress. While showing little entrepreneurial talent themselves, they support and are sometimes even willing to finance proposed innovations in the hope of finding greater opportunities for profit-making. This hope is not, of course, always fulfilled. One of Falilou Mbacké's brothers, Bassirou, was persuaded in 1947 to participate in a French project designed to test the feasibility of mechanized production of peanuts under Senegalese conditions. He supplied funds and the labor services of 250 of his disciples for the experimental work that was carried out under the supervision of French agricultural engineers on a 15,000-hectare plot near Boulel, north of Kaffrine. The project, known as Bloc Experimental d'Arachides, ended as a failure in 1953, leaving Bassirou with a large deficit, which he, however, was able to absorb without undue difficulty.[29] That Mourid leaders are open to innovation and willing to take risks does not mean that they do not appreciate the importance

28. "L'Ecole Franco-Mouride de Diourbel," *Bulletin de l'Enseignement de l'Afrique Occidentale Française,* no. 80 (Dakar, 1932), pp. 241–42.
29. J. C. Froelich, "Archaïsme et modernisme: Les Musulmans noirs et le Progrès," *Cahiers de l'Institut de Science Economique Appliquée,* vol. 3, supp. no. 120 (Paris, 1961), p. 90.

of traditions, which they generally respect—unless they interfere with the production of monetary revenue. The cultivation of traditional subsistence crops, such as millet, generates little enthusiasm among them. They want to see it kept at a minimum because it diverts resources from money-earning activities. There is perhaps no more forceful way to convey the Mourid elite's appreciation of the social benefits that may be derived from a rising monetary income and of its single-mindedness in the pursuit of monetary gain than to reproduce, in its stark simplicity, the statement which Modou Khabane, one of the Mourid elite's wealthiest members, used to justify his opposition to subsistence cultivation: "Money begets money, and that is good because it provides the most effective means of increasing the welfare of the Mourid community."

Weber's Hypothesis

A comparison between Calvinism as analyzed by Max Weber and Mouridism brings out some amazing similarities. There are, of course, also many differences. The social organization of the Mourids is totally unlike that of the Protestant dissenters of Western Europe and North America. Certain basic Calvinist concepts, such as, for example, predestination, do not appear in Mourid theology. Weber's central interest, however, lay in the economic consequences of Calvinist beliefs, and it is in relation to these consequences that Calvinism and Mouridism appear to be virtually identical.

The Protestant Ethic and the Spirit of Capitalism was, as Weber himself tells us, an attempt to lay bare what he believed were "the motive forces in the expansion of modern capitalism," or in contemporary parlance, the key factors in the economic development of the Western world.[30] While Weber implicitly accepted the thesis of the British classical economists that economic development requires a steady supply of labor and capital, he doubted their view that purely economic incentives, such as higher wages and profits, could always be counted upon to produce it. That view, Weber contended, had to assume a human interest in economic acquisition as an end in itself and not as a means to an end. Such an attitude was indeed common in

30. Max Weber, *The Protestant Ethic and the Spirit of Capitalism*, trans. by Talcott Parsons (New York: Scribner's, 1958), p. 68.

modern Western countries, but it was also "unnatural" and needed explaining. "A man does not 'by nature' wish to earn more and more money," he wrote, "but simply to live as he is accustomed to live and to earn as much as is necessary for that purpose."[31]

Weber argued that the prevailing attitude toward economic acquisition in modern Western countries had been shaped by the Protestant Reformation, especially Calvinism. He noted that it was particularly pronounced in Protestant countries and that it was in those countries that economic expansion had taken place most rapidly. In them, ceaseless toil and systematic investment had not been originally intended for the sake of material acquisition as the ultimate goal; they had served a religious purpose.

Calvin had taught that salvation could not be achieved through good works, because God had determined from eternity whom He would save and whom He would not. The world existed for no other purpose but to glorify God; the elected Christian was in it solely to increase the glory of God, and his social activity had to be directed exclusively to that end. It followed from the doctrine of predestination that a man could neither know nor influence his fate. He could only hope that he was in a state of grace and behave accordingly, by attending with the utmost diligence to whatever social task engaged his energies. There could be no room in his life for leisure and enjoyment; to indulge in them, even to a small extent, would be a symptom of lack of grace. "The fulfillment of worldly duties" was, as Weber put it, "the only way to live acceptably to God."[32]

What Calvinism thus required of its followers was ascetic conduct in a form hitherto unknown to the Christian world. Asceticism had, of course, been practiced by Christians for centuries, but in its traditional form it had meant separation from mundane concerns, especially from the irreligious distractions of customary social life, through withdrawal into convents and monasteries; whereas Calvinism called for continuous involvement in, not withdrawal from, worldly activities as a matter of religious duty. Thus, unlike traditional Christian ethics which had sought to restrain acquisitive activity, Calvinism encouraged it. Yet, while putting a stamp of religious approval on economic acquisition, Calvinism condemned unnecessary consumption and ostentatious behavior. "The superior indulgence of the *seigneur* and the parvenu

31. Ibid., p. 60.
32. Ibid., p. 81.

ostentation of the *nouveau riche,*" said Weber in emphasizing this point, were "equally detestable" to it.[33] Tawney, who strongly supported Weber's ideas on the influence of religion on economic behavior, also stressed this theme. "The enemy of Calvinism," he stated, was "not the accumulation of riches, but their misuse for purposes of self-indulgence or ostentation."[34] The accumulation of wealth was primarily intended to enhance the welfare of the community. "The pious man," wrote Calvin in the *Institutes,* "owes to his brethren all that it is in his power to give."[35] Calvinist asceticism, therefore, meant money-earning activity combined with abstention from self-indulgence for the benefit of the community. But this intramundane asceticism, which Weber called the "Protestant ethic," is also, as we have seen, the central feature of Mouridism.

It seemed obvious to Weber that an ethic calling for limitation of consumption combined with continuous work and reinvestment of profit, once it is inculcated into the masses, would lead to capital accumulation and economic development. Economic incentives alone could not be expected to yield the same results, because they were not as reliable and effective as the psychological sanctions that an ethic based on religion places upon the maintenance of the attitudes required by it so long as the religious belief is alive.[36] Weber did not, of course, pretend that the economic development of the Western world could be simply explained as the consequence of the Reformation. He readily admitted that other factors had entered into it.[37] But none could match the emergence of Protestant asceticism in importance. "The religious valuation of restless, continuous, systematic work in a worldly calling" had provided, he claimed, "the most powerful conceivable lever" for rapid economic expansion.[38]

The Mourid case, however, does not support this claim by Weber, even though there can be no doubt that Mouridism has served as a positive force in the Senegalese economy. Indeed, the extraordinary role that Mouridism has played there adds weight to Weber's argument about the superiority of religious ethics to economic inducements in promoting capital accumulation. Nevertheless, it must be observed

33. Ibid., p. 163.
34. R. H. Tawney, *Religion and the Rise of Capitalism* (New York: New American Library, 1947), pp. 93–94.
35. Quoted by Tawney, *Rise of Capitalism,* p. 104.
36. Weber, *Protestant Ethic,* p. 197.
37. Ibid., p. 91.
38. Ibid., p. 172.

that while Senegal has grown faster economically than some countries, it has lagged behind other countries in tropical Africa, when, according to Weber's logic, it should have outperformed all of them.

This failure of the Senegalese economy, notwithstanding the salutary effect of Mouridism on capital accumulation, suggests that Weber, and the classical economists on whose basic ideas he relied, erred in holding capital accumulation to be the most important element in economic development. Perhaps Schumpeter was right in stressing innovation as the critical variable. Perhaps there is more than one critical variable. Whatever the truth in that regard, the only inference that can reasonably be drawn from the Mourid case is that capital accumulation is not as important as has so often been maintained and that Weber, consequently, overstated the impact of the Protestant Reformation on the economic development of Western Europe.